A Summer Classic

A SUMMER CLASSIC

THE BEW WHITE STORY

An Entrepreneur's Tale of Love, Life and Business

CHRISTOPHER TAUNTON

A Summer Classic: The Bew White Story

Union Hill Publishing
200 Union Hill Drive, Suite 200
Birmingham, AL 35209

1 2 3 4 5 6 7 8 9 10

Printed in the United States of America

To Bew and his family ~

Whatever else this book is,
may it first and foremost be a blessing to the White family

CONTENTS

FOREWORD

"EVERY autobiographer must secretly believe he has triumphed in life," wrote playwright Arthur Miller. So, when over a plate of barbeque, William Bew White III asked me to write his biography—that is, his autobiography by proxy—I was initially taken aback. Though dear to me, Bew, as friends call him, is not a man who has changed the course of history. He is not a famed entertainer or statesman. He did not create cold fusion. Nor has he commanded victorious armies on the field of battle. Isn't an autobiography a bit pretentious?

But that is taking the narrow view of autobiographies and who deserve them. Indeed, by such a standard, very few would ever be written. But there are other reasons for autobiographies. Who among us does not wish that he knew more about his forebears? Most of us know something of our parents' stories, less about our grandparents, and by the time we reach our great-grandparents, their memories have faded into oblivion.

Who were they? What were their hopes and dreams? What were their struggles and fears? I, for one, think it would be nice to know such things about my ancestors. And if some choose to invest in expensive family portraits of those who, in little more than a generation, will be all but forgotten, why not invest in something that fleshes out those people in a way that mere paint on canvas cannot?

And, as Arthur Miller suggests, Bew's story did meet this autobiographical criterion: he had triumphed in life—*and he knew it.*

"Larry, I can't believe I'm on the Auburn University Business School Advisory Board—" He then named several Fortune 500 executives. "These people are big shots! They're captains of industry! I'm just a small fish!"

"No, Bew," I said. "You're a big shot, too." I gestured at him with my fork, barbeque speared on its prongs. "You're a captain of industry as important as any of them."

He let that sink in, and then added: "Yeah, I guess I am. I'm just being humble."

This is classic Bew White. Funny. Unpredictable. Jarringly honest. To those who don't know him, this vignette might sound like the boasting of an obnoxious or arrogant man. All I can say is that he is nothing of the sort.

This anecdote is best understood in the light of the best fictional equivalent to Bew White: Steve Carrell's Michael Scott character in the hit comedy series *The Office*. If I didn't know better, I would swear the writers of that series knew Bew. Michael Scott is abrupt, politically incorrect, amusing, forgiving, occasionally (and unintentionally) offensive, unexpectedly gracious, and is a fundamentally decent human being. This describes Bew.

Bew's story also meets a second autobiographical criterion that is absolutely necessary if such an undertaking is to be worth the effort: he's interesting. Bew is a colorful character. Quite literally. And if I, a colorblind man, think that, I can only imagine the impression he makes on others. He is, simply put—although there is nothing simple about him—flamboyant. And friends who have known him much longer than I will tell you he's been that way his whole life.

That flamboyant character became the basis of his triumph in a kind of fashion industry. When his father presented him with the opportunity to become an Alabama dog food manufacturing magnate, Bew figuratively tugged the lapels of his trademark seersucker suitcoat and walked away. He knew what he wanted, and he pursued it—how shall I put it?—*doggedly.*

But life isn't all peaks and no valleys. Bew will be the first to tell you that. As Oliver Cromwell, a great statesman and general worthy of many biographies, once famously observed as he sat for his own portrait: "Paint me as I am, warts and all." If I was to do this biography, I warned Bew, it would have to be warts and all. As an author and columnist, I well know that a good story arc must have tension, conflict, and then resolution. I mean, how is one to appreciate the mountaintop if he's never been in the valley? And Bew readily concurred, not least because his life has seen a number of valleys.

And herein lies the value of this book to you, dear reader. This is not the story of a man's straight-line success of going from rags to riches. As one of Bew's friends observed, "Bew started life on third base." Indeed, he did. Knowing more than most about his own ancestors, Bew White is descended from an aristocracy of sorts. Even so, his story is a zigzag. If he started on third, mistakes and misfortunes would send him back to second and first bases. Undaunted, he kept swinging and pursuing his own version of the American Dream.

And that's where the tension enters the story. The American Dream can ring hollow if a man is left to enjoy the mountaintop alone and, worse, if he is spiritually empty when he gets there. Bew was both alone and empty. And he had to ruthlessly reassess his own life at a time when he should have been enjoying the fruits of his labors.

This is a book that every ambitious young man and woman would do well to read; seasoned businessmen and women will recognize something of their own successes and failures in a life that has had as many ups and downs as a turbulent stock market; and wives will see their own husbands in these pages as well as their own frustrations with the men they love. We can only hope they possess the character of Bew's wife, Wendy, whose own story leavens this loaf. Astute readers will deduce that she is the quiet, unassuming anchor that gives this narrative its heartbeat.

And yet, this was not a story that I could write. Already under contract for a book with my own publisher, I could not countenance starting another. Instead, I directed Bew to a budding author with whom I am well acquainted: my middle son, Christopher. Having recently finished graduate school, I knew he would leap at such an opportunity, and he was well-prepared to do it. He had served as my own research assistant for my previous books and had closely observed how books were written. Furthermore, his temperament was perfectly suited to this project where he would, in the absence of an extensive family archive, have to interview Bew and his many family members and friends to develop the story's arc. What Christopher lacked in life experience, I could provide as the narrative unfolded in his manuscript.

What follows is a little gem that I hope generations of Whites will come to appreciate as a portrait of a forbear to whom they owe much. I also hope the young — young men most of all — will make use of the wisdom this book offers as they set out in search of their own triumphs.

Larry Alex Taunton
Duck River Ranch, October 2020

PROLOGUE

IT WAS a cool southern evening on the White farm in Boligee, Alabama. Situated in the fertile Black Belt of west Alabama, the farm's thousand acres spill out across plain and valley along the Tombigbee Waterway. The fall leaves were still in the process of migrating from branch to earth. Tomorrow, hunters would probe the estate, filling the air with birdshot as dogs ran their prey to ground at the annual dove shoot. But this evening was a quiet one. This evening Bew sat before a large stone fireplace on the farmhouse's screened-in porch enjoying a Cuban cigar with his friends.

Lost in thought, Bew watched as his old college roommate Michael Young held the room in rapt attention. Michael, an actor by profession, was a natural *raconteur.*

"So, all the passengers have disembarked from the plane, and still, the 'Bear' is nowhere to be seen," he said dramatically, his audience leaning forward with bated breath. "Finally, we see the 'Bear' exit the plane with a man supporting him on either side—he's drunk!"

Auburn fan Jim Rotch, Bew's friend, and, on many an occasion, lawyer, is clearly enjoying this embarrassing story about the legendary football coach of Auburn's cross-state rival, the University of Alabama. In another chair sits Bob, a Navy Seal and Bew's long-time hunting and fishing guide. Though his blood ran crimson and white – Alabama's team colors – he, too, was grinning with a cigar clamped between his teeth.

Bew took a long drag on his cigar and exhaled contentedly. What a life. At the age of 69, he was living out his dream. His luxury furniture company, Summer Classics, had grown to a net worth of more than $100 million. The company's footprint was visible across the country and overseas.

Then there was Wendy. Standing mere feet away, she was his college sweetheart and the love of his life. She was his rock and his strength. He looked over his shoulder and watched her as she animatedly talked with Darlene Rotch. Wendy glanced outside and caught his gaze. She smiled. It was a smile full of warmth and love.

"Lord, what have I done to deserve this woman?" Bew wondered.

For Bew, it seemed as if all the planets had aligned. His business had surpassed even his own high expectations and ambitions. Summer Classics was on the cutting-edge of the luxury furniture market. With more than thirty years of history behind it, Summer Classics had garnered a dedicated customer following. With its overseas furniture production and an in-house cushion manufacturing operation, Summer Classics had all it needed to meet the demands of the furniture market. And with stores in 13 states, its market was growing.

But most significant to Bew was he finally had a successor. His son William Bew White IV served alongside him as the president of Gabriella White, their parent company set over Summer Classics. William's vision aided Summer Classics in its increasing growth. He had initiated several significant changes—most notably, the founding of Gabby (named after Bew's mother), a subsidiary of Gabriella White, the holding company, that catered to the indoor furniture market. This division proved to be a smashing success. The future looked bright and secure.

Bew was brought out of his reverie by the laughter in the room.

"My producer is signaling 'Cut! Cut!' So, we wrap up the interview," Michael was finishing a story. "It's one of the only *Kids Are People, Too* interviews we never aired."

As Bob playfully presented a formal defense of "the Bear," Bew rose and walked into the house. He stepped aside to let Darlene pass outside. Coming to Wendy's side, Bew helped her clean the kitchen. As they returned the last of the clean dishes to their cabinet, Wendy considered her unusually reflective husband.

"Is everything ok?" She asked.

Closing the cabinet, Bew went to Wendy and embraced her. "Everything is *great.*"

But it wasn't always like this . . .

CHAPTER 1

"THE PARABLE OF THE RICH FOOL"

"But God said to him, 'You fool! This very night your life will be demanded from you. Then who will get what you have prepared for yourself?' - Luke 12:20

"LIE DOWN, Mr. White! Lie down!"

Surrounded by six nurses, Bew was in Atlanta's Piedmont Hospital. The nurses were all action. He gasped for air. Feeling his life ebbing from him, he desperately longed for the presence of his wife. Craning his neck, he tried to sit up. "Lie down!"

Four floors down, Wendy jammed the elevator button. "Open! Open! Open!" Finally, the door opened, and she jostled past the exiting passengers, ignoring their angry glares. She pushed the button for the fourth floor and impatiently watched the doors close. She looked at her phone again, reading Bew's texts.

"Help!"

"What's up?" she had replied.

"I don't know, and the nurse won't answer. This may be it?"

She watched the elevator display announce its ascent. "No. Oh, Lord, save him!"

Back in the room, Bew was panicking. "Where's my wife? Where is…"

"Mr. White, lie still!"

He was overwhelmed with a crushing feeling of failure and loneliness. Would he die in this bed alone? Never seeing Wendy again? What a mess! What had he done to her? The person he loved more than anyone in the world would be left in his disastrous wake. "You selfish bastard!" he said to himself. "How could you do this to her?"

Just down the hall, Wendy ran with the swiftness of a track star towards Bew's room. As she ran past the nurses' station, she shouted, "My husband says he needs help and that y'all won't come!" She ran into the room and saw Bew surrounded by nurses.

Seeing Wendy enter the room, Bew spoke frantically, "Wendy! I love you! I'm so sorry! I'm going to die! I'm so sorry! I'm so sorry! I'm so sorry!"

"Keep him down!" The nurses pushed Bew down.

Wendy stayed in his line of sight and kept calm as best she could. "That's okay, darling. I love you. You're going to be fine. Don't worry, everything is going to be okay. Everything is going to be okay." She was trying to convince herself as much as she was trying to convince him.

"No, no, no, it's not okay. I'm dying. I'm going to die. I'm sorry, Wendy. I'm so sorry."

"Honey, you didn't do anything. There's no need—"

"Put that in his IV. Push him down! Push him down!" a nurse commanded.

Another nurse spoke as she held him down, "You're going to be okay. You're going to be okay."

"No, I'm not! I am dead! I know I am dead! I have a minute or so. I feel it! Seconds!" He was turning white. His heartbeat was slowing.

Wendy's eyes welled with tears as she watched her husband fighting for life. She'd do anything to keep him alive. "Anything, Lord!"

"We have to take him to ICU! Take him to ICU!"

Bew snapped, "ICU? Are you guys kidding me? I am so

dead! I won't make it to the elevator! I have only a minute or two! We'll never make it to the elevator and then wherever the heck ICU is! Oh, God this is it!"

"His blood pressure is 70/30. Get the dopamine!"

The nurses began lowering his bed so that his head was lower than his heart. He was losing sight of Wendy. "Wendy, I'm sorry. I'm so sorry. I'll never see you again. You're beautiful, you're everything, you're my life." Bew's vision was blurred with tears. His heart was full of fear and regret.

"Hold him," a nurse commanded.

Wendy stood to the side, watching in stunned silence. One of the nurses, a young man, looked up. Wendy gave a hopeful look. In response, his face was grim. He dropped his gaze. Wendy's heart sank.

"Wendy! I love you!"

"Honey, I love you. It's okay. It's okay."

"Mrs. White..." the nurse spoke imploringly.

Wendy understood. She stepped out into the hallway to give the nurses space to work. Out in the hall, all was calm and orderly. Only in a hospital could there be death and disorder in one room, and peace and order in the next. Down the hall, a man holding flowers softly knocked on a door and entered.

Inside the room, Bew thought of what he was leaving behind. It wasn't supposed to end this way. He had so many plans. He had constantly lived for the future - his eyes always set to what could be, what should be. Now, what had been? What had he lived for? It was over, and he didn't get to finish.

Out in the hall, tears streamed down Wendy's cheeks. "Where's my wife?" She heard behind her. She closed her eyes. Then she did what she had been taught to do—she *prayed*.

THE YOUNG MAN ABOUT TOWN

"Apparel oft proclaims the man."
– Polonius in Shakespeare's "Hamlet"

IT WAS like a scene out of *Forrest Gump*, but for the fact that Forrest went to The University of Alabama, and this was Auburn. William "Billy" Bew White III ran as fast as his legs could carry him. A laughing Dennis Johnson ran close behind him with an outstretched cattle prod. Several other fraternity brothers followed. "Hey Billy, you're not finished with your push-ups!"

The year was 1968. Enrolled as a freshman at Auburn University, Bew had pledged with the fraternity Sigma Alpha Epsilon (SAE). A graduate of the Darlington (boarding) School in Rome, Georgia, he had enjoyed the attentions of the fraternities SAE and Kappa Alpha. Much to his delight, Darlington alums in both fraternities had literally fought over him during "rush." Who could blame him for enjoying the attention? It was nice to feel wanted. For a variety of reasons, Bew decided to pledge with SAE. ("If you pledge with SAE, I'll pay for it," Bew Sr., an SAE alum himself, had said.)

Now, after receiving the electric shock of a cattle prod to his buttocks, Bew was having second thoughts. It was SAE's "Hell Week," the period designated for the hazing of new members. The stark difference between this week and the previous one was jarring. To get him to join, the fraternity had begun by fawning over him. But now that he was in, they treated him like trash. What had he gotten himself into?

Hiding behind the "party barn" just beyond the lake, Bew watched as Dennis and the others turned back to the lakeside fraternity house in search of other pledges. Ever since his middle school years at Mountain Brook Junior High School—an experience he had hated—Bew's school experience had vastly improved. In stark contrast to the cliques and the bullying of that school, Darlington had been a pleasant—and even cherished—time. He found that he generally liked his classmates and they generally liked him. Living at the preparatory school, Darlington students got along with one another, their teachers, and the authorities of the school. In the Darlington years, Bew had come into his own.

Now, at eighteen years old, Bew stood six feet and an inch tall, and had a slender build of 135 pounds. With two years of experience as a salesman at the haberdashery Richard's of Mountain Brook, he always presented a fashionable, well-kept appearance. His black hair was always combed, and his face was always clean shaven. With a pair of black, thick frame, rectangular glasses—the style of the day—he could play the serious part when he wanted to, but those who knew Bew knew him to be good-humored and upbeat. For him, life held opportunity and excitement.

BEW WAS BORN ON JUNE 12, 1950 to William Bew White II and Gabriella "Gay" Comer White in Birmingham, Alabama.

He had three sisters: Gillian, Toody, and Bevelle. If Southern aristocracy exists, then Bew was born into it. He was the great-grandson of Braxton Bragg Comer, governor and then senator of Alabama, and founder of the Alabama-based Fortune 500 textile company Avondale Mills. On top of this, Bew was the son of Bew Sr.—a lawyer in the law firm Bradley, Arant, Rose & White. Born into this hard-working, well-established, business-conscious family, Bew's future seemed to be charted for him. He had two clear career paths before him: law or the textile industry.

His path was made clearer by his early sales experience as a teenager working summers and Christmases at Richard's of Mountain Brook. Located on Petticoat Lane in Mountain Brook Village, Richard's resided in an old Tudor-style building with bay, leaded glass windows on either side of an impressive oak door with a leaded glass coat of arms. Richard's was a very traditional, "your father's" kind of haberdashery. Its reps, clubs and foulards were all proudly labeled "Made in England, Expressly for Richard's." With its mahogany tables and suits of armor, Richard's had a traditional style and class which was well suited to the pretentions of the Mountain Brook community.

Bew's experience at Richard's helped shape the direction of his life. Richard entrusted Bew with the responsibilities of a floor salesman, and Bew rose to the challenge. With a compelling personality, a good work ethic and a growing knowledge of fabric, weave, fit and pattern, Bew discovered he had a knack for sales and a good sense of fashion. On top of this, he enjoyed the work.

His path was made clearer still by his own father's counsel. Bew Sr. was a father typical of his generation. Like Ward Cleaver of *Leave It to Beaver* fame, his children recall him in his morning ritual—a ritual that they dared not disturb—sitting at breakfast with the *Birmingham Post-Herald* (working the crossword puzzle) and a cup of coffee. Though Bew Sr. could be formal, and not demonstratively affectionate towards his children, they did not doubt his love for them. Bew Sr. was a dutiful father, raising his children and guiding them as best he knew how. Now

that Bew was coming into manhood, Bew Sr. took this task all
the more seriously. Based on his long experience as a lawyer
immersed in the professional world, Bew Sr. directed his son
away from law. Bew recalls his father telling him, "Law is not
what it once was. It's no fun anymore. It has become a lawsuit
business." Bew Sr. also had observed in his son what Bew was
coming to see himself: "You can sell! Do that!" So with his own
growing enjoyment of sales and fashion along with some fatherly advice, Bew enrolled in textile school at Auburn and took
aim at the family business, Avondale Mills.

BEW TRUDGED CAUTIOUSLY back towards the SAE house,
fearing what might lie ahead. Sadly for him, more of the same
awaited him. Not long after, he would find himself with other
poor pledges crawling on hands and knees through a dark,
muddy drainpipe. Such was hazing, and such is human nature.
This is the fraternity's inversion of The Golden Rule: *do unto others as has been done unto you.* This had been done to these fraternity
brothers as pledges, and so they would do the same to these new
pledges, and on it goes until this very day. Yet, despite things
as they were in this moment, life—more specifically, God in
heaven—would continue to smile upon the young Bew White.
Though it was not without further hardships, Hell Week did
come and go, and soon, the rest of Bew's collegiate experience
began.

Bew lived with another freshman, John Mills, in an apartment on Gay Street just across from the Auburn campus. Neighboring the apartment complex was a dry cleaner where Bew did
all his laundry (even his underwear). Most of his classes were
within walking distance. When he wasn't on foot, he drove his
navy blue Camaro.

For Bew, the semester went smoothly. He found that Darlington had prepared him well academically. His college classes

were focused on material he had already learned in high school. This freed him to enjoy his social life, his favorite part of life at Auburn. Like most college students, he lived for the weekend. He loved the parties in the SAE party barn. SAE was known for having the best parties on campus.

But, more than anything, Bew looked forward to the Auburn football games. Every gameday Bew, his fraternity brothers and their dates would dress up (the guys would wear a coat and tie and the girls wore dresses) and go to the game. On this day, the whole campus would buzz with activity. In the vicinity surrounding the stadium, crowds of Auburn students, alumni and families gathered in excited fanfare. Fans of the opposing team, strengthened with the hope that their team might triumph over the Tigers, walked boldly among them. As the battle between the two teams was fought on the gridiron, so, too, the war of words between the two fanbases. Finding strength in numbers, Bew and his fraternity brothers fed off of this environment. It was a thrilling way to pass a Saturday.

In 1968, the Auburn Tigers' head coach Ralph "Shug" Jordan was in his eighteenth season. Well-beloved, Shug had won Auburn's first national championship in 1957, and to this day he remains the winningest coach in Auburn football history. There were few things that Auburn students took more pride in than their football team. Indeed, to understand southern culture, one must understand the significance of football in the state of Alabama. Two of the nation's richest traditions are represented in the two football teams the Auburn Tigers and the Alabama Crimson Tide. The cultures of these universities were essentially formed around football. A "good week" or a "bad week" for the students would largely be dependent upon the outcome of that week's football game.

All in all, Bew's first semester was a fine start to college. Bew enjoyed the Greek life on campus, he did well in school, and he was establishing a name for himself. Nonetheless, when Christmas break came, Bew welcomed it. He was glad to go home to see his family again.

Home was in Mountain Brook on Cherokee Road next to the Mountain Brook Club golf course. The Whites had lived in this house since 1954. Then, just a short walk across the course lived Bew's grandparents Gillian and Hugh Comer – affectionately called Mimo and Perks by the grandchildren. A five-minute drive from the house lived his other grandparents Mary Lee White and William Bew White. With so many family members —immediate and extended—living so close together, family had always played a significant part in Bew's life.

Now, as the kids were all growing up and going their own way, Christmas had come to be all the more meaningful. Christmas brought the White family together. It brought Toody and Gillian back from Converse College in Spartanburg, South Carolina and Bew back from Auburn, Alabama. Christmas meant Christmas break for Bevelle, the youngest of the White children—a student at Brook Hill School for Girls (this is now the Altamont School), and so the last White child living at home. It was a time that Bew's parents "Gay" and Bew Sr. cherished.

For Bew, Christmas also meant going to work at Richard's of Mountain Brook, where he had worked summers and Christmases since he was 16. It is there that Bew learned a lesson that would serve him well in business the rest of his life.

Richard's was staffed that Christmas by Bew and two others —Richard, the shop owner and an unabashed anglophile, and a Englishman Bew knew as "The Colonel." Customer traffic was generally slow, and when it was slow, it was Bew and the Colonel's custom to play chess. Bew had learned much of the game from the Colonel, and Bew made a quick study.

"Check."

Bew smiled as he removed his hand from the rook. The Colonel's forehead creased as he frowned. He moved his Queen into a defensive position. At that moment, a customer walked through the door. Richard looked up from some papers behind the counter and signaled the Colonel and Bew. Glad for the reprieve, the Colonel directed Bew to the customer.

"Billy." He nodded.

Rising, Bew moved his bishop and whispered, "Check mate."

Stunned, the Colonel scanned the board to verify this claim. He saw he was beaten.

"Damn," he muttered under his breath. The pupil had beaten the master.

"Good afternoon, sir. How can I help you?" Bew asked, walking towards the college-aged customer who was looking through a pile of ties.

"Do you have any wide ties?" the customer asked.

Richard walked up, "We've got plenty of ties. All English made. Come take a look at some of these." The young man followed Richard but after a quick glance at the ties, he shook his head.

"Any wide ties?"

"We do not have any 'wide ties.'" Richard practically said this with pride. Then he nodded at Bew.

"Sir, if you'll follow me, I'll direct you to a store down the road that sells 'wide ties.'" Bew led the customer out of the store. After Bew returned, he walked to Richard behind the counter. "Have you considered selling wide ties?"

"No. It's only a fad," Richard replied curtly.

"I don't think so. At Auburn, it's what everyone is wearing," Bew observed.

"It's not what my customers wear. Besides, the style won't last."

"Okay."

Bew dropped the subject but took the lesson to heart. He was learning to read market trends.

Christmas was eventful. Bew enjoyed his days with family. He also enjoyed time with friends he had made in Auburn whose homes were Birmingham, too. But the days passed quickly, and in no time, the White home saw the departure of Bew and his sisters. It was time for another semester.

With the subtraction of Auburn football on the weekends, the spring semester of '69 proceeded much as the fall semester had, with Auburn largely insulated from the turmoil that characterized so many other campuses during the Vietnam War. He continued to excel academically, and while Bew tended to enjoy Greek life, sadly, there was still some hazing. On one cold winter day, Dennis Johnson, who had previously chased Bew with a cattle prod, made Bew pose like the Statue of Liberty in the freezing SAE lake until he couldn't move his legs. SAE brothers had to help carry Bew out. Despite this, Bew did not let the hazing hold him back. He still enjoyed attending the SAE parties on the weekend. He enjoyed going to the spring rodeo, where liquid courage spurred some students to bull ride. He enjoyed the dam sliding on inner tubes.

Bew, along with every other able-bodied male enrolled at Auburn (and at many other universities around the country), was required to be in the Reserve Officers' Training Corps (ROTC). Several times a week, in uniform, Bew and the others participated in drilling and marching. Mostly there was a lot of marching. This participation in the ROTC added little color to Bew's experience at Auburn. It was normal and expected.

While Bew was never what one might describe as "studious," this was no reflection of his intelligence. Bew was sharp. Indeed, he finished his freshman year with a 4.0 GPA. Because of this, Bew was honored at Auburn as a Squire. To be a Squire was to be honored among the top ten men in the freshman class. It was a high honor indeed for the young man. It was in this group that Bew came to know Taylor Boyd. This was the beginning of a friendship that was to be lifelong.

Taylor and Bew had been in many of the same circles. Both were in Auburn's textile school. With Bew in SAE and Taylor in Kappa Sig, the two were frequently in the same social circles. But it was as Squires that they became friends.

The two connected on many levels. They both had a similar upbeat, even-keeled approach to life. They shared similar experiences at Auburn. While Taylor had not grown up with a family in the textile business like Bew, he had a brother who worked as an engineer and was faring quite well with the work.

Both Bew and Taylor had similar goals. They both wanted to make a lot of money. But for the present, little else was on their minds except enjoying their college lives.

Summer break of 1969 entailed a return to work at Richard's. With many fellow Auburn students in Birmingham over the summer, there was no shortage of SAE parties and other social activities with the fraternities and sororities. When he wasn't working, he enjoyed cruising around in his Camaro, joining in the fun. Bew was also very much an active participant on the dating scene. Bew often picked up his date and went to the parties or went to drive-in movies. Dates were almost always a group activity. Friends were always finding dates for friends, and Bew was no exception to this. He enjoyed helping his friends find a date. Toody appreciated this about her brother. He was always good in helping her find a date to join in the fun as well.

For some years, the Whites had vacationed at Ponte Vedra Beach, Florida every summer. Bew and his sisters always looked forward to this time. Gay loved the beach. Bew Sr. however, was not a lover of the coast. As a member on the board of Southern Airways, Bew Sr. could fly for free. While the family vacationed there, he often came and went, staying in Ponte Vedra for a few days, flying back to Birmingham, and perhaps returning to Ponte Vedra at some later date.

Bew, Gillian, Toody, and Bevelle all invited friends to vacation with them. Not only would they be joined by several friends, but they had come to Ponte Vedra often enough that they had friends there. Over the years, they had even had summer romances.

As members of the Ponte Vedra Inn & Surf Club, they enjoyed all the perks that came with membership – the restaurants, the pool, and the beach front. During the day, they would enjoy sitting in the comfortable beach furniture on the patios overlooking the ocean. Everyone enjoyed sunning by the pool and on the beach, swimming, walking, and Bew enjoyed fishing. At night, they enjoyed staying up late talking around bonfires. It was a wonderful time.

At the start of his sophomore year at Auburn, Bew moved out of his apartment into the SAE House, rooming with Billy Weeks—a sophomore with Robert Redford-like good looks. A fraternity house not unlike those which are common to campuses with a vibrant Greek life, the SAE House had a great room with a commons area on one side and a game room on the other, a kitchen, and its dorm rooms with a community bathroom. Like the other fraternities on campus, SAE had its own cook and house mother. It was unique in that it was the only fraternity with a lake.

Bew was glad to start another year at Auburn which found him more established within the fraternity and with a comfortable routine. He did not find his classes too challenging but neither were they the simple reviews of his high school material. He continued to throw himself into Auburn's Greek life, and he continued to enjoy the dating scene. All were glad to welcome back another season of Auburn football. Much to Bew's enjoyment, Shug's Tigers led by the talents of future Heisman winner Pat Sullivan would go on to enjoy an 8-3 season, and most significantly, a 49-26 win over the Alabama Crimson Tide at Legion Field.

Of no one could Polonius' maxim "Apparel oft proclaims the man" be said more than of Bew White. Even from youth, he was known for his dapper look. As an admirer of Ralph Lauren and an experienced salesman of men's clothing, he never failed to dress stylishly. Confident, he often wore brightly colored clothing comparable to the style of Vineyard Vines today. This is a habit Bew would maintain for the rest of his life, and it proclaimed something of the man the boy would become. Indeed, had he not become a designer of furniture one can well imagine him following in Lauren's footsteps as a designer—and salesman, since he was first and foremost a salesman—of men's clothing.

The fall semester of 1969, with the escalation of war in Vietnam at its zenith, would be remembered for the Draft Lottery on December 1. It was instituted under President Nixon in response to the perceived inequities of the draft system of choosing older men first. The Draft Lottery was a random selective process to determine the order of conscription for 1970 for men born between January 1, 1944 and December 31, 1950. Numbers were assigned on the basis of birthdates and last names.

The evening of December 1, 1969 was memorable. Auburn students sat in groups before televisions and radios listening to hear if their number was called. In the SAE House, it was standing room only with students filling the great room and spilling into the hallways. Those closer to the TV shouted birthdates so that others standing in the hallways could hear if they had been drafted. Fortunately for Bew, he was not called. Everyone remembers the heavy drinking that followed. If they were going to get drafted, they weren't going to be sober for it.

The following semester, Bew began working at the Auburn haberdashery Sons & Harwell on College Street, near the Toomer's Corner Oaks. With his long experience at Richard's of Mountain Brook, he was a great fit for Sons & Harwell. Bew was a hard worker. Most days he went directly from class to work. Sometimes he even worked weekends when the store needed an extra hand. It was a good job for him that meshed well with his class and social schedule. He was grateful for the work, and even more grateful for the funding it provided for his active social life. He would keep this job through his senior year at Auburn. To fill his absence at Richard's, Bew helped Lee Hart, a friend at Auburn, get a job there over Christmas break. Bew did not then know that she would one day repay the favor.

Bew's sophomore year ended on a difficult note. He had been dating a girl from Birmingham for some time now. She had often come to see him at Auburn, joining him for parties and football games. But things changed between them, and they broke up. For the first time since his early days at Auburn, Bew was without a girlfriend. It was at this time, in the final weeks of the spring semester in 1970, that Lee Hart repaid the favor.

Bew picked up a wide tie and held it next to the suit a customer was holding.

"This tie will go perfectly with that suit."

The customer was persuaded, and soon, another satisfied customer left Sons & Harwell with a suit and tie. The door had hardly shut before it opened again. In walked Lee Hart. Lee was an attractive brunette who liked to wear skirts and ribbons.

"Hey Billy!"

"Lee! What brings you here?"

"Well, I've been thinking. I have a friend you should take to the party this weekend. She's one of my sorority sisters."

"I don't know, Lee. You know I just broke up with my girlfriend."

"I know. That's why I was thinking of you. She just broke up with her boyfriend."

"Well, what's her name?" Bew asked, getting a little curious.

"Her name is Wendy Jane Wall."

"I don't know her."

"She's great. I think you two would have a fun time."

Bew thought for a moment, and then said, "All right, Lee. If she will, I will."

Lee beamed. "Oh, I've told her all about you! She already said she would if you would."

Bew was simultaneously alarmed and flattered by this revelation. "What did you tell her?"

"Oh, nothing much. I just told her that you're a fun guy." Amused by Bew's visible discomfort, Lee laughed with her infectious laugh.

Bew smiled, "Well, that's true."

Lee chuckled, "Anyway, I'll tell her that you'll pick her up at the AOPi House at 7, okay? That's when the rest of us are going."

Bew went on the alert as a customer walked in. "Sounds good. Thanks, Lee. I better get back to work."

"Bye, Billy."

"Bye, Lee."

That weekend Bew picked up Wendy as instructed and they went to the SAE party together. Wendy was the same year as Bew. Formerly the head cheerleader at Banks High School in East Lake, Alabama, Wendy was a petite, attractive brunette with a demure demeanor. Her curly, shoulder length hair showed that special southern-born care. In Bew's current circumstances, she was the perfect date. She had a warm, quiet personality. She listened to his stories and jokes attentively, and she seemed to enjoy them. As for Wendy, Bew suited her fine for a date. Like Bew, she was just looking to have a fun time. She enjoyed his personality and his gentlemanly manner.

This wasn't love at first sight. Neither one of them was looking for that at the moment anyway. In fact, neither one of them found the date all that remarkable. Their present interests were simple: neither wanted anything more than a pleasant time.

Bew's sophomore year came to a close. That summer, Bew got a job delivering Coca-Cola in a delivery truck to customers around Birmingham. It was, he says, the worst job he ever had. He would deliver the wooden cases of Coca-Cola to companies around town. If the money collected was incorrect, he was made to pay the difference out of his own pocket. Yet, there were some perks to the job. Bew made deliveries to the company where Wendy worked part-time. He would make his delivery and then take the opportunity to visit with Wendy.

Bew and Wendy went out on a few more dates that summer, but neither dated the other exclusively. They were not looking for anything serious. All the same, the two went out together more regularly than they did with others. Then, one day, they had an argument. Bew asked Wendy to help him find one of his friends a date. She declined. A quarrel followed, and the relationship, it seemed, was over.

The summer months passed. As autumn approached, Bew was even more active socially because he was the SAE rush chairman. He even planned SAE parties in Birmingham and elsewhere in Alabama. In this role, another trait developed for

Bew that would remain with him: he loved event planning. Bew found all the details of event planning and hosting to be of great interest. He was constantly mindful of what needed to be done, what was done well, and what could be done better. He took his role as rush chairman seriously.

One party that summer was particularly memorable for him. The party was hosted jointly by the Auburn and Alabama SAE chapters at the Hollywood Country Club on Lakeshore Drive (this is now a Marriott Hotel). The music for the party was provided by Suzie Storm and the Stormtroopers – the crush of many young men. It was a huge party. Bew doesn't remember another party quite like it in college. In the course of the evening, Bew noticed that another famous personality graced them with his presence: the famous former quarterback for the Alabama Crimson Tide and the current quarterback for the New York Jets, Joe Namath. The relationship between Joe Namath and Suzie Storm had been highly publicized. Namath was accompanied by a burly man (Bew thought the man looked like a bodyguard). Bew and the other students were starstruck. Then, all of a sudden, a fight broke out among some of the students. The fight grew, and the party devolved into a massive brawl. Bew wasn't sure how the fight began, but the very presence of so many Auburn and Alabama students in the same room was surely a chief ingredient. Bew quickly departed before things got worse, but he had thoroughly enjoyed himself that night.

For the most part, Bew's summer went on in a routine way. He continued to date, but he was not dating anyone exclusively. He also continued delivering Coca-Colas but for one significant difference: he and Wendy didn't talk. But one SAE party in the start of fall changed everything for Bew and Wendy.

"Thanks, Dennis." Wendy walked through the door held open by her date, Dennis Johnson.

Dennis followed behind and made a beeline for a group of SAE seniors. Wendy followed, hearing them exchange greetings and back slaps. She scanned the room. Her eyes passed over a young man standing behind a table at the entrance to the room.

She gave him a second glance. It was Billy White. As rush chairman, he was exchanging words of greeting to some newcomers when he felt her gaze. Bew turned, and their eyes met. Wendy held his gaze for a couple of seconds before following after Dennis. "He's cuter than I remember." She thought to herself.

In that moment, everything else faded into the background for Bew. He watched Wendy walk to Dennis—*Dennis!*—the jerk who had been the bane of his early fraternity existence.

"I'm such an idiot! She's beautiful. How could I have ever let her go? And what the heck is she doing with him?" If it had been Wendy Wall's purpose to make her former beau jealous, and Wendy remains mum on this subject to this day, she could not have chosen a better date to do it.

Bew's date, a leggy blond, walked up. "Hey Billy, I'm going to get something to drink. You want anything?"

"Thanks. I'm all right," Bew replied distractedly.

"Okay."

Bew watched Wendy, throwing her head back in laughter, as Dennis told her and his friends some exaggerated story of his heroics. In that moment, Bew wished he had a cattle prod of his own. "I am such an idiot! But him?" His competitive fires were stoked to white hot.

"Hey Billy! Good party, huh?" It was Taylor Boyd.

"Hey. Yeah," Bew replied. "Awesome."

Taylor could see that his friend was distracted. He followed Bew's gaze.

"Hey, it's Wendy!" Taylor paused and started to put things together. "Is she with Dennis now?"

The look on Bew's face should have been enough. "What do you think?" Bew said, deeply annoyed by the question.

Taylor let out a whistle. "Well, come join us when you get the chance." Taylor went to join his date. "But they do look good together, Bew. You gotta admit it," Taylor said, slapping his friend on the back in an effort to provoke him to action.

The evening wore on. Bew tried to enjoy himself, but he just couldn't get Wendy off his mind. He wanted to look happy, too.

He told a few jokes of his own, cuddled his date, and affected an air of confident indifference, but it was all a façade masking his real feelings. Finally, Bew determined he had to do something. His moment came as his date was occupied in conversation with her sorority sisters. Finding Wendy in a group of girls, Bew walked over and tapped her on the shoulder.

"Hi Wendy!" he said as if just noticing her for the first time.

Wendy turned around. "Hi!" She smiled. Relief rushed over Bew—she seemed glad to see him.

"You look great tonight!" Bew complimented her genuinely.

"Thanks!" Wendy blushed.

Bew braced. Looking over her shoulder, Bew could see Dennis about two cattle prod-lengths away. But, to his surprise, Dennis didn't seem to care. Dennis turned away in disinterest and resumed his conversation.

Probably hazing some other poor schmuck, Bew thought. *The bastard.* Bew looked at Wendy again. There was a momentary awkward silence.

"Hey, Wendy?" Bew asked nervously.

"Yes?" she replied with held breath.

"Can I call you?" Her answer, here in the presence of a rival, would make him or break him.

"Yes," she said smiling, as if knowing the direction of his thoughts and offering him the confidence he so desperately needed.

It was a singular moment. "Okay," Bew said. Outwardly, he appeared calm and confident, as if this was the answer he had expected to receive all along. Inwardly, however, he was all high-fives and fist pumps.

Bew withdrew politely and rejoined his date. He felt like he was walking on clouds. With that, one of the best seasons in Bew's life had begun.

As might be guessed, Bew did call Wendy, and as their junior year at Auburn began, the two resumed their relationship. Even though the two had dated some in the summer, it was like they were rediscovering each other − seeing one another in a new light. Wendy loved Bew's quirky sense of humor, his upbeat personality, and his eccentric style. Bew loved the way Wendy made him feel. She was supportive, kind and uplifting. Within weeks, Bew "lavaliered" Wendy. This was a long-held tradition in the collegiate Greek system, where a guy presented his lavalier—the pendant displaying the Greek letters of his fraternity—to the girl he was dating as he might a class ring or letterman's jacket. If a girl accepted the lavalier, she would wear it to show that she was "going steady" with a member of this fraternity. Wendy did accept, and the match was made.

Bew's friends and family noticed the change Wendy brought in him. Taylor thought Wendy was one of the kindest people he had ever met. He could tell that Bew did not take Wendy for granted. Bew knew how fortunate he was to have her. He often sang her praises.

Toody remembers one occasion when she was visiting her brother at Auburn. The two of them sat in Bew's Camaro talking as Wendy walked over to them.

"Wendy, have you met my sister Toody?" Bew asked. The three of them chatted briefly. Toody liked Wendy's cheerfulness. As the conversation concluded, Bew said, "I'll see you tonight."

"See you tonight, Billy." Wendy said. "Nice to see you, Toody!"

Soon after Wendy had left, Bew turned to his sister. "Isn't she a doll?"

That is how Bew thought of her. Wendy was a doll. His family thought so too. When the rest of Bew's family met her over Thanksgiving break, they instantly fell in love with her. His siblings and parents frequently told him: "You had better not lose that girl!" Bew was determined that he would not.

Not long after the break, Bew picked Wendy up in his car at the AOPi house in Marguerite P. Toomer Hall. On Bew's earnings, he could take her out for a nice date typically – not an expensive one, but a nice one. This night Bew could tell that something was bothering Wendy. When he tried to get her to laugh, she wouldn't laugh. Any conversation felt forced. This went on all night. It was a miserable date.

Finally, on the car ride home, Bew said, "Wendy, something is wrong. What's bothering you?" Wendy sat in silence. "Wendy? What's wrong?" More silence. "Wendy, I can see that something is wrong."

"It's nothing," She finally replied with some effort.

"No, it's not nothing. What's wrong?" Bew parked the car a block away from the AOPi House.

"I can't..." she started to say but stopped. "It's nothing." Bew began to drive again and parked in front of the AOPi House.

"Wendy, you need to tell me what's wrong."

Wendy took a deep breath. "Remember my ex, the guy I used to date?"

"Of course."

"Well, he called me over the break and asked me to marry him."

Bew's jaw dropped. "What?" Then, composing himself, he said, "Well, that's easy to answer! Say no! You're dating me."

Wendy was looking down at her shoes. A tear rolled down her cheek. "Well, I used to think I loved him. I want to make sure I'm not making a mistake."

"What are you going to do?" Bew asked.

"I guess I'm going to date both of you to make sure," Wendy replied.

"Okay. Then give me back the lavalier."

Wendy returned the lavalier and got out of the car.

Bew little understood the difficulty of Wendy's circumstances. In the summer between their sophomore year and junior year, Wendy's father had suffered a heart attack and passed away at the age of forty-three. On top of this, she had come out of a long and serious relationship. After the passing of her father, Wendy wasn't sure that she would return to Auburn. She had seriously considered staying home with her mother. But her mother insisted that Wendy return to the university and finish her degree, assuring Wendy that she would be all right. It was a tumultuous time for Wendy, but she did a good job of hiding her turmoil from her friends and from Bew. Now that her ex had called her, it served to aggravate the tumult in her heart.

What was actually only a period of a few weeks seemed like a decade to Bew. He and Wendy's ex took turns dating Wendy. Bew was miserable. "What chance have I got against this guy?" He thought. "He wants to marry her. I just want to date her." Though still going out with Wendy whenever he could – whenever it was his turn—he went on other dates, just to try to move on. But he couldn't. He didn't want to be with any of them. He wanted to be with Wendy.

When Christmas break came, Bew was still in the midst of his misery. On one evening, Bevelle recalls overhearing a conversation between Bew and their cousin Bobby Yoe. Ever since they had been children, it had been customary for Bew, his siblings and his cousins to spend time together at their grandparents' house across the golf course. Even when everyone grew up, they would go there often over school breaks. Now, over this Christmas break, several of them had met there for dinner one night. After dinner, Bobby—who was on break from Middlebury in Vermont —and Bew went to visit in the den. Bew's little sister, Bevelle just "happened" to be passing by as she overheard Bew talking emotionally with Bobby.

"Bobby, I've never loved a girl like this. Wendy, she's amazing. She's beautiful. I can't lose her." Bobby listened attentively with sympathy. "I've tried to move on, but I can't. I'm trying to date this other girl, but I can't be with her. I don't want to hurt her, but it's just that I can't stop thinking about Wendy."

The eavesdropping Bevelle listened intently as the two talked—as Bew poured out his heart to Bobby Yoe. She was moved. "This has got to be one of the sweetest things I have ever heard a guy say," she thought.

Christmas came and went, but Bew felt no Yuletide cheer. Trying to help him out, one of his friends set him up on a date with a girl who was a sorority sister of Wendy's. Like Wendy, she lived in East Lake also. So, on Christmas night, Bew took her to the local movie theater to see *Love Story* starring Ali McGraw and Ryan O'Neal. There something happened that Bew would not discover until 2018.

Bew and his date entered the theater. He looked around and found seats in one of the front rows. Unbeknownst to him, in one of the back rows sat Wendy with her date. Startled, she watched as Bew entered with her sorority sister. A pain filled Wendy's heart.

Her? she thought.

Struck with jealousy, she realized she might be losing Bew. In that moment, she made up her mind. She couldn't lose him. She knew what she needed to do. She just hoped she wasn't too late. That very night, Wendy broke-off her relationship with this would-be husband, and then she called Bew.

"Billy!" Bevelle called out. "It's for you."

Bew came downstairs and walked to the phone. "Who is it?" he whispered.

"It's Wendy." Bevelle said smiling.

Bew's heart skipped a beat, but he immediately suppressed his feelings of excitement. He knew he was only going to get hurt. He took the phone.

"Hello? Wendy?" he said hesitantly.

"I want to be with you, Billy. I know now. I love you. I love you, Billy. Will you take me back?" Wendy pled.

Bew exhaled in relief. "Take you back? Yes, yes, Wendy. Of course. I love you too." Emotional fist pumps again.

Bew did not return his lavalier to Wendy. He went a step further —he "pinned" Wendy. According to collegiate tradition, the giving and receiving of a fraternity pin symbolized an even greater commitment than the giving and receiving of a lavalier. For many it was even considered a pre-engagement gesture. Wendy accepted Bew's pin, and she proudly wore it, happy to be "Billy's girl."

The remainder of Bew's days at Auburn were happy and exciting. They were largely defined by his and Wendy's relationship—they saw each other almost every day. Bew loved having

Wendy by his side.

This time also saw a couple of living changes for Bew—first he moved to a house at the corner of Opelika Road and Saugahatchee Road across from a McDonald's, and finally, he lived in a cinder block house (though it could hardly be called a house) on Opelika Road with a friend and recent SAE pledge Michael Young.

Whenever he could, Bew would go to spend time hunting and fishing at the family farm in Boligee. Bew's friends often accompanied him on these excursions. These friends included Danny Lawrence (known to his friends as "Golden Eagle" due to his suave blonde hair), Bew's roommate Michael Young – who had grown up in the Philippines, and Taylor Boyd. To this day, they all enjoy recollecting these trips.

In the fall of '71, Bew and Wendy were getting much more serious. At this point, both felt confident that this relationship was probably leading to marriage. They were starting to imagine a future together. Wendy expected Bew to pop the question soon, but she wasn't sure when. Over the breaks, the two spent a lot of time with each other and their families. Bew's family liked Wendy, and Bew got on quite well with Wendy's mother and her brother Billy and sisters Toni and Lisa. That December, the two enjoyed Christmas together.

Bew rose from the dinner table, signaling Wendy. "I had better get you home."

Wendy rose from the table. "Mr. White, Mrs. White, thank you for dinner." Wendy embraced Bew's sisters.

"Merry Christmas!" Bevelle called out as Bew and Wendy walked out the front door.

"Merry Christmas!" Wendy called back.

Bew and Wendy drove back to East Lake in contented silence. Bew held his hand out, and Wendy clasped it, squeezing it warmly.

"Your family is so nice to me," Wendy said.

"Oh, they love you," Bew replied. They continued to drive in silence. Wendy sensed there was something on Bew's mind.

CHAPTER 2

She felt a slight tremor in Bew's hand. They pulled into her driveway.

"Do you want to come in for a moment?" Wendy asked.

"Wendy…" Bew turned to look at her. "I have a Christmas gift for you. Open the glove compartment."

Holding her breath, Wendy opened the glove compartment. Her eyes immediately fell upon a small box. She pulled it out. "Billy…"

Bew took it from her hand and opened it. "Wendy, will you marry me?"

Wendy's eyes welled with tears. "Yes! Yes! Yes, I'll marry you, Billy!"

Bew took the ring and slipped it onto her finger. Wendy looked at it glowingly, and the two kissed and embraced. Both Bew and Wendy were overflowing with happiness.

"I have to tell my family!" Wendy and Bew got out of the car, and the two went into the house.

"Mom! Mom! We're engaged!" Wendy shouted.

CHAPTER 3

NEW YORK,
NEW YORK!

"Make your mark in New York and you are a made man."
- Mark Twain

BEW AND WENDY were married on July 29, 1972. The wedding was in Canterbury United Methodist Church, a large traditional church in Mountain Brook. It was an intimate affair with family and close friends. The groom's party comprised of Alex Jones, Hammond Cobb, Billy Wall, Billy Weeks, Richard Howell (the ring bearer and son of Richard from Richard's of Mountain Brook), Bobby Yoe, Danny Lawrence, Brock Jones, John Mears, and Bew's father—the best man. In Wendy's bridal party were Lisa Wall, Jody Wood, Dari Scroggins (the flower girl), Beverly Dollar, Bevelle White, and Toni Wall—the maid of honor.

Michael Young, Bew's Auburn roommate, remembers the wedding fondly, recalling how Bew asked him to be an usher for the wedding.

"He asked me to come to his house and hold his hand through it, so to speak. This has always been our friendship."

Michael was honored to be there for his friend, supporting him through the week leading up to the wedding and serving as usher. He also didn't mind seeing Toody—whom he had a crush on at the time.

The ceremony was simple and sweet. Bew and Wendy stood at the altar facing the pastor and wedding officiant as Bew Sr. stood at Bew's right and Toni stood at Wendy's left. Their faces beamed with joy, all savoring the moment. Bew and Wendy said their "I dos" in the sight of God and their family and friends.

BEFORE THE END OF their senior year at Auburn, Bew had been hired to work for Avondale Mills in New York City. After their honeymoon, Bew flew to New York to find them a place to live and to get settled in his job. Wendy would join him soon after. In New York City, Bew found an apartment in a building called Tudor City. As they still couldn't move into the apartment for a couple of weeks, Avondale Mills generously paid for Wendy and Bew to stay in the Plaza Hotel—one of NYC's nicest hotels—for two weeks. Wendy packed her things, said goodbye to her mother, and flew up to join her husband.

Bew and Wendy were extremely grateful for the generosity of Avondale Mills. A French Renaissance chateau-style building the Plaza Hotel was iconic. Since its opening decades earlier, the hotel had long been a favorite among the rich and famous. Within its walls have stayed notables such as Miles Davis, Andy Williams, Truman Capote, and The Beatles. The façade of the hotel appears in the film *The Way We Were* starring Barbara Streisand and Robert Redford. Settling in their room, Bew wondered if he might one day be listed among the hotel's notable guests.

Bew and Wendy were also grateful that the hotel was only a short bus ride to work. Bew had already begun his work at Avondale Mills and Wendy was beginning her job at the Wool Bureau as a receptionist. Someone from Avondale Mills knew the former receptionist who was moving back to Alabama. The receptionist recommended Wendy for her replacement, and after an interview, the Wool Bureau hired her.

Bew and Wendy were glad when two weeks had passed, and they could move into their new apartment in Tudor City on the corner of 1st Avenue and 42nd Street across from the U.N. building. The apartment cost $333 a month. It was a single bedroom, single bath with a living room and a very small kitchen. In the living room, they had a TV and a king-sized sleeper sofa, which they could use for guests. The efficiency kitchen had a small refrigerator, a cook top, a sink and a small oven. With arms extended, you could touch both sides of the kitchen.

With their jobs, they both quickly settled into a routine. In the morning, Wendy took the bus to the Wool Bureau located at the corner of 40th and Lexington Ave. Bew took the bus to the Avondale Mills office on 40th and Broadway. As he grew familiar with the route, he sometimes chose to walk, joining hundreds of others walking to work. His route took him past Grand Central Station, where he enjoyed watching crowds of people pour out of the terminal. Getting nearer to work, he would walk by—never through—Bryant Park, a place known to be a drug hang out.

While Avondale Mills was headquartered in Sylacauga, Alabama, it had several other offices – in Greensboro, North Carolina and in Atlanta (both had only one salesman), along with an office in Chicago and the NYC one where Bew worked. The NYC office covered all territory in the Northeast from Virginia up. Most of the Avondale Mills salesmen just had accounts in New York City, but a few of them, including Bew, were responsible for sales in other territories as well. Bew's territory included Ohio, Michigan, western Pennsylvania, and upstate New York.

When it came to his job, Bew enjoyed the selling. It brought him into contact with so many interesting people. But the travel could be difficult. It was a lot for a young man of twenty-two to take on. As an Alabama native, he found the often-snowy driving conditions to be difficult. He might be stuck in his hotel and have to reschedule meetings. These trips were quite lonely so he would try to make friends and invite them to come join him for dinner, but frequently people were unavailable.

Bew and the other Avondale Mills salesmen found themselves in an interesting position. In the 1970s, there was a period of inflation. Prices were going up, and so cotton prices went up, too. Trying to get ahead of these rising prices, many companies were buying in much larger quantities. Avondale Mills sold out of fabric two years in advance. Because of this, the company was selling by allotment, which meant they could tell the buyer how much they could get. They were not sure if they could offer enough product, but it was great business. The company made money hand over fist. But, as a result, there was little that Bew and his fellow salesmen could actually sell. Primarily, they sold excess fabric from overruns, seconds, cancellations and double knits which were quickly going out of style.

Bew maintained his accounts and made new accounts by traveling to see clients in his territories. Frequently, a client might not know if they needed fabric until a salesman came, at which time a client might reup their order. This was Bew's job. He would maintain accounts, visiting these clients in person in Cleveland, Detroit, Pittsburgh or elsewhere. He would also research the surrounding area and cold-call different companies, hoping to gain new accounts. For the most part, Bew's trips were successful. He did well retaining his accounts, and occasionally getting new ones.

On Sundays, Bew and Wendy started going to Fifth Avenue Presbyterian Church, a beautiful, old Gothic-style church situated in Midtown Manhattan. After church, it became their habit to go to Patricia Murphy's for brunch where they enjoyed the Yorkshire pudding and mimosas. Every now and then the two of them would go to Roast Beef & Brew. They especially enjoyed going there for the all-you-can-drink special (with the choice of wine, beer, or sangria). They would get the prime rib, a baked potato, and the salad bar, and they would drink all the sangria they could handle. Even decades later, Bew and Wendy look back on these evenings with fondness. It was evenings like this that helped keep them going through difficult and often lonely days. They still laugh, recalling how their trips home were always an adventure on such nights.

On one cold, snowy winter night, as Bew was walking back from work to Tudor City, wearing a suit and tie with leather shoes, he slipped on an ice patch next to the entrance of Prospect Tower. He hit the ground hard enough that he was knocked out. Bew lay on the cold pavement.

Inside, as the time passed, Wendy grew concerned. Bew was almost always home by this time. Dinner was ready and would soon be getting cold.

As Bew lay out cold, people passed by without stopping. When he came to but was still dazed, he watched as people shuffled around him. Touching his head, he could already feel a bump rising. He slowly rose to his feet and walked home in amazement that no one had bothered to help him as he lay out cold on the curb.

"Billy! Thank God! Where have you been?" Wendy breathed a sigh of relief as she embraced him. She took a step back. "You're wet. And dirty." She began to brush him off.

Bew recounted what had happened to him outside. Both of them were somewhat shaken by this incident and were taken aback by the response of New Yorkers. It left them longing for the southern kindness of home.

That Christmas, Bew's parents flew Bew and Wendy back to Birmingham. They were grateful and happy to be in Birmingham. They were surprised by how much they had missed the landscape – the trees and the grass. It was nice to visit with family and friends. Family had been such a part of their lives. It was something they had mostly taken for granted until things changed. They found the time rejuvenating but far too brief.

Not long after their return to New York, Mimo Comer and Bevelle came up for a visit. They stayed at the Plaza Hotel. Mimo took Bevelle, Bew and Wendy to a matinee play. After the play, she invited them to join her that evening at Trader Vic's – the Polynesian restaurant in the basement of the Plaza Hotel.

That night, they met Mimo and Bevelle in the lobby, and together they walked into Trader Vic's. As they arrived, the maître d' greeted them, "Good evening, Mrs. Comer. I put you right over here next to the President." They followed the maître d' with raised eyebrows.

Bew turned to the maître d', "The President? As in, the president of the hotel?"

"No, sir."

"Richard Nixon?"

"Yes."

As they came to their table, sure enough—there sat President Richard Nixon along with his wife Pat and daughter Tricia Cox. They sat down at their table - all of them in shock.

"That's... That's President Nixon!" Wendy whispered in disbelief.

"I'm going to go talk to him," Bew said, beginning to rise from his seat.

"No. Don't," Wendy urged.

"I'm going to do it."

"Billy!" Mimo hissed.

Wendy clutched Bew's wrist. "Please, no."

Bew reluctantly resumed his seat.

In the course of their meal, Wendy and Bevelle got up to go to the restroom. A moment later, Tricia rose from her table and walked to the restroom close behind them. Reporters swarmed Tricia asking about the meal, about their drinks, and about every detail they could think of. When Wendy and Bevelle returned to the table, Bew and Mimo asked them about their experience. As Wendy told them, she reached into her bag to get some lipstick. With her hand in the bag, she looked up and saw the heads of several men around the restaurant rapidly turn and fix their gaze on her. She froze. They continued to watch her. She drew her hand slowly from the bag with the lipstick, dramatically holding it out before bringing it to her face. Satisfied, the secret servicemen assumed a more casual position. Wendy exhaled in a gasp. Bew, Mimo and Bevelle softly chuckled.

This year saw many changes for Bew and Wendy. Realizing how much they missed the trees and grass, they started to take the train to Rye, New York on the weekends. They would take the hour train ride to this beautiful, small coastal town in Westchester County. They loved walking through the beautiful suburban neighborhoods and along trails by the water and through the natural park.

Wendy got a new job as secretary at the advertising agency Benton & Bowles. While she had enjoyed the people at the Wool Bureau, the work had been dull. She was glad to finally have interesting work to do. The days at Benton & Bowles were filled with activity as she performed various duties for the business agency.

One of their weekend excursions to Rye coincided with the Westchester Classic golf tournament. On a whim, Bew and Wendy decided to attend. They went to the ticketing window, and fortunately, there were still tickets. As they stood in the crowd watching each golfer tee off, Bew recognized Hubert Green. Green was a rising star in the PGA. In the years to come, he would go on to win the 1977 US Open, the 1985 PGA Championship, and enjoy a career that landed him in the World Golf Hall of Fame in 2007. While most knew Hubert for his professional achievements, Bew knew him personally from Birmingham. Hubert had been a familiar face at the White residence as he had dated Bew's sister Gillian for a time. In the course of the event, Hubert recognized Bew, and the three chatted warmly. Bew and Wendy managed to attend again the following day after receiving free tickets from a kind gentleman. This weekend became one of their favorite memories from their time living in New York City.

Later that year, Bew and Wendy found a condo in Nyack, New York. It felt more like a home. It was nearly twice the size of their apartment in Tudor City—and less expensive! It had a larger living room, one-and-a-half baths and a larger dining room. On top of all this, it overlooked the Hudson River.

In their new condo, Bew and Wendy enjoyed being somewhat removed from NYC, but their commute to work across the Tappan Zee Bridge was nearly unbearable. To ease the commute to work, Wendy got a new job at Honig and Associates – a marketing research agency in White Plains, New York. Here, she helped take down information from polls and surveys. She enjoyed the work.

Right around this time, Bew had to travel to Detroit. On the agenda for this trip, he had an especially important appointment. He had been quite pleased to discover that Kmart—which was fast becoming the largest retailer in the country—was headquartered within his territory in Troy, Michigan. He scheduled an appointment ahead of time to line up with his trip to Detroit.

Driving his rental car to the Kmart headquarters, Bew was impressed by what he saw. The complex sprawled over 200 acres. It was a state-of-the-art complex, consisting of several interlocking modernist towers in a chocolate-brown hue. As he entered, he was met by a receptionist – the only receptionist for the whole building – who directed Bew to a lobby further in the building. He marveled at their operation. There were fabrics in one building, men's wear in another, and women's wear in still another. Bew came into the lobby and sat down, waiting to be called. He had an appointment with Kmart executive Richard Archibald. He waited for more than an hour. Finally, an older man wearing a green visor came to get Bew.

"Mr. White. Right this way."

Bew picked up his briefcase and followed the man to Archibald's office. The man opened the door, let Bew in, and left. Bew entered confidently and swung into his sales pitch.

"Thank you for taking the time to meet with me, Mr. Archibald." Bew introduced himself, gave a brief history of Avondale Mills, and he started to open his suitcase and pull out some swatches of fabric. "I can offer you some great prices on these fabrics."

Archibald cut Bew off. "I don't want to see your stuff! You guys screwed us five years ago!" He then proceeded to cuss Bew out. Bew stood in stunned silence. The meeting was over in less than five minutes. Archibald spoke into his intercom. "Please show Mr. White out."

The man with the green visor held the door open for Bew. Bew walked through, bewildered.

"Good day!" Archibald called after them as the door closed.

They walked for a time in silence down the hall. Finally, Bew spoke, "Well, that didn't go the way I had hoped."

The man chuckled. "So it would seem."

"But I would still like to call y'all."

"Don't waste your time."

When Bew returned to NYC, he determined that he wasn't giving up. He didn't know what had happened between Kmart and Avondale Mills, but he felt sure they could do business together again. Bew started sending letters to Archibald. In these letters, he included swatches of different fabrics. He told Archibald he didn't know what had happened in the past, but he hoped they could do business. The prices Avondale Mills offered were competitive prices.

In this time, the country was afflicted by the 1973 oil crisis. Richard Nixon had ordered an air drop to supply Israel in the Yom Kippur War—the Arab-Israeli War. In retaliation, OPEC declared an oil embargo against all nations—including the U.S. —perceived to be supporting Israel. Bew and Wendy remember the government giving gas by allotment – limiting the gas that people could get at a time. Oil prices soared and car lines at gas stations extended far into the streets. Bew and Wendy dreaded the long waits for gas and the terrible traffic the lines caused throughout the city. Traffic on the Tappan Zee Bridge was already dreadful for Bew's carpool every day, but the oil crisis caused it to be almost unbearable.

Bew went into work day after day, fighting the traffic on the bridge and riding the train from Tarrytown into the city. Day after day, he continued to send the letters to Archibald.

In the evenings, Bew and Wendy were always glad to kick up their feet and rest. Bew would often watch one of his favorite TV shows *Kolchak: The Night Stalker* with Darren McGavin, and Wendy would join him.

One day, Bud Svenson, the vice president of the flannel mill, came to Bew in the office. "Bew, see if you can sell this to Kmart." He handed Bew swatches of flannel. Bew's superiors knew of his persistent letters to Kmart, and they admired this.

"Yes, sir." Bew took the swatches, and he mailed them that afternoon.

The following Monday, while Bew was working at his desk, his phone rang. He answered it.

"This is Dick Archibald," said the voice on the other end of the line.

Bew sat up straight. "Mr. Archibald!"

"Can you get me a million yards of this flannel?"

"I don't know, but I'll find out right away."

"Give me a call back as soon as you know." The phone call ended.

Bew went straight to Bud Svenson's office. "I just got off the phone with Dick Archibald from Kmart. He wants to know if he can get a million yards of that flannel. He wants me to call him back with an answer." Bew spoke excitedly.

"Yes. He can't pick his patterns, but we can sell him an assortment," Bud replied.

Bew called Archibald back and relayed this information. "Let me come see you in Troy," Bew added.

"All right. How soon can you come?"

They set an appointment for the following week.

Bew went to Troy and met with Archibald. They arrived upon an agreement. Avondale Mills could sell Kmart fabric at thirty-five cents a yard. This was a good deal for Kmart. They could turn around and sell the fabric in their stores at sixty cents a yard, giving Kmart a great profit margin. Bew returned to NYC a hero. This was a major deal for Avondale Mills.

A couple of weeks later, Bew came into the office, walking

by the receptionist.

"Mr. White, you have some mail. I put it on your desk," the receptionist said smiling.

"Thank you," Bew said.

He walked towards his desk in the bullpen. As he walked, many looked up from their desks and smiled at him. There at his desk sat a large pile of envelopes. "What...?" Bew grabbed one and opened it. It was an order from a local Kmart store in Michigan. He proceeded to open others. They were all orders from Kmart stores around the country. Apparently, Archibald had directed stores to make their individual orders with Bew. He beamed.

Bew walked into Bud's office with an armful of these envelopes and dropped them on the VP's desk.

"What the...?" Bud sat back in surprise.

"These are all orders from Kmart stores." Bew turned around and walked out.

"Wait! Bew!" Bud called after him.

"I have more!" Bew called back. He returned with another armful of envelopes four more times.

As Bew came to work in the following days, a pile of letters —orders from Kmarts—were often waiting for him on his desk. Day after day this happened. Finally, Bew went to the reception-ist and asked her to take the letters directly to Bud Svennson's office to make logistics easier.

Bew's income almost immediately doubled after this. He and Wendy felt like they were walking on clouds. It was surreal. Bew learned a lesson that would always serve him: never give up. Even when chances seem slim, don't give up because hard work and persistence can pay off eventually.

With this boost in income, all sorts of options opened for Bew and Wendy. That year, Bew joined the prestigious New York Athletic Club. Located in Central Park South, Manhattan, the NY Athletic Club is a twenty-four-floor building with ev-erything from two restaurants and a cocktail lounge to a train-ing floor with basketball courts, boxing rings, and a swimming pool. This was a huge change for him. He and Wendy could go there to play tennis, enjoy the swimming pool, and use the sauna. They also enjoyed going to the club's summer facility on Travers Island in New Rochelle, NY on weekends whenever time and finances allowed. This all did much to increase Bew's morale.

As 1974 began with increased stability, their horizon broadened, and Bew and Wendy started considering more changes in their life. They began to dream of having a home, and they spent many a weekend exploring New York suburbia. They were discouraged to find that many neighborhoods of Westchester were still far from affordable. Finding a home in New York that was within commuting distance to NYC seemed to be out of the question.

Bew and Wendy's desire to move grew when they learned that Wendy was pregnant. They had talked about it, and now it was finally happening—their family was growing. They were thrilled to be having a baby. With this news, they continued their efforts. At the recommendation of one of Bew's clients, they took their search to Wilton, Connecticut.

In Wilton—a town 25 miles northeast of Rye—Bew and Wendy found everything they loved about Rye—tree-lined streets, grassy parks, quaint shops and restaurants—all the cozy feeling of home. Bew imagined himself finally being able to own a dog and go for weekend jogs in these neighborhoods. Yes, the morning commutes would be longer, but this was a price well worth paying. They soon found a ranch-style house, and they happily joined suburbia.

Bew and Wendy embraced their new lifestyle. Their new house sat on two acres of well-forested land with a stone fence all around. They loved the trees and the open air. They could walk and jog in the neighborhoods over the weekends. They finally got a dog—"Wadsworth," an Old English Sheepdog— that could accompany Bew on his jogs. Driving once again became an enjoyable experience—as it almost never was in the city. They could drive into town to eat or to shop. These were all welcome changes.

Bew's daily commute to work in NYC was about one hour and forty-five minutes one way. In the mornings, he would catch the 6:45 train, arriving in NYC at 8:00. On the train ride in, Bew would always read the New York Times. He especially looked forward to reading the news on Mondays, never failing to be amazed at how much had happened over the weekend. He would arrive at the office around 8:15. As he was often the first one there, he would flip on all the lights and go to his desk. At the end of the day, he would take the 5:45 train back to Wilton. As he and many other businessmen took the same commute day after day, they taught themselves to play bridge to pass the time on the train rides home. Bew would return home most evenings around 7 PM.

As the weeks passed, Bew and Wendy became familiar with the area. After trying a couple of churches, they started going to Wilton Congregational Church. On the weekends, they loved going to the estate sales, where they purchased antiques such as leather books, antique cabinets, and dining sets. They also enjoyed going into Norwalk, located along the Norwalk River. Here, they shopped for furniture and clothing, often going to the estate liquidators where old furniture was stacked everywhere. In Norwalk, they discovered a new soup and salad restaurant called The Partridge—a place they frequented for dinner.

Wendy had continued her work during the pregnancy, but after a few months of this, work and the long commute had begun to overwhelm her. With Bew's job improving as it was, Wendy decided to leave her job and stay home. It was a great relief to her that she could do this.

So that Wendy could have a car to drive in Wilton, Bew bought a "station car" – a car solely for the purpose of driving to and from the train station. He purchased a VW Beetle for a mere three hundred dollars. It was cheap for good reason. Most noticeably, the car had a hole in the floor next to the wheel base. On wet days, whenever he drove over a puddle, water would splash up into the car onto him. He got a piece of cardboard to cover the hole, but often the cardboard would fly up and he would still get wet unless he held it in place with his foot. He got into a rhythm, cycling one foot between the clutch, the brake and the gas and with the other foot he held the cardboard in place. Every ride was an adventure.

While Bew and Wendy found better community in suburbia than in the city, they still felt quite lonely. They had many acquaintances but few friends and often thought of Birmingham and of family. It was difficult being so far from Alabama especially in the midst of Wendy's pregnancy. If they had lived closer, no doubt family would have stepped in and been a help.

If the baby was a boy, Wendy asked if they could name him after Bew and his dad. But Bew felt that there was no need for yet another William Bew White. They could not come to an agreement on this.

As Wendy was due any day, they had to stay in Connecticut for Christmas. On Christmas day, Wendy received a wastebasket for the baby's room and a candlestick from family. Bew received a silk robe from China that didn't fit. They deeply felt what they were missing this Christmas, and this only added to their loneliness.

When the due date came and went, Bew drove Wendy around Wilton, going up and down hills to induce labor. He wondered if Wendy might even consider taking castor oil. They were ready for the baby. Then, on a snowy weekend, on January 11, Wendy went into labor. Bew drove her directly to the Norwalk Hospital in his VW Beattle.

At the hospital, Bew and Wendy waited for hours. The nurses and doctors wanted to wait until Wendy was sufficiently dilated, but they waited too long. Taking Wendy to the operating room, they managed to safely deliver the baby—a boy—using forceps.

Wendy woke up from the anesthesia around 9 the next morning and asked Bew, "What did we have?"

"It's a boy!" Bew proudly answered.

Bew and Wendy beamed with happiness. Sitting in a hospital chair, Bew held his son. He was moved beyond words. He turned to his exhausted wife lying in the hospital bed. They felt such love for one another and for this new addition to their family.

"Please, can we give him your name?" Wendy pleaded.

Bew looked at his son. "William Bew White IV." He considered the name silently and grew emotional. He looked at his wife. Nodding, he said, "Yes."

William Bew White IV was born on January 12, 1975. Bew and Wendy could not have been more pleased. Their new son bore the name of his father, his grandfather, and his great-grandfather.

For Bew, work continued to go well. In the past year, he had nearly tripled his volume. His clients had come to know him, and they had come to trust him and appreciate his professionalism. Over the weekends, Bew helped Wendy with William as much as he could. He also still enjoyed going for long jogs, taking their black sheepdog mix Wadsworth with him.

One week that May, Bew suddenly became very sick and had to go to the hospital for three nights. While he was in the hospital, Wendy and William stayed with him as much as possible. One day, while she was at the hospital, she decided to get a pregnancy test. It was four months after William's birth, and she had a suspicion that she might be pregnant again. In those few days in the hospital, Bew and Wendy learned that Bew had gotten sick from too much stress, and that Wendy was pregnant with their second child. They were shocked and thrilled.

With a baby under six months old and another one on the way, Bew and Wendy did little that summer. When he could, Bew enjoyed fishing at Wilton Lake with John Cella. While he does not recall ever catching anything, he always enjoyed the fellowship and the peace and quiet in this beautiful setting. Bew and Wendy also enjoyed going to the Wilton pool now and again (for the short period in which it was warm enough to do this). That summer, they did manage to go to Birmingham briefly. Their family showered William with attention. They had him christened in Birmingham with his cousin Braxton. It was nice to be in Birmingham, but such a trip was a lot to undergo for their little family. When the time came, they were glad to return to their home in Wilton.

At Avondale Mills, Bew still spent much of his time traveling, and when he was in New York City, he often took his clients out to lunch. For these lunches and for all his trips, he did not have a company credit card. Everything was paid for in cash. He had a book for keeping track of all expenses. On one occasion, this proved to be problematic.

"Bew, thank you for meeting with me, and thank you for lunch. I'll talk to my people. We plan to order soon," Bew's client said.

"My pleasure!" They shook hands. Bew signaled for the check. Reaching for his money, he took the check from the waiter, and then went pale. Bew looked at his customer and tried to talk.

"Is everything all right?" the client asked Bew.

"I hate to ask this… I'm so sorry. I don't have enough to pay for the meal." Bew stammered. They both sat there awkwardly. The customer understood what Bew was asking. Bew felt such shame and embarrassment. The customer took out his wallet, trying to hide his own resentment at this request. "Thank you. I'll pay you back. I promise I'll get the money and pay you back."

The rest of that day Bew felt miserable. He felt so embarrassed to have to ask his client to pay. Still a young man, he hated how it reflected upon his own professionalism. He looked incompetent. When he returned home, Wendy could tell that something was greatly bothering her husband.

"Honey, what's wrong?"

Bew related that afternoon's incident. "It was humiliating." He didn't want it to bother him so much.

Wendy tried to comfort Bew. "It's not your fault."

That fall saw a welcome change for Bew. Michael Young, Bew's old college roommate, had just graduated from Auburn and moved to New York City to start a career in show business. The only people in NYC Michael knew were Bew and Wendy. Michael's parents were not pleased with their son's decision. Michael struggled to make it in NYC. For his first two-and-a-half years, he made hardly any money, but he refused to ask his parents for financial aid as this would be like admitting defeat. Michael was glad for Bew's friendship during this time. Whenever one of Bew's clients wasn't able to go to lunch, Bew would call Michael and take him out to lunch at the NY Athletic Club. Michael was grateful for the free meal, and he was happy to have a friend in New York—someone to hear his stories.

Little did the two realize what an encouragement they were for one another. Michael looked up to Bew. In Bew, Michael saw a successful businessman with a family and a home. Michael was grateful for Bew's generosity and his encouragement. Bew believed Michael had a bright career ahead of him. He told Michael how he would find someone and find a home one day – all things Michael longed for. Michael felt like he had nothing going for him in his career in these times. Reflecting years later, Michael said, "Bew was my big cheerleader. At that point, I don't know that I believed him, but boy, it made me feel good."

Similarly recalling these times, Bew reflected, "I had no friends then until Michael Young came." Bew was glad to have his old roommate in New York. Michael was interesting and talented. He loved Michael's stories. He sincerely believed his friend had a bright future ahead of him. He was excited to see what Michael would accomplish.

While Michael was still getting settled in NYC, Bew and Wendy would have him out on some weekends for a night or two in Wilton. Wendy knew how important this friendship was to her husband, and she was pleased to see them having a good time together. Michael was glad for the fellowship, too, and a homecooked meal. They both cherished these times.

In the winter of the following year—Friday, February 26th to be exact—Wendy, more than nine months pregnant, felt the beginnings of labor pains. She called the hospital. When they heard the period of time between each contraction, they encouraged her to wait if she could. She waited. Bew returned from work in the middle of the afternoon that day. When Wendy told Bew she was having contractions, he panicked.

"Get in the car! Let's go!" Bew grabbed his keys.

"Let's wait just a little longer," Wendy said.

Bew sat down with William, nervously bobbing him up and down on his bouncing knee. He flipped on the TV to pass the time. He couldn't help but start laughing as he watched Don Rickles ruthlessly and impartially roast celebrities on The Dean Martin Celebrity Roast.

"Billy, it's time," Wendy said. Bew looked at her. "Billy, we need to go now," she said with more emphasis. Bew leapt to his feet and helped Wendy get into their Chevrolet Monte Carlo. After leaving William in the care of a babysitter, Bew drove at high speeds towards Norwalk Hospital.

"Billy! Don't kill us!" Wendy said, bracing herself in her seat.

"Wendy! You're in labor! You could have the baby any minute," Bew replied seriously.

"I'll be okay. I think we still have plenty of time. Slow down!"

After arriving at the hospital in one piece, they entered, and Wendy was admitted. Bew sat beside Wendy as the nurses came in and out. Sensing that things were not as urgent as he had first thought, Bew considered William's birth. He had waited hours. Experience had taught him that this would be a long night. "Wendy? Are you all right?" He rested his hand on Wendy's hand.

"I'm all right," Wendy replied.

"Do you think it's going to be a while?" Bew asked.

"I think so."

"Okay, will you be all right if I go finish watching Don Rickles in the waiting room? One of the nurses can come get me."

"Of course," Wendy said.

In the waiting room, Bew and other soon-to-be fathers

laughed hysterically as Don Rickles roasted Frank Sinatra. When the program finished, he rose and walked back to the room, still wiping tears of laughter from his eyes, and there he saw his wife holding a baby girl. Gabriella Walker White was born on February 27, 1976. Just like her mother, Walker was a small baby, weighing in at six pounds and thirteen ounces.

Bew rushed to Wendy's side. "Wendy… She's already… No one came to get me." He struggled to find words. He felt overwhelmed.

Wendy said nothing for a moment. She just held Walker, rocking her back and forth. Bew stammered, not knowing what to say. Then, Wendy whispered, "Do you want to hold her?"

Going silent, Bew nodded. He took their daughter into his arms. Gazing into her eyes as she looked back at him, his heart was filled with love and such pride for his baby girl. "She's beautiful," he said with emotion. He sat down with her in the chair next to the bed. He couldn't take his eyes off of her.

"That's your daddy," Wendy said. "That's your daddy." Wendy thanked God as she took in the sight of her husband holding their daughter.

On a bright spring Sunday, a couple of months after Walker's birth, Bew and Wendy had Walker christened at Wilton Congregational Church. She looked beautiful in her christening gown. They took a photograph to commemorate this day. Bew and Wendy stood in the sunshine beside the white church. Wearing a black suit and a silver tie, Bew held William, who was fourteen months old and now had a good head of hair. Next to Bew, Wendy stood in a pink dress holding the newly christened and now sleeping Walker. Wendy smiled down at her baby girl, watching her peacefully sleep.

That fall, Bew sold the Volkswagen Beetle for one hundred and fifty dollars and purchased a postal Jeep belonging to his cousin Jim Tullis for $600. Equipped with left-hand drive (which was unusual for a postal office jeep), this was his new "station car." He loved it. It wasn't much, but it had character and he enjoyed its rustic look. William loved it too. Wendy has saved a picture in which William sits in the parked jeep with his hands on the steering wheel and his legs dangling a foot from the Jeep's floor. Having watched his father drive, William has the look of one who knew precisely what he was doing.

Needing additional room for their growing family, Bew and Wendy found another house in Wilton for sale. They began to plan how they would renovate it. Wendy made plans to re-paint the kitchen and generally make the house into their home. Their lives continued to change, they continued to adapt. As their family grew, Wendy felt strongly that she needed to give motherhood her full attention.

"You make the money, and I'll take care of the kids," Wendy told her husband.

Bew happily agreed to this. He was thankful to have a wife who wanted to raise their children as she did, and he felt secure and confident about his own work. Though frustrated that he had been passed over for promotion (many of his coworkers had been promoted around him), Bew liked his job, and he knew he was good at it. He and Wendy made a good team.

One morning, while Bew was working at his desk, Dick Maher appeared in the doorway of the executive office.

"Bew, can you come to my office?"

Not knowing whether he should be fearful or excited, it was with some trepidation that Bew rose from his desk and went to Maher's office.

"Take a seat," Maher said.

Bew sat down. "Bew, you're being promoted," Maher declared. Bew sat up. "You're being promoted to assistant vice president of merchandising in Birmingham."

Bew was stunned. "Is that all right?" Maher asked.

"Absolutely!" Bew replied.

Bew called Wendy from his desk. "Wendy, Avondale Mills has promoted me to assistant vice president of merchandising in—get ready – Birmingham!"

"Birmingham?" Wendy said in amazement. "My goodness! We just bought a new house in Wilton!"

"I know!" Bew said with equal amazement. "I'm just as surprised as you." There was silence on both ends.

"Well…" Wendy said, almost laughing.

"Well." Bew responded. "I guess we're moving again!"

"We're moving to Birmingham!" Wendy said joyfully.

THE
RETURN

"It's a thing to see when a boy comes home."
- John Steinbeck in *The Grapes of Wrath*

BEW AND WENDY immediately put their new house back on the market. It sold within two weeks. They were thrilled to be going back to Birmingham. They missed their family and friends, and they missed the South. And they were returning to them and to it as something different from the boy and girl who had gone to the Big Apple in search of their fortune. New York had matured them. But it had done more than that for Bew. Like the fairytale of Jack and the Beanstalk, young Bew had gone to town and returned home with magic beans—though he didn't yet know it. As it has done for so many before him and since, New York had given him a glimpse of his own potential. He would draw from the well of that experience for years to come.

Bew was simultaneously excited and nervous about his new job. He was excited to be joining management. He aspired to be president of the company one day. For now, though, he was nervous because he had received no job description. He hoped he would be up to whatever lay ahead.

With two very young children and a (recently purchased) Chevy Vega with a tendency to overheat, the drive to Birmingham was a stressful one. Bew stopped often to put antifreeze into the leaky radiator. Nearly the entire car ride, as Bew remembers it, the children cried. Besides the occasional necessary stops, the Vega did not break down. In two days' time, they arrived safely in Birmingham at the house of Bew's childhood. For the time being, they would move in with his parents.

After moving in and settling the family as best they could, Bew got right to work. While Avondale Mills had most of its operations located in Sylacauga, it also had offices in Mountain Brook. Bew's office was in Office Park in Mountain Brook. He worked here with three other people: his boss, Manny Goldstein, another vice president of merchandising, Barry Grimes, and a secretary.

Because Bew had received no job description, he found himself often learning his job on the fly. Most of his work kept him in Birmingham, but he still had to travel as well. He was given the responsibility for one of Avondale Mills's biggest accounts – the Levi account in San Francisco. This would require him to travel to San Francisco every two to three weeks.

His work also took him to the mills in Sylacauga. Most weeks, he would go to the biggest mill which made a million yards a week. He wanted to learn the business and understand their operations better. He spent much of his time with the production manager. All the mills ran 24/7. Bew would sit with the manager, asking him to explain all the work he was doing.

When Bew was away working most days, Wendy and the kids stayed at home with Gay. They all did their best to settle into a routine. For Gay, who had been an empty nester for some years now, this was a dramatic change to her domestic environment. Wendy was keenly aware of this. She knew this needed to be as temporary as possible – for everyone's sake. In a month's time, Wendy told Bew it was time to go. They needed a place of their own. For his part, Bew hated to move out because it meant he would have to start paying rent. But he conceded.

They moved to the Sharpsburg Manor Apartments in Irondale. It wasn't much, but Bew and Wendy were happy to have their own place again.

As the VP of Merchandising, Bew thought he was responsible for telling the mills what fabrics they were going to make. He expected to be more involved in design. Because of this assumption, he often gave the designers directions – either in person or from the Teletype in Office Park. The designers resented this. They didn't feel answerable to him for their work. They thought he was cocky and taking advantage of his family ties. Soon, they complained to Manny, who in turn rebuked Bew.

"These aren't very friendly," Manny told Bew. He held a number of teletypes in his hand – teletypes from Bew to the mill.

"They're factual," Bew replied.

"They're not friendly," Manny repeated.

"Tell me how you want me to do it then." Bew asked.

"Say 'please' and 'thank you' more."

"Okay, I can do that," Bew conceded. "Is 'please' and 'thank you' enough?"

"Yes," Manny said as he turned and walked out of Bew's office.

In this regard, Bew struggled. Considering his age, he had acquired a great deal of sales experience. But he had no management skills. Manny was right. Bew was abrupt, demanding, and given to firing off harsh missives to subordinates. Perhaps it didn't seem that way in New York. It was simply how things were done there. How many were the times that his own bosses had addressed him in this manner? But he wasn't in New York anymore. In the South, social grace is as important in the office as it is in the parlor, and Bew had to relearn this aspect of southern life.

Bew always enjoyed making calls on the Levi account in San Francisco. He stayed in the elegant Stanford Court Hotel. With Avondale Mills picking up the bill for the business lunches, his client often chose Tadich Grill, one of the oldest and most prestigious restaurants in California. To Bew's horror, he ordered whatever else struck his fancy. On another occasion, Levi's head of kid's wear ordered and drank an entire bottle of Dom Pérignon. To the money-conscious Bew, this was intolerable.

Back in Birmingham, Bew continued to instruct the mills in design. Taking Manny's words to heart, Bew's relations with the mills improved. The mills were recognizing Bew's sincere desire to understand operations. They also recognized that his sales experience gave him a fair grasp of market trends. When orders were fulfilled and they needed to produce for inventory, the mills sometimes asked Bew for instructions.

Bew recalls the first time this happened. He had come to observe the production at the mill when the operations manager called him over. "All right, Bew, tell us what we need to produce. We need to make a million yards. You tell us what to make."

"You want me to make that decision?" Bew asked nervously.

"That's right," the operations manager nodded. "You decide."

"I'm only twenty-six years old," Bew thought. He looked around the mill. If he wanted to improve his management skills, this kind of responsibility was an important step.

"Okay," he said resolutely.

Soon, Bew and Wendy bought a house near their apartment on Wilderness Road. They were pleased with their current lot in life. They had a home. They enjoyed their Birmingham community. They were happy with their little family. Bew's job was going well. If he could ask for anything more, he wished for a swift rise in management.

One Tuesday evening the White family sat around the dinner table at Mimo's.

"Billy, how are things at work?" Bew Sr. asked.

"It's going alright," Bew shrugged. "I had hoped it would involve more management. I'm grateful for the job, but sometimes, I just feel like another salesman."

"You know, I could talk to George. He works with a lot of businesses. He may know of some opportunities." Bew Sr.

was talking about George Jones. George had been Bew Sr. and Gay's accountant for some time now, and recently, he had become Bew's accountant as well. George also happened to be good friends with Danny Lawrence.

Bew considered for a moment, "Sure. There's no harm in asking," he said indifferently.

The next Tuesday evening, Bew Sr. told Bew that he had asked George if he knew of any possible business opportunities for Bew. Indeed, George did know someone that was looking to sell their business, Bama Feeds, a dog food company in Tuscaloosa. George said he could arrange for Bew and Bew Sr. to go see it that weekend if they were interested. The idea excited Bew. It wasn't fashion or design, but it might be his chance at ownership in a company.

That weekend, Bew and his father drove up to Tuscaloosa to look at Bama Feeds. They found it to be a fairly sizable operation. The current owner guided them around, explaining the operations of the company. Walking through a warehouse, Bew Sr., who owned several hunting dogs himself, grew excited. He loved dogs.

"I see a lot of potential here," Bew Sr. said to Bew as he dramatically slapped his hand on a stack of dog food bags.

Bew scanned the warehouse silently. He watched as several mice scampered behind a shelf in the corner. While he wasn't sure what he had expected—it was dog food after all—this wasn't it.

Following the direction of his son's gaze and thinking, Bew Sr. said, "This is dog food. They aren't running Tadich Grill, son."

The two drove back to Birmingham in silence while Bew reflected. Finally, Bew broke the silence, "I do want to be in ownership, but I don't think this is it. I know nothing about the business."

"You could learn," Bew Sr. interrupted.

"I know I could, but it lacks that artistic element that I want. I know you love dogs, but for me, I think I need to be involved in design of some sort."

"I can understand that. You and I are different there. You probably do need that," Bew Sr. replied understandingly. "Do you still want to keep looking for other business opportunities? I can keep an ear to the ground."

"I would appreciate that."

At the start of a new year, Bew was presented with another business opportunity. Bew Sr. was introduced to David Anderson by one of his clients. It so happened that they were all members of the Mountain Brook Country Club. Anderson was the president of an OEM (Original Equipment Manufacturing) company headquartered in Trussville called Blooming Industries. He needed someone to invest in his company and run his company's sales. In return, Anderson offered partial ownership of Blooming Industries. Bew Sr. was excited for his son. This seemed like a great fit for Bew. The fact that David Anderson served on the board of First National Bank of Alabama, the largest bank in the state, served to further impress Bew Sr. He arranged for Bew and Anderson to meet.

When Bew met David Anderson for himself, he was impressed immediately. Anderson was charming, persuasive and good looking. He was clearly well-off and well-respected.

"Bew, I'm glad to finally meet you," Anderson warmly shook Bew's hand. "Your father has spoken highly of you and your abilities."

"Nice to meet you, Mr. Anderson," Bew said as they shook hands.

"Please. Call me David." They seated themselves. "Bew, I'll get straight to the point. I think you and I could be business partners. I hear you're looking to get into ownership, and I am looking for someone to take over my sales. If you invest in this company, I'll give you partial ownership and make you the vice president of sales. With your background in sales at Avondale Mills, you are more than qualified for the job."

Bew was excited by the possibility to get into ownership. He expressed that he was highly interested in taking Anderson up on his offer. Anderson proceeded to tell Bew about the business.

Blooming Industries was an OEM company. Blooming manufactured and sold specific products—often smaller pieces of a product—for companies that either could not manufacture, or did not want to manufacture, that product. These companies would then take these products and sell them under their own brand name. Bew was especially interested when he heard that Anderson was looking to break into the furniture market.

This was nearly everything Bew had been hoping for. He could use his sales background. He would be involved in design. Most importantly, he would have ownership. Bew asked Anderson if he could take some time to consider things. Anderson encouraged Bew to take all the time he needed.

Bew did take his time. While this opportunity held great appeal for him, he was hesitant to leave Avondale Mills. He had a good job right now, and he had reason to believe he was on an upward ascent. As things turned out, he did not have to wait long to find out.

Only a couple of weeks later, on a Monday morning, Manny called Bew into his office. "Bew, I have good news for you. You're being promoted."

Bew lit up. It was finally happening.

"Avondale Mills wants you to take over the North Carolina office along with its territory. This includes a pay raise – sixty-five thousand a year. Congratulations." Manny was genuinely pleased to relay this information.

Bew was surprised. This felt like a demotion— he was being taken out of management. He felt his dream being crushed—he would likely never be the president of Avondale Mills. "I'm being taken out of management?" Bew spoke carefully, doing his best not to betray his disappointment.

Manny smiled. Ignoring Bew's question, he said, "You're a great salesman, Bew! You should take this. Have you ever been to Greensboro? It's a real nice place to raise a family."

Bew was conflicted, but he smiled, "I'm grateful. When am I supposed to start?"

"Right away," Manny spoke enthusiastically. "You'll start next week."

With this 'promotion,' Bew's dream of being the president of Avondale Mills was crushed. He realized that the company's ownership was going to his cousins. Bew accepted his new posting, but he also kept the door open to Blooming Industries – just in case.

Bew started in Greensboro the following week. Right away, he liked the city. It was very similar to Birmingham. The city was small, and its suburban neighborhoods were quaint. For the time being, he would rent an apartment while Wendy stayed in Birmingham with William and Walker. He promised to find them a nice house soon.

Bew ran the Greensboro territory ably. He answered to Jack Long, who had previously run the Greensboro office. Bew was the only salesman in the office, and a secretary worked with him.

As days turned into weeks, Bew longed for Wendy and the children to finally join him. As his house search had yet produced no results, he asked Wendy to come up to help him. Wendy's mother went to stay with Walker and William, and Wendy came to Greensboro for a few days. As Wendy and Bew drove through various neighborhoods and looked at the houses, they had a shared excitement. They had little difficulty imagining the happy existence their family might have there. This weekend still produced no hard results, but it gave them a vision for a future that they liked.

But Bew's enthusiasm was soon dampened by some sudden and unpleasant exchanges with his boss. In the days that followed, Bew was regularly greeted with obscenity-strewn teletypes. Some days Long even called Bew to chew him out over the phone. These conversations left Bew confused and angered. Perhaps Long, who had previously held Bew's post, was unsatisfied with Bew's handling of the job. Perhaps Long was discontented with his new role as Bew's supervisor. Bew never quite knew what was upsetting Long. Whatever the case, Bew's enthusiasm for the job was quickly dwindling. He called David Anderson.

"David, this is Bew White. I'm sorry I have taken so long to get back with you. Is your offer still on the table?"

"Bew, how are you doing? Yes, of course. My offer stands if you're interested," David spoke with warmth.

"I'm interested. Can I come see you at your office soon?" Bew could hardly hide his eagerness.

"Tell you what. How about you and your wife come to our house for dinner this Friday?"

"Thank you! Wendy and I would be delighted." Bew was disarmed by this gracious invitation.

That weekend, Bew and Wendy pulled up to the Anderson house on Mountain Brook Parkway. It was a beautiful mansion. "Good grief. This guy is *rich.*" Bew was in awe.

"It's beautiful," Wendy said in amazement.

David's wife Mary greeted them at the door and whisked them inside. David greeted them both with a broad grin. "Bew!" David shook Bew's hand like they were good friends that had not seen each other in a long time. "And this must be your wife! You didn't tell you were married to Miss America." Wendy blushed.

As the evening wore on, Bew and Wendy were charmed by David and Mary's warmth and hospitality. Eventually, the dinner's conversation turned towards business.

"Bew, if you give me twenty-five thousand, I'll give you twenty-five percent of the company," David said as he refilled Bew's wine glass.

Bew shifted in his chair. That he could own a quarter of the company right away greatly interested him. He nodded to show that he liked what he was hearing.

"I just need you to take over my sales. I can't think of anyone better qualified for this position than you, Bew."

"David, I am very interested."

"Marvelous! Come on out to the plant in Trussville and I'll show you the operation."

The next week, Bew returned to Greensboro where he once again faced the wrath of Long.

"Where the hell were you this weekend? I tried to reach

you," Long demanded over the phone.

"I was in Birmingham, spending time with my family," Bew said with resignation. At this point he had given up fighting back. He drifted into thought as Long exploded in clear dissatisfaction at this response. Bew thought about dinner at the Andersons. He recollected the warmth of David and his wife. As Long berated him, Bew warmed more and more to the idea of working for Blooming Industries.

The following weekend, Bew and his father – his trusted advisor in these matters – paid a visit to the Blooming Industries plant in Trussville. Bew and Bew Sr. were pleased with what they saw. Blooming Industries was not a remarkable operation, but it showed promise. Bew was greatly attracted to the idea that he could be responsible for taking the company to new heights.

Bew was satisfied by what he had seen. He also liked the idea of staying in Birmingham. It would be nice for his family to set down roots there among family and friends. After taking a loan of $25,000 from the First National Bank of Alabama, Bew called Anderson, and they made plans to make the deal official. Bew then wrote a nice letter to Donald Comer III, the CEO of Avondale Mills, giving his two weeks' notice and expressing his gratitude for the job.

Two weeks later, Bew started as the vice president of sales for Blooming Industries. His salary was forty thousand less than his salary at Avondale Mills, but he felt confident that he could live on this with the help of what he would make in commission. He was thrilled to be back in management. He got to work setting up a sales team.

The next month, Bew had to travel to North Carolina for the High Point Market—a market which took place every six months, once in April and once in October. High Point is the largest furniture market in the world. The market has over twelve million square feet of show space, and it attracts tens of thousands of attendees from around the world, including retail buyers, interior designers, architects, and others involved in the furniture industry. It was Bew's responsibility to go to High

Point to run Blooming Industries' showroom.

Bew traveled to Greensboro where he stayed with Terry Romine. The two had worked together and become friends only a few months earlier while Bew was living in Greensboro. They enjoyed going to dinner and catching up. Afterwards, Bew turned in early for the night so he could rise early and prepare the Blooming Industries showroom.

The next morning when Bew arrived at High Point, the showroom was locked. He went to the High Point office. "Hey, can you help me out? I'm with Blooming Industries. Our showroom is locked."

"You haven't paid your rent," the man replied.

"What?" Bew said in surprise.

"You haven't paid your rent," the man repeated.

Bew walked to the nearest pay phone and called David Anderson. "David, this is Bew. They won't let me into the showroom because we haven't paid our rent."

"I'll handle it right away. I'll wire the money." David did not seem to be even remotely concerned.

"Okay. Thanks." Bew hung up the phone. "This is a disaster," he thought.

High Point received the rent and unlocked the showroom for Bew. Bew was dumbstruck by this blunder. How could David forget to pay rent for the most important furniture market in the industry?

Before long, High Point was busy with thousands of attendees. Bew worked the showroom with the help of a couple of more experienced Blooming Industries sales reps. It would take some time for him to learn how to talk to his new customers, but thankfully, he always made a quick study.

In the coming weeks, Bew's travel for Blooming Industries greatly increased. He traveled to markets around the country and he visited his sales reps to help them sell to their clients. In any given month, Bew could be away for weeks at a time.

When summer arrived, Bew felt exhausted. He was tired of being on the road so much. He, Wendy and the children did get to spend some time at Ponte Vedra with Bew's parents that summer. He also joined the Mountain Brook Country Club, paying the initiation fee as a junior member. He and Wendy spent time at the club whenever they could manage it. Despite all this, he found little in the way of real rest that summer. In July, he had to go to the market in Atlanta along with his usual travel.

After five months of working for Blooming Industries, Bew became aware of some critical problems with the company.

"Shit," Bew heard the controller for Blooming Industries, Rex, swear from the adjacent office. A string of further obscenities followed. Bew rose from his desk and walked into Rex's office.

"Is something wrong?" Bew asked. The two of them got on well.

Rex ran his fingers through his hair with both hands. "We're late on our payments."

"What do you mean?" Bew was confused. "Did we forget to pay?"

"I didn't forget." He held up a letter. "This is a notice saying we are late in paying the building's rent. I know I sent them the check for this payment."

"Maybe we can just write another check?" Bew offered.

"Bew, this isn't the first time this has happened. This could be really bad," Rex said seriously.

"Go talk to David about it," Bew said.

"I would, but he's at Palm Beach." Rex was exasperated.

Bew went back to his office. Trying to suppress a rising fear, he poured himself all the more vigorously into his work.

Out of necessity, Bew became increasingly involved in the plant's production. Blooming Industries had no director of operations. This responsibility properly fell to David Anderson, but David gave the operations little of his attention. As a result, Bew was often unimpressed with the quality of production. Even though he had little to no experience here, as a salesman he cared about the quality of the products he was selling. It was a bumpy process. He felt his own inexperience and ineptitude in this part of the business. Bew called this the beginning of his 'MBA of mistakes.' He learned by trial and error, but the fact remained that he did learn.

Later that fall, Bew was sitting at his desk when Rex stormed by. "Rex!" Bew called after him. "What are you doing?"

Rex wheeled around and leaned forward with both hands on Bew's desk. "Bew, his checks are bouncing. They are f-ing bouncing," Rex hissed.

"What?" Bew was struggling to comprehend.

"All those late payments. I *did* send those checks. They're bouncing at the First National Bank of Alabama." Rex was fuming.

"That can't be. He's on the board." Bew's mouth was agape.

"I can't take this. I'm going to confront him right now. This is unacceptable." Rex gritted his teeth.

"Good. Good!" Bew urged as Rex resumed his march to David's office. He heard Rex speak in a raised voice, but whatever conversation followed decreased in volume.

Not long later, Rex returned, looking appeased.

"Well?" Bew asked. "How did it go?"

"I confronted him. He's aware of the problem. I think it's going to be all right."

"That's a relief." Bew was grateful that Rex had confronted David and he continued his work hopefully.

After a couple weeks on the road, Bew returned to find Blooming Industries' operations were in shambles. Quality was poor. Shipments were late. To make things even worse, David was again gone to Palm Beach. Bew felt close to despairing. He resolved that he would confront David upon his return. He found his opportunity a few days later.

"David," Bew spoke, striding into David's office. "We really need your help here. We're having major issues with our shipments. We're…"

David held his hands up. "I know. I'm sorry. Mary loves Palm Beach, and I love my wife. You know how it goes," he smiled, hoping to elicit Bew's sympathy. Bew only frowned.

"What am I supposed to do, David? I can't run our sales team *and* operations. I need your help," Bew spoke imploringly. David spoke more seriously now. "I'm sorry. I promise I'll be here." Bew was silent and skeptical. "Well, I guess we have work to do! Let's get to it!" David said cheerily, very much wanting to end this tense conversation.

In the following days, Bew saw a marked improvement in operations. David's presence and involvement greatly increased the company's morale. Bew was greatly encouraged, and with this general improvement, he felt more confident in his own work.

The next week, he dared to let his despair give way to optimism. He knew there was still a lot of work ahead, but the work did not feel insurmountable as it had only the week before. He greeted his coworkers cheerily. "Good morning, Rex," Bew said as he sauntered by. Rex sat at his desk with his head in his hands. "Rex? Is everything all right?"

"No. Definitely not," Rex muttered. "More late payments. The checks bounced. Again."

"Where- where is he?" Bew was shaking. He started towards David's office.

"He's not here," Rex said just before Bew went through the door. "David hasn't come in."

"I'll talk to him when he does," Bew declared resolutely.

"Bew, I don't think-" Rex started to say, but Bew interrupted. "He promised. He promised he would be here." Bew wanted to trust David.

"David does whatever the hell he wants," Rex said in disgust.

Bew walked off, not wanting to believe this. David had promised.

Bew grew anxious when David did not come in that day, the next day, or even the next. When David did not come in at all that week, he gave up. He faced the fact that David had lied— he had gone to Palm Beach again.

Bew had always liked David. The two of them had never

exchanged a cross word. But now Bew saw that this was all a façade. Not only was the man incompetent as a CEO, he was also unethical and untrustworthy. While the company was bleeding out, David raised not a finger to save it. He escaped to Palm Beach while Blooming Industries slowly capsized. Bew realized that Blooming Industries would inevitably collapse. He knew he had to get out before the company pulled him and everyone else down with it. He began to form an exit strategy.

NEVER LET A FAILURE GO TO WASTE

"The only real mistake is the one from which we learn nothing."
- Henry Ford

BEW HAD ONLY been with Blooming Industries seven months when he decided to leave. Bew wished now that he had remained with Avondale Mills. At the time, he had weighed the risks as slight against his own abilities. He was determined to own and run a successful company. Now, faced with the prospect of unemployment, his aspirations seemed foolish. He would even endure the anger of Long in return for stability right now.

Bew was struggling to keep his head above water. He had mistakenly thought that he could support his family on this salary, but he had difficulty caring for them and paying the mortgage. He feared they might have to make some serious lifestyle changes soon. Finances became so tight that Wendy could not even go to the grocery store. This was more than she could bear.

"We're going to run out of food," Wendy told Bew anxiously one night. "I can't buy orange juice. I can't buy milk for the kids. What am I going to do?"

Bew could hear the anguish in Wendy's voice. He sat at the kitchen table with his head in his hands. "I'm working, baby.

I'm trying my best."

"How are we going to feed our children?" Wendy asked in despair.

"I'll figure something out." Bew knew he was running out of time. He had to act now.

To make ends meet, he started looking to sell his Avondale Mills stock. When Bew Sr. became aware that Bew was considering this, he intervened. "Don't do that. I'll lend you money." Bew and his father came to an agreement for a loan of $1459. It felt like he was taking a loan of ten thousand. It was an extremely difficult conversation. When even this loan proved insufficient, Bew began to live on a credit card. He desperately wanted to be free from this situation, but he felt helpless. The immediate needs of his family took precedent.

Another month went by, and still, the late payments and the delayed shipments continued for Blooming Industries. Anderson showed no concern. Bew continued to travel to markets and work his territory for the company, but whatever energies he had left to him he put to forming a plan. In the end, he decided his best option was doing the one thing he knew how to do – he would start a sales rep company.

At markets, he started to put out feelers. He needed a team of sales reps around the country for his company. He would serve as sales manager, offering their services to companies. These companies would pay a ten percent commission on all sales. Bew would get three percent and the sales reps would take seven percent. He was pleasantly surprised to find that there was widespread interest in his idea.

Around this time Bew Sr. approached Bew regarding an upcoming merger between Southern Airways and North Central Airlines. The board of Southern Airways was discussing a new name for the airline after the merger. He asked for Bew's help. The two spoke over the phone.

"Hey Billy, I've told you about this merger. Right now, the board is trying to think of a name. Could you come up with a name for the airline? You're really good at this stuff," Bew Sr. said.

Not much later, Bew came back with a name along with a logo—'Vista Airlines.' "It means 'looking over the next horizon.' They'll never have to change it." Bew was quite pleased with his idea. Bew Sr. took it to the board.

He called Bew later that week with the board's decision. "They decided to call it Republic Airlines."

"Ugh. That's a terrible name," Bew said in disappointment.

"Well, it's what they wanted," Bew Sr. replied.

Bew was suddenly struck with an idea. "Can I take the name?"

Bew Sr. was aware of Bew's latest venture. "Yeah. I think so. Check and see."

This was how Bew named his new company 'The Vista Corporation.' He trademarked the name and kept the logo too.

After nine months of working for Blooming Industries, Bew finally mustered the courage to take a leap of faith. It was time to begin The Vista Corporation. On one of those rare occasions that found Anderson in his office, he decided to finally inform Anderson of his plan.

"David," Bew walked into David's office and approached his desk. "I need to talk with you about something."

David looked up smiling. "Sure. Take a seat." He gestured to a chair.

Bew sat down with his hands folded on his lap. "David, Blooming Industries can't afford me. I'm leaving to start a sales company called The Vista Corporation. I'll work off of straight commission now. I'll be the sales manager for a number of sales reps around the country. I can continue to sell Blooming Industries' products along with other lines. You only need to pay me commission—ten percent commission, three for me and seven for my sales reps. Also, I'll personally take the territory where we don't have a rep."

Anderson could not have gotten a better deal. He no longer needed to pay Bew's salary, he got to keep Bew's twenty-five thousand dollar investment, and he only had to pay Bew's commission. David amiably accepted the proposal.

So, in 1979, at the age of twenty-eight, Bew took his leave of Blooming Industries and began The Vista Corporation. He worked tirelessly to get his business underway and made arrangements with sales reps he knew all over the country. He picked up lines through his contacts from Blooming Industries and introduced himself to companies, telling them he was the president of The Vista Corporation. Once a few bigger companies signed on, other companies began to follow. Within several weeks, Bew picked up nearly a dozen lines.

Bew's target companies were smaller, unestablished companies—companies that needed help putting a sales team together. These companies needed someone to pick up their line and help put them on the map. In addition to sales, Bew also offered to help with product design. The biggest draw for smaller companies was that they could get all this without paying a salary.

Among the sales reps that Bew hired were some old friends and business acquaintances. Bew hired Terry Romine, his friend in Greensboro, from Wrangler, who took over territories in the northeast. He also hired Sonny Harwell from Sons and Harwell. He had maintained a friendship with Sonny and his brother Donnie—the owners of the store—since his time working there at Auburn. When he started Vista, Sonny called him and asked if he could work for Vista. Bew hired Sonny, and he proved to be a great salesman.

Bew was pleased. Everything was developing nicely. With two young children at home, he now felt the great need for an office. After a short search, he found a space for rent by the founder of Meadowcraft – one of his father's friends – William McTyeire Jr. The space was on the second floor of a building on Culver Lane in Mountain Brook Village. Rent was $135 a month. Just having an office with a phone to make his phone calls was a massive boon to his business.

Wendy started to work with Bew at the office. With her experience in New York City, she gave him valuable secretarial help at The Vista Corporation. While their maid watched William and Walker, Wendy came to work at the office three days a week from 9 AM to 1 PM. Bew was glad for her help.

In the early days of Vista, Bew felt like he was spinning plates. There was so much to be done. Most basically and importantly, he needed to sell. He had to travel now more than ever to sell in his own vast southeast territory, help his sales reps sell in their territories, and attend all the markets. He made every day count. In another month's time, he brought his lines to twenty.

In the spring, Bew picked up Central Manufacturing Company—a line that would prove to be very significant. He found Central Manufacturing at the Atlanta Gift Market. As he usually did, he was making the rounds, studying the various products on display, when he came across the Central Manufacturing booth. He watched as people lined up to buy a baker's rack. "Boy, I could sell those," Bew thought.

In this way, Bew met the owner of Central Manufacturing —Daren Brooks. Bew and Daren were very different. Daren was stocky, ruddy faced and bearded—a "good old boy" from small town Alabama. On the other hand, Bew was a slender, clean shaven and fashion-conscious blue blood from Mountain Brook. Daren enjoyed letting loose in the evenings, sloshing bourbon and meeting women while Bew preferred a stirring conversation over a glass of scotch. Yet, both recognized in one another that same drive to succeed. Right away, they knew they could do business together. Bew and Daren arranged to meet at Central's plant in Ensley, Alabama the following week.

When Bew and Daren met, both were clearly invested in working together. As the two talked, Daren grew excited. Bew convinced Daren that he could think bigger. Vista could do more than just sell in Birmingham—Vista could sell their product all over the country. Vista could put Central Manufacturing's name on the map. As for Bew, he was excited to pick up Central's line. He knew a hot item when he saw it. He could not wait to sell these baker's racks.

As Bew had hoped, the baker's rack sold wonderfully. Everyone wanted it. Bew sold it to small dealers and to larger retailers such as Haverty's and Jefferson Home. The baker's rack became Vista's best-selling item. In a short time, Bew heard from retailers that they needed to reorder their stock. Bew couldn't believe his good fortune.

When summer came, Bew and Wendy were very grateful for the kindness of Danny Lawrence. Danny, who had been living in Hilton Head, South Carolina, offered the Whites the use of his condo. This was a retreat they were able to enjoy for many summers. At the condo, they spent their time in various ways—on the beach, playing tennis in the nearby tennis courts and simply resting together. Still a bachelor, Danny liked to join them and play with them whenever he could. They all especially enjoyed going together to Harbor Town to hear Gregg Russell, who performed there under an old oak tree every summer. With a sound similar to James Taylor and a very deliberate family-orientation to his music, it was something Bew, Wendy and their children always looked forward to. These summers were precious times for their family.

Vista continued its upward trend through the year and into the new decade. Bew soon managed to add several more significant lines. One week, while in attendance at an unfinished wood show in Las Vegas, Bew became acquainted with Pete Smith, the owner of Sonoma Wood Products. A long-haired hippie living on a boat in Sausalito, Pete liked Bew and the work Bew was doing. After a sales meeting in Sonoma, California, Pete gave Vista the Sonoma line.

With Pete's help, Bew managed to make contact with Bernie Marcus, the co-founder of The Home Depot. The two of them met in Atlanta, where Home Depot had recently been established. Considering Vista's lines, Bernie was drawn to Sonoma's wooden bunk beds. They made a deal, and Home Depot purchased a truck load of the beds. This was a highly profitable deal for Bew.

In the time to come, Home Depot and Bernie Marcus would become one of Bew's best accounts. This was also a significant relationship for Bew. Bew and Bernie had almost monthly business appointments in Atlanta. Soon, these appointments became lunch meetings. Bew always looked forward to these meetings. Bernie was very amiable, and he was a living treasure trove of business wisdom for the aspiring and ambitious Bew. Bernie even encouraged Bew to invest in Home Depot's stock. To this day, Wendy likes to remind her husband how he passed on this opportunity.

When it came to traveling Bew tended to go by car. That said, he still flew relatively often. As a result, he was quite familiar with the Birmingham Airport and those who worked there. One day, as Bew was getting his ticket at the Southern Airways counter, Lonnie, who always worked the counter, said to him, "Bew, you don't have to buy the ticket. You know that, right?"

Bew definitely did not know this. "No. You'll just write me a ticket?"

"Yeah. Your father is on the board of directors. You can fly free."

Bew put his wallet away. "Hell yeah!"

Bew was thrilled. He was always concerned about travel costs each year. While he did not travel more than was usual, he flew for free for the next six months.

Sadly for Bew, his free flying came to an end when Bew Sr. learned of the arrangement. Bew Sr. was displeased. He often flew from Birmingham himself, and he likely heard about Bew's free flying through conversation with Lonnie. He confronted Bew right away. "Do not do that ever again."

"Well, I am your son," Bew replied weakly. He knew he was standing on thin ice.

"No. I can't take advantage of the company I work for," Bew Sr. was emphatic.

"Okay." They dropped the subject. "Damn," Bew thought ruefully. "I should have done that a lot more while I had the chance."

Traveling weeks at a time, Bew felt the toll this was taking on his family. He wished there was more time in the day – time enough for his work and his family. Whenever he returned home from his trips, Walker was always the first to greet him by rushing outside to meet him. This always meant a lot to him. "Walkie Stalk!" he would say as he scooped her into his arms. As he walked inside with Walker, he would greet William who was often playing his Atari. Bew was amazed at how quickly his children were growing up. Right now, he had to get the company to a place where it was sustainable. This would mean a lot of effort up front, but one day soon, he hoped, he could spend more time at home.

Bew had to spend long hours and many weeks away from home, but he was pleased to see his hard work paying off. In 1980, he would make fifty thousand dollars, and he was on track to make much more. He now had as many as twenty-four lines. Unfortunately, in a major setback, he was soon forced to drop many of them.

Most of Vista's lines were smaller companies. This had been Vista's niche from the start. Bew knew that the services of The Vista Corporation naturally appealed to smaller companies because they could not afford to hire their own salesmen. What Bew had not taken into consideration was that this meant many of these companies also lacked the funds to pay Vista as well. Many still owed Bew commission from the previous year – commission, as it so happened, that he would never receive. He started dropping lines. One of the lines was Blooming Industries. He felt relieved to finally cut ties with this part of his past.

As this problem persisted, Bew finally decided to do something. He called a company that was late in paying him $8000 in commission. "Hey, did you know you owe me about eight thousand in commission checks?"

"Oh. Yeah, yeah. We are going to pay you, but we're having cashflow problems right now."

Cashflow problems—Bew heard this time and again. In one such phone call, he came to a realization. "So, I'm a payable? You don't consider me as an employee?" His shock grew as he came to grips with this reality.

"Yeah, you're a 1099."

Bew realized that he was being treated not like an employee, as he had assumed, but rather like one of so many other payables. He knew this meant that companies would buy their materials such as wood and metal for their furniture production—things they required to do business—long before they paid his commission. Vista was just a payable in a stack of bills. He soon had a phrase for this phenomenon: "I'm in the hat." These companies would go into "the hat"—the stack of bills—and pick out somebody they had to pay. They just might pull Vista out of the hat, or they might not.

Early in the winter of 1981, Bew was surprised to learn that Wendy was pregnant. He had just returned home early after a week on the road. As was his custom, he offered to make Wendy a drink. She requested a white wine spritzer—something she never drank. Bew knew right away—Wendy must be pregnant.

"No. That's not possible." He blurted out.

"Yes." Wendy nodded her head.

Bew was in shock. "Oh my... We can't even afford two children. I can't even pay the mortgage. What are we going to do?" Bew ran his fingers through his hair. This is how he learned that Wendy was pregnant with their third child, Wynne.

Left with far fewer but more significant lines, Bew continued to work hard. He felt the stress of the unpaid commission. Unfortunately, Sonoma – one of his best lines – proved to be yet another company that was late in paying his commission. He called them to try to settle his payment. "Where is my money?"

Sonoma's controller gave Bew the response he dreaded. "Well, we're having cashflow problems."

Bew's voice raised several decibels. "Don't put me in your cashflow problems. I'm your sales person. I should be considered like your employee."

"Well, it doesn't work that way," the controller replied apologetically.

Not again. Bew could not handle this happening again. "I'm going to talk to your boss. Who writes the checks? This is crazy. I am not going to be a payable."

"I'm sorry. That's the way it is."

Bew felt like things were slipping away. He had worked too hard for this to end in failure. In his frustration, he was much less flexible. With the pregnancy, Wendy was frequently unable to work in the office. Bew needed more help. He would complain to her. "You need to be there today. I need you to do this." He would often say such things to her as he left home in the morning. Finally, Wendy made a decision.

One morning, as Bew stressed his need for her help, Wendy informed him, "You need to get somebody else to do this. I didn't sign up for this. I need to take care of the kids."

This was not what Bew wanted to hear. "Somebody else? Then I have to pay someone."

Wendy held her ground. "I need to take care of the kids."

Without a reply, Bew stormed out of the house.

At his office that day, Bew called the employment agency Snelling & Snelling. He was connected with someone who could help him with recruitment. Her name was Amy Strowman. "Mr. White, could you describe for me what sort of person you are looking to hire?"

"I want a female. I want her to be between the ages of twenty-five and thirty. I want someone who is single. I want her to be Jewish."

There was a momentary silence on the other end. Finally, Amy replied, "I can't write any of that. You can't request that."

Bew was unperturbed. "Fine. You know what I want."

Amy sent six different women to meet with Bew, and none of them met Bew's requirements. Finally, Amy went to his office to meet with him. She sat across from him with notepad in hand. "Mr. White, I am here to find out what sort of person you are looking for." She touched her pen to the page, ready for notation.

"What I'm needing is..." Bew thought for a moment. "I'm really needing someone like you. Would you be interested in doing this?"

It dawned on Amy that she did, in fact, meet all of Bew's

requirements – she was female (obviously), of the right age, single and Jewish. She looked up from her notepad, considering his offer. "Yeah. I think I would," she said with reservation.

"Can I hire you?" Bew was serious. Right there, Bew and Amy negotiated, and she agreed to come work for him. Amy left Snelling & Snelling, and Bew hired her full-time.

Further into the pregnancy, Bew and Wendy received some alarming news from Wendy's doctor. The doctor told them that the pregnancy would be very high risk. They were overcome with worry and grief. That night, they had a difficult conversation.

Bew lay in bed, staring at the ceiling. He could not sleep and knew she was awake next to him. He broke the silence. "Wendy, what do we do? I can't lose you."

"I've been praying and praying. I don't know what else to do." Wendy whispered. More silence. Then, "I'm going to go talk with Pastor Hay."

Bew put his arms around her. "Yes. Do that."

Bew and Wendy had recently started attending Covenant Presbyterian, a PCA church planted only a few years earlier. Later that week, Wendy met with the pastor of Covenant Presbyterian, Dr. Bill Hay. The congregation especially loved their pastor for his kindhearted and compassionate nature. He was not judgmental, and he was very conscientious to offer sound, biblical wisdom and words of Christian comfort.

When it came to matters of faith, Bew often looked to Wendy. He knew his wife to be a woman of prayer and devotion. He admired her for this. When he was troubled or anxious, Wendy and her faith served as a rock and support to him. Now, in this moment, he looked to her again for this support. When he returned home from work that day, he was anxious to hear about her meeting with Dr. Hay.

When he saw Wendy in the kitchen, he immediately noticed a change in her demeanor. "So? How did your meeting with Bill Hay go?"

"Wonderful. I know God is in control. He is watching over me and the baby," Wendy answered.

"I'm afraid. You know what the doctor said," Bew pressed.

"I am too. We must keep praying," Wendy spoke confidently. "I trust God to take care of us."

Bew embraced Wendy. Later, in the darkness and stillness of their bedroom, he prayed, "God, keep them safe. I can't lose her. Please, God."

As Wynne's birth approached, Bew was stressed for additional reasons. He did not currently have any health insurance. Bew talked to Daren, and he helped Bew apply for health insurance through Central Manufacturing. Bew got an insurance card in the mail but he was terrified that it might not work. Without this, he would have no way to pay the hospital.

On September 5, 1981, Bew and Wendy's prayers were answered. Wynne Comer White was born a beautiful and healthy baby. Also, much to Bew's relief, his insurance card worked, and he was able to pay for the medical expenses. Bew and Wendy thanked God for his goodness and protection.

CHAPTER 6

TRIAL
AND ERROR

*"The most important thing to do if you find yourself
in a hole is to stop digging."*
- The First Law of Holes

WHEN IT CAME to his own abilities, Bew was an optimist. His business had faced its share of problems, but he felt sure he could put The Vista Corporation in the best possible place to succeed. There was no problem that enough hard work and determination could not resolve. As it happened, events would seem to confirm this for him. In the year of 1982, Bew picked up the Mallin line—a line that proved to be Vista's most significant one yet.

During a cold call visit to an outdoor furniture store in Mississippi, Bew was approached by another sales rep there. "Dude, you can't sell this stuff," the rep said, commenting on Vista's lines. "You'll never make any money like this. Here, I sell this line." Introducing himself as Allen Alterman, he handed Bew a catalog. The line belonged to an outdoor furniture manufacturer called Mallin. Bew was interested.

"They just opened a plant in Atlanta," Allen continued. "What territory do you work?"

Bew told him.

"Okay, it just so happens that they're looking for a rep in your territory. This is the guy to call – Mike Mallin. Go see him now." The rep handed Bew a card.

"Thank you. I'll give him a call." Bew took the card, and the two parted ways.

Bew called Mike Mallin from his office the next day. Mike confirmed that they were looking for a rep in Bew's territory. They met the following week. Mike was duly impressed and agreed to give Bew Mallin's line.

Mallin was significant to Bew for several reasons. Not only would it prove to be a profitable line, but it was also Bew's first real venture into outdoor furniture. This was something he had wanted ever since his time at Blooming Industries.

Bew knew that there were great possibilities that came with a line like this. After speaking with some reps on the west coast, he learned they were making as much as three hundred thousand dollars a year with it. He wondered if he could match such figures in his own Mallin sales.

Later that year, as he was going to see a client in Columbus, Georgia, he decided to try something new. As a rule, he passed over small towns. Since all his other lines were contemporary, he could sell in big cities only. But on a whim, he decided to stop in Dadeville, Alabama to see if he could sell Mallin to a small account. Much to his surprise, he ended up selling ten sets of furniture to a furniture store there. When he did this, he realized the Mallin line was quite different from every other. With this line, he could now make these stops in small towns and sell furniture en route to selling in big cities.

This was transformative to Bew's work. He had finally found his way into the outdoor furniture market, and success had fallen into his lap. In addition to this, he observed that there was very little in the way of competition in this niche. Mallin would become Bew's best seller.

In the meantime, he also continued to sell Central's line. This remained an extremely profitable relationship for both. In this year alone, Bew had made well over one hundred thousand from this. He sold everything Central made. Recently, they had started making cast iron park benches with wood slats. Bew had great success selling them. After showing them to Bernie Marcus in one of their monthly lunches, Home Depot started buying truckloads of the benches. This was yet another major deal between Home Depot and Bew.

Suddenly, Bew got sick with the flu. He was almost completely bedridden for two weeks. When the flu passed, he immediately checked in with Amy. "Has anyone called since I've been sick?"

"No. No one called."

Bew was alarmed. "No one? We should have gotten reorders during that time."

"No. No calls and no reorders."

Bew immediately called Haverty's. "Hi, this is Bew White. How's your stock of baker's racks?"

"Hi, Bew. Yeah, we ran out of stock."

"Why didn't you call to reorder?"

"Because we knew you would call."

Bew took their order and ended the call. He was shocked by what he had heard. He realized The Vista Corporation was far too dependent on him. He had to get the company to a place where it ran more independently.

All the while, Central continued to thrive. To match high demand, their production was rapidly outgrowing their facility. They moved to a property in Pelham on Hinds Street – a quonset hut warehouse of forty-six thousand square feet – far larger than their plant in Fairfield. This new facility suited Central's purposes, giving them adequate space for production with room for further growth.

Central had come a long way since Bew had first started working with them in 1979. Their expansion was greatly owing to Bew's sales. Given this, it seemed quite natural when Daren approached Bew with a business proposal. He offered Bew fifty percent of the property for ten thousand dollars. Central would pay the rent on the note. This sounded like a good deal to Bew.

He accepted.

Bew rode his success into another year. He felt like he was in his prime. After working tirelessly with his Mallin and Central lines, he was making close to $200,000 a year. He was proud of what he had achieved with The Vista Corporation. He had come far since his days with Blooming Industries. It was around this time that Bew set a new goal: he would be a millionaire by the age of forty.

In the following weeks, Bew invested more of his time in Central. He watched as their volume grew exponentially. Home Depot had negotiated larger orders with Central for a discounted price on the benches – the price dropped from $110 to $85. Daren was thrilled with these orders. He did everything he could to cut down the price and increase his volume. Bew began to notice how Daren was often tight for cash because all his money was tied up in receivables and inventory, but since he could always count on getting his commission, he dismissed these concerns.

Sadly, Central was actually in a very poor way. From all outward appearances, business seemed to be better than ever. They were fulfilling massive orders for Home Depot. But Daren had fallen into an all-too-common snare: He had become enamored with increasing volume. Home Depot showed a willingness to make orders as high as a million dollars at a time, but Central had to lower their prices. Daren thought he was making a fortune with such orders, but he was actually running his company into the ground. Their prices had become less than their costs.

In the end, Central lowered the price of their benches from $110 to $27. Bew wondered how Central was sustaining itself with such prices. He tried to voice his concern to Daren, but Daren assured him that all was well.

Eventually, Bew discovered that Daren was hiding the truth. Things were far worse than he could have suspected. Daren had a dangerously high credit with South Trust Bank. He had even been creating false invoices and putting them on his credit line. Finally, Daren did not even have enough money to pay payroll taxes. Bew learned all of this when it was too late. Daren went bankrupt.

Bew was floored. Because he owned half of Central's building, he was summoned to a meeting with Daren and his lawyer along with representatives from South Trust Bank. Bew came with his father representing him.

They all met together at the law firm Bradley, Arant, Rose & White. The dominating personality of the meeting was Daren's lawyer, Jim Rotch. It so happened that Jim and Bew Sr. worked together. In many ways, Jim considered Bew Sr. to be his mentor.

At the outset of the meeting, Jim explained that he would be representing Daren and South Trust. Bew was shocked. He had never seen someone do this. He did not even know this was possible. Both Daren and South Trust were content with their representation.

Knowing that negotiation is all about leverage, Jim advised Daren to invite South Trust to take their best shot. This was Daren's leverage: he had nothing to lose. Bew was amazed as he watched Jim save Daren. Jim got South Trust to agree to give money to Daren to pay off his American Express card.

"This guy is a genius." Bew thought as he watched Jim work the room. After the meeting, Bew made a call, "Jim, this is Bew. Would you be my lawyer?"

"You have your father," Jim replied.

"Well, he is free, but he isn't really because he often gives me a hard time for something I'm doing. I need someone who will give me advice without personal attachment."

Jim agreed to become Bew's lawyer. Bew then called his dad. "I want Jim to be my lawyer now."

"You know you're going to have to pay him." Bew Sr. replied.

"Yeah, I'm fine with that. Now you don't have to worry about getting involved with my business, and it doesn't affect you personally."

"Okay."

For Bew, this was a welcome change. Bew Sr. was more conservative than Bew when it came to business. Bew wanted to be able to work without getting his father mad about something he had done. He felt that Jim better understood his business. Like Bew, Jim was entrepreneurial. In fact, Jim had lost money to investments. This was important to Bew because it meant Jim understood that business required risks.

This was one good result from the meeting, but Bew was soon hit with the hard consequences. As Daren was bankrupt, the ownership of the building was turned over to Bew. This was a huge setback. As a sales rep, Bew had no use for owning a building. He was worried about the payments. His note payment was $5400 (after tax). This meant Bew needed close to $7000 a month to keep a building he did not want in the first place. He immediately put the building up for rent.

Over the next several months, he had two different renters. The first one had to leave when he was unable to pay rent. Bew rented to a second person with a small company. Again, this person was unable to pay rent. Bew was getting desperate. He lacked the funds to pay for the building from his own sales, and renting the building was producing nothing. He evicted the renter and took the renter's equipment as payment for rent. The renter sued Vista.

The lawsuit was a jury trial. The renter got a trial lawyer, and Bew had his insurance company lawyer. Bew lost. He felt sure the trial was lost the moment the jury learned that he was from Mountain Brook. The assumption was Bew was wealthy. He could pay. His insurance company had to pay $20,000. They dropped him after the trial.

To Bew's dismay, misfortune was followed by misfortune. The First National Bank of Alabama threatened to close Bew's loan unless he paid his debt forthwith. Desperation drove Bew to quick action. He took a loan from South Trust Bank equal to the amount of his loan at First National. Taking a check with him, Bew went to pay off his loan and close his account at the First National Bank of Alabama. Assuming Bew would only pay interest on the loan, they were taken aback. They asked him to reconsider, but Bew's mind was made up. "I kind of felt like y'all were getting ready to close my loan. I didn't really appreciate that treatment. I'm done. I'm paying it all off." In effect, he had just transferred his account and loan to South Trust.

Even this act could not spare Bew from a rapid financial decline. By now, he had a negative net worth of $230,000. Jim Davis, the CEO of Jemison Investments and owner of the Pelham building, regularly called Bew, emphasizing the urgency of his mortgage payment. Bew had been stalling, but he knew he could stall no longer. He arranged a meeting with Jim. He was desperate to get out from underneath this overwhelming burden. He told Jim to either take the building or let him pay interest only. Much to his relief, Jim agreed to the latter.

Following this meeting, Bew considered his earlier goal of being a millionaire by the age of forty. In one year, his fortunes —literally and figuratively—had changed dramatically. He felt foolish for setting such a goal.

That summer, one of Bew's friends, Richard Waters, approached him with a generous offer. The two had known each other since elementary school. Richard was aware that times were difficult for Bew. He told Bew that he owned a building on Highlands Avenue that had available space that Bew and Amy were welcome to use for free. Bew accepted Richard's offer with gratitude. It was a porch with high glass windows on a Victorian-style house.

When a third renter failed to pay rent on the Pelham building that fall, Bew stopped renting the building altogether. Knowing he had to fill it up somehow, he began to look for opportunities. He found one that December. Bew had just returned from work when he noticed that their dining room table had new mirror placemats. He had seen these before at friends' houses and at dinner parties. He was noticing the trend.

The next day, Bew met with Nelson Glass in downtown Birmingham. He took a glass placemat from home and showed it to them. He asked them how much it would cost to make glass placemats for The Vista Corporation. They quoted Bew a fair price. He realized he could have great profit margins with these. This was how he could pay the building's rent.

In the January Atlanta Gift Market of 1985, Bew filled their showroom—a showroom which had come to him along with the Pelham building—with Vista glass mirror placemats and Vista mirrors. These new products generated a fair amount of interest at the market and sold well. Bew was thrilled with this. He resolved to find more products to fill his warehouse and to sell in his showroom.

Recently, Bew had observed the rise of outdoor umbrellas. Many of his accounts were selling or looking to sell them. More particularly, many of his customers were asking for umbrella bases. He learned that many were buying umbrella bases from a company called Diversified Products. Headquartered in Opelika, Alabama, Diversified Products was one of several businesses belonging to the entrepreneurial Fob James, the former governor of Alabama. Bew asked Diversified Products if they could make colored bases for Vista. They agreed. With this, Bew started a new line and called it 'The Base Company.' It would soon become highly profitable for Vista.

That spring, Bew and Amy moved their office again. Richard told them that the newly constructed building next door also belonged to him. He asked them if they wanted to move their office there, again rent-free. Bew and Amy accepted. They were happy to move out of the porch, which had no heat or air conditioning.

By 1986, Bew's position became stronger. He found his footing once again. While his salary was small, business was great. At first, Bew had gotten into manufacturing out of desperation to pay the Pelham building's rent, but this did far more than pay the building's rent. In addition to this, Vista sales were as good as ever. By now, Bew's sales for Mallin over the past few years exceeded two million.

In these times, Amy often was left to run Vista's day-to-day operations while Bew was gone working on the road. Bew knew he could always trust her with these responsibilities. Amy appreciated this trust. He gave her the freedom to work in a capacity where she was making major decisions, often daily. She considered Bew a great mentor. He was not controlling, open to new processes and methods, and allowed her to make mistakes and learn.

Amy also played another important role for Bew. He was an effective and driven businessman, but he also had the habit of speaking without a filter. She helped smooth out situations where he had caused some friction. Also, she was not afraid to push back against him when the situation might call for it. At one market, she recalled they were talking to a group of salesmen. Mid-conversation, without a word, Bew handed her his empty Coca-Cola bottle. Amy glared at him and said, "Excuse me? The garbage can is right there." Bew complied.

One day, Amy suggested that they hire another person. "Bew, I can't do it all. It's too much. I know somebody. She's a legal assistant at Sirote."

Bew recognized that this hire had been necessary for some time now. He agreed. "Okay, let's bring her in."

When Honie came into the office to see Bew, their meeting was not so much an interview as it was a pitch. Straddling his chair, he pitched Honie on Vista and on his many business ideas. She felt she understood Bew's drive and his vision. Bew sensed this, and he duly hired her.

While Vista had gone through some major changes, Bew still worked as closely as he could with his other reps around the country. One of these sales reps was in Seattle. He called Bew that spring to tell him that he had been talking with a major Dutch furniture company named IKEA. IKEA was opening a store in Seattle in a couple of months. Bew had never heard of IKEA, but he agreed to come to Seattle for the store's grand opening. When he went a couple of months later, he was greatly impressed. IKEA's furniture display was beyond any he had seen.

Upon his return to Birmingham, he received a call from this same sales rep.

"Bew, IKEA called to buy an order of Amisco bunk beds." Amisco was a Canadian company Bew had picked up at High Point several years earlier.

"What's the size of the order?" Bew asked excitedly.

"It's an $80,000 order with a backup order of another $80,000," the rep said jubilantly.

"Wow. That's huge."

This was Vista's largest order to date. Bew was thrilled, but he felt some slight misgivings. The order seemed too big. Bew sensed this sales rep might be resentful at splitting commission on the deal. Vista's sales reps knew the deal – for their Vista sales they would receive seven percent commission and Bew would receive three percent.

In the following year, Bew suffered a terrible blow. His outlook on Vista changed entirely. While the company was not as he had originally conceived, it still mostly followed the model on which it had been founded. Manufacturing was a new step for Vista, but Bew still saw himself primarily as a sales rep and the head of a sales rep company. Certainly, he had suffered setbacks, but he felt that Vista was finally settling into a groove. He was mistaken.

Bew had profited nicely from the IKEA-Amisco deal. All of the Vista sales reps working with Amisco resented him for this. They decided jointly to cut him out of all future deals. Amisco sales had grown to nearly $200,000 a month. They no longer wanted to share the commission with Bew. This endeavor was headed up by the sales rep in Seattle who had orchestrated the Amisco sale with IKEA. These reps approached Amisco and asked the company to make all future deals with them only. Amisco agreed.

When Bew learned of this, he was outraged that Amisco and his sales reps had swindled him. He warned his reps not to do this. He told them that they were just "screwing themselves."

They ignored him. They moved forward without him. Amisco became nervous that Bew might sue the company as they were in clear violation of contract. The Amisco sales manager called Bew to try to settle the conflict peacefully, but Bew would not have it.

Bew consulted with Jim Rotch who advised him against pursuing a lawsuit. The lawsuit would cost at least $100,000. It was not worth the trouble. Bew was displeased, but he agreed. Amisco still owed him commission. He demanded they pay it, and they quickly did. He finally agreed to let Amisco out of the contract and then dropped their line.

This was a major blow, and it proved the insurmountable shortcomings of this business model. Further growth was impossible for The Vista Corporation. This sort of model – the division of commission between Bew and his sales reps – only worked with smaller numbers. The better a line sold, the bigger the numbers became, which increased the likelihood that his reps would cut him out. Bew knew that the Vista model would no longer work for him.

From this moment forward, Bew decided he would stop traveling all over the U.S. to help his reps sell. Now, he would sell in his territory only. He would also spend more time manufacturing and selling his own products. He had a building to keep up. Bew did not consult anyone in this, he simply made the change.

SUMMER CLASSICS

"Man, I'm sure glad I didn't go to work at Bama Feeds.
I'd be selling dog food – or out of business."
- Bew White

THE YEAR OF 1987 was a significant one for Bew. After the Amisco debacle, Bew turned his focus to Vista's manufacturing. This latest venture proved to be quite profitable. Bew knew Vista needed to continue growing its own line. While the company was changing in this regard, Bew would continue to rep for reliable lines such as Mallin, and he would rep for Vista.

Significantly, ever since the Base Company's start in 1985, Bew had finally taken on a greater role in product design which he had long desired. He felt validated in the recent success of his base designs and was full of ideas. He felt he knew the market and the trends and was ready to design more Vista products.

Bew reached out to David Traylor and his business partner Bill Davis—unfinished furniture manufacturers in Birmingham. He had seen their work, and he was duly impressed. He asked David if they would start manufacturing cypress Chippendale furniture for Vista according to his designs. David told Bew they could do it, but Bew would have to paint the furniture himself. They came to an agreement. Soon, David and Bill were making

Vista Chippendale planters and benches. Then, Bew had these products delivered to the warehouse to be painted, stocked, and shipped.

He found another manufacturer in Clanton, Alabama who agreed to make Vista Adirondack chairs. These chairs were all manufactured out of Tupelo wood. They were knock-down, ready-to-assemble chairs. Bew bought them at a very cheap price. Unfortunately, he soon learned the chairs were also cheaply made—they all rotted quickly. He was disappointed. He added this to his MBA of mistakes to learn for the future.

Though Bew had cut back on how widely he was traveling, he was still gone nearly as often in his territory in order to keep the business going. He was also just as busy with markets all year long. As Bew traveled and worked the markets, he picked up more new products. He got into wicker. He discovered a customer at Myrtle Beach whose wicker furniture he could buy and sell. He also discovered Chippendale planters at an unfinished wood dealer's place in South Carolina. He made a deal with the dealer and soon started buying them by the truckload. Vista would paint them and sell them. He sold all of these products in the Vista line.

Bew had also begun doing something new with the Mallin line. He started buying their product and stocking it in Pelham. He did this to have better control over the whole sale – the inventory and the decision concerning who got it. With all his Mallin sales, Bew could now have a quicker turnaround, and he had a better profit margin.

Bew could not know, but this same year, one of his sales stops in Spartanburg, South Carolina would change the direction of his career and his company. He made a stop at Stuckey Brothers Furniture Company. Bew was familiar with Stuckey Brothers, as he had done much business with them in the past. This day, as he walked around their basement, his eyes fell upon some white Adirondack chairs. Chairs like this were hard to find. He wanted some for himself. As Bew got closer to the chairs, he read the scripty logo on the hangtag - Summer Classics. At that moment, the store owner Curtis Hart walked down the stairs. He walked to Bew with extended hand. "Hey, Bew. How's it going?"

Bew shook his hand. "Hey, Curtis. What's this 'Summer Classics' stuff?"

"Oh. That's me."

"What do you mean 'me?' You're a retailer." In these days, it was extremely rare that a company did manufacturing *and* owned retail stores. Ethan Allen was one of the only companies that was doing this at the time.

"Well, I have this guy across town making these Adirondack chairs out of cherry wood and painting them for me. Then I sell them."

"I love that name—Summer Classics. How did you think of that?"

Curtis shrugged, "I don't know. I just thought it was a good name."

"It is a *great* name," Bew spoke with emphasis. "I love it."

Later, as Bew drove back to Birmingham, he thought about the name on the hangtag – Summer Classics. "I love that name," Bew thought. "That could be something."

When Bew returned to his office, he spoke to a lawyer, Thad Long, about trademarking the name. After further inquiry, Thad informed Bew about "first use"—he couldn't have the name unless Curtis signed the name over to him or else abandoned it. Bew insisted the lawyer check on the trademark all the same. This was a mail-in form process which would take weeks, maybe months. Bew waited eagerly for the results.

Earlier in the year, Bew and Wendy had begun looking to move. They acted promptly when a house on Cherokee Road went on the market that fall. Though it required some fixing up, Bew quite liked it. It was only two houses down from Bew's parents. Bew quickly closed on the house. Much to Wendy's annoyance, he also agreed to rent out their house on Wilderness Road before their new house was ready for them. Because of this, Bew and his family had to move into an apartment at Rime

Garden Inn for a little over a month while their new house was being fixed up.

Bew and Wendy remember this time well. While living in the Rime Garden Inn, Bew and Wendy became quite sick – so sick that Wendy's mom had to stay with them to take care of them and the kids. They also recall that Christmas well. While they could not stay in the new house, they did put up a Christmas tree. They put gifts under the tree on Christmas Eve. On Christmas day, they took the kids to the new house to celebrate. "Look, Santa came to our house!" Bew and Wendy told the kids. They were very happy when the renovations were finished and they could move into their new home.

In the spring of the following year, when pollen visibly coated trees, cars and everything in the open air, Bew finally got the call he had been waiting for – Thad told him that Summer Classics was not trademarked. Straightway, Bew acted on this information and called Curtis at Stuckey Brothers.

"Hi, this is Bew White. Are you doing anything with that 'Summer Classics' thing?"

"No. The guy across town who was making it for me went out of business. I'm not doing anything with it anymore," Curtis replied.

"Can I have it?" Bew asked.

"Sure," Curtis said indifferently.

"Great! I'm going to send you something. Will you sign it and send it back to me?"

"No problem."

Bew sent Curtis the proper form and Curtis sent it back with his signature, legally signing the name over to Bew. So Bew got the name Summer Classics. He made a scripty logo. He was now ready to have a proper go at outdoor furniture.

"Honie!" Bew dropped a folder on Honie's desk. "I want you to look at these and tell me what you think."

Honie opened the folder which contained his handwritten Summer Classics logo. Then, there was a stack of outdoor furniture drawings and sketches. It was the Summer Classics line.

Bew had long wanted to make his own outdoor furniture. He had been working in the outdoor business long enough to know the market well and was greatly underwhelmed by the products he saw. As he saw it, most outdoor furniture was primarily functional and comfort driven. The industry was rife with poor design. It lacked beauty. None of the furniture was anything he particularly wanted at his own home. Bew wanted to create furniture that was beautiful to look at—furniture that transformed an outdoor living space.

The office was buzzing with excitement. Work was never slow at Vista, but now, everyone was filled with a new energy. Bew's drive and enthusiasm were contagious. Everyone was champing at the bit, eager to see Bew's vision come to life.

Bew reached out to David Trailer and gave him his designs. David agreed to start manufacturing Summer Classics cypress outdoor furniture. Per Bew's designs, they made two collections. The first collection was the Ponte Vedra collection. They produced another collection called Windsor. These included several different dining chairs and Adirondack chairs. They also produced a white fifty-four inch octagon table. They built all this furniture and Bew had it painted and stocked at the warehouse. He was ready to take his Summer Classics line to market and on the road.

Around this time, Bew hired Neal Morgan. Neal had just graduated from college and was looking for work. He got connected with Bew through his friendship with Billy Kruger—one of Vista's dock workers. Bew initially brought Neal on board to move the books from the old green ledger sheets onto Peachtree (the accounting software of the day). But, soon after, recognizing the young man's abilities, he asked Neal to take over Vista's shipping operation. Neal would remain with the company for the next three decades.

In the following weeks and months, Vista was busier than ever with the work of painting the Summer Classics furniture, stocking it, selling it, and shipping it. They had Summer Classics booths at market, and they sold the furniture to clients on the road. Bew also handed the Summer Classics line to one of Vista's reps.

Casual Market in Chicago was especially memorable this year. It was in this moment that Bew's business went international. While making his rounds at the market, he was drawn to the wooden umbrellas of Sombra. They had a wooden spider system and a canvas top. Ordinarily, such umbrellas sold for $500, but Sombra was selling them for $100. Bew was astounded. "How do you do that? I could sell the hell out of these," he addressed the man running Sombra's booth. The two soon exchanged names. This was Juan Cabesa. Juan was Chilean, and all his umbrellas were manufactured in Chile and shipped to Costa Mesa, California, where Juan operated his business. Bew wanted these umbrellas. Soon, an agreement was reached, and Bew became a Sombra distributor.

"You buy containers, and you ship on the east coast. I'll ship everything on the west coast," Juan told him.

Soon enough, Bew was receiving these umbrellas by the container and shipping them from Pelham all across the east coast. Vista had to handle this, the new Summer Classics line along with their usual stocking, selling and shipping of umbrella bases and Mallin furniture. Vista's production was growing rapidly, and they found that their work required them to go back and forth between their office in Downtown Birmingham and the warehouse in Pelham almost every day. At year end, Amy had a suggestion. What if they moved their office to Pelham? Considering how frequently they went out there to check on shipments and operations, it would be more efficient. This made good sense to Bew. He agreed.

In the new year of 1989, Bew, Amy and Honie thanked Richard Waters for generously letting them use his building space, and they moved to Pelham. It was nice to have one centralized place of work. This was one major improvement, but initially, the office conditions were poor, to say the least. Many days, Amy and Honie had to literally wipe mouse droppings off of their desks.

Business was good for Bew, but one thing was not changing—he still traveled weeks which added up to months through the course of a year. For years now, he had been trying to cut down on his traveling. He regretted all that he was missing at home. For example, every January he was at the Atlanta Market and every January he missed William's birthday. He had three young children at home who were growing up quickly. Wendy and the children needed him to be home. At a company party, Wendy asked Honie and Amy, "When can you get Bew off the road?" She said this in a teasing manner, but in reality, she was pleading with them. Wendy wanted her husband at home. Bew felt this. He promised her he would try to make it happen.

This was easier said than done. The business was extremely dependent upon Bew. He had learned this the hard way, and it frightened him. He felt the great burden of creating a business that was sustainable. He feared that if he let up even a little, the company would fail. He knew he had to do something to make the business depend less on him. Bew determined that he had to get off the road—for good. This meant Vista needed to make a radical change.

Bew stressed this to his team and had their support. They loved his family, and they wanted to help him. With this in mind, they all did everything they could to make Summer Classics monetize to a certain place that Bew could get off the road from now on.

In this period, there were several other companies that had just started going in a similar direction as Vista with outdoor furniture—companies such as Restoration Hardware. Bew was well acquainted with many of these companies including Gardener's Eden, Plow and Hearth, Saks Fifth Avenue, Neiman Marcus, and Crate and Barrel. Bew asked Honie to make a concerted effort to get Summer Classics into their home catalogs. He wanted to distance himself from the mom-and-pop outdoor furniture of the day. Summer Classics was high-end furniture for high end living. These home catalogs targeted just the kind of clientele that Bew wanted to reach.

Honie made a point of getting to know these companies, befriending those who worked there. Soon, several companies, such as Gardener's Eden (a subsidiary of Williams Sonoma), agreed to put Summer Classics in their home catalogs. They admired the beauty and quality of Summer Classics furniture.

In these days, Bew did the photography himself. He would load up some furniture and go to a place such as the Birmingham Botanical Gardens to set up the furniture. To help make everything as elegant as possible, he would take dishes and other accessories from home. After seeing him do this a time or two, Wendy intervened.

"Billy! What are you doing?" Wendy asked crossly as she watched Bew pick up a stack of dishes.

"I just need these for some photography. I promise to take care of them." As Bew spoke the stack of dishes swayed in his hands. He quickly rebalanced.

Wendy winced. "This is nuts! Here, give them to me." Bew withdrew. "I'll help you."

Hearing this, Bew gladly handed her the dishes. He knew he was out of his depth here. "Thank you!" He gave her a peck on the cheek. "You're a lifesaver."

Wendy mumbled something under her breath as she carried the dishes out to the car. With Wendy's help (she was especially gifted with flower arrangements), Bew was able to frame beautiful and appealing scenes with Summer Classics furniture for the home catalogs.

As a few businesses picked up Summer Classics for their home catalogs, more started to reach out to Vista. They loved what they saw of Summer Classics and wanted the line in their own catalogs. This was all great business for Vista. Getting into so many of these home catalogs helped establish the Summer Classics brand. The brand benefitted by its association with these companies, and it reached its target audience from a wider platform. Summer Classics was becoming more than just your ordinary outdoor furniture line. The line had emotion. People felt a connection to the product because it represented a certain way of living.

This is exactly what Bew had wanted all along. He was interested in creating more than just a product—he was interested in a lifestyle. When people looked at Summer Classics furniture, Bew wanted them to see what he envisioned—beautifully furnished spaces where they might share memorable moments with their friends, family and loved ones.

Up to this point, Vista's production had been a means to pay for the Pelham building. Bew had always paid his salary out of his sales commission. Finally, Summer Classics was getting to a place where Bew could pay his salary from its sales. He decided it was time to start resigning his lines.

He decided he would get off the road by January, 1990 which was only months away. When he called his lines to tell them that he would get off the road by this date, many asked him to reconsider, but he was resolute.

As January neared, something happened which validated Bew's decision to get off the road and push Summer Classics. Indeed, he saw that he needed to go yet further. Bew was at his desk when the receptionist walked into his office.

"Mr. White, lately, whenever people call, I answer the phone, 'The Vista Corporation.' They say 'Is this Summer Classics?' How should I respond?"

She had Bew's full attention. "How do you answer?"

"I say that this is Vista."

Bew smiled. He had a wonderful sense of clarity. This was a sign. "From now on, I want you to answer the phone as 'Summer Classics.' Let me know how that goes."

"Okay."

As the receptionist walked out, Bew leaned back in his chair. He knew now that Summer Classics was the future. He did not consciously decide that Vista must be subsumed into Summer Classics, but Summer Classics now so dominated his focus that this would inevitably come to pass.

That long-awaited January day in 1990 came and went. Bew called all his lines. "This is my last day on the road," he told them. They still asked him to reconsider. He would not. "No. I'm done," he reiterated. Some believed he would eventually return, but he did not.

Yet another even more significant January day came. Bew said his goodbyes and left work early. He was taking the rest of the day off. As he drove home, he felt exuberant. He was done with the long trips. He was finished with the constant loneliness. He would not have to face rejection after rejection as a sales rep often must. He was ready to be home and to spend time with his wife and children. He parked the car in the driveway, walked through the door, and shouted, "Happy birthday, William!"

GO *SOUTH,* YOUNG MAN

"Go forth to meet the shadowy future without fear
and with a manly heart."
- Henry Wadsworth Longfellow

BEW FELT VALIDATED regarding his decision to get off the road and give Summer Classics the lion's share of his attention. Not only was the Summer Classics line selling well, it was quickly gaining a reputation for its quality, beauty in design, and comfort. Bew and his team knew their future depended on the success of this line.

For it to succeed, Bew knew he had a lot of work to do. He had to put Summer Classics in front of people in home catalogs and at markets. This was impressed on him all the more when he decided to take Summer Classics back from his Vista rep. To his horror, this rep had not only done poorly with the line, he had taken the line all the way to zero. Bew was furious.

Thankfully, Bew could take solace in the fact that Summer Classics was already selling in the home catalogs of Gardener's Eden, Plow and Hearth, Neiman Marcus, Saks Fifth Avenue, Crate & Barrel, Restoration Hardware, John Deere, and Frontgate. This was no small achievement. As a result, orders were steadily coming in, and their production volume was increasing.

This kept David Traylor and Bill Davis busy manufacturing and Bew's team busy with the painting and shipping.

In addition to all this, Bew continued to work with Juan Cabesa in Costa Mesa and the factory in Chile. Bew was beginning to view this relationship as increasingly significant. Since the time he started this partnership in 1988, the market umbrellas had sold quite well. Recently, Bew was becoming aware of the fact that Juan's relations with the factory were tense. Indeed, tensions had just come to a head when the Chilean factory burned down. Juan claimed the fire was deliberate. He suspected they did it to get insurance money. Bew didn't know what to make of all this.

Coincidentally, Bew and Wendy were going to Chile in March of that very year for the wedding of Bew's friend and college roommate Michael Young. Michael, who was now a familiar personality on ESPN and MSNBC, was getting married to Cecilia Bolocco, a recent winner of Miss Universe (the first Chilean to win this most prestigious of beauty pageants). In Chile, Cecilia was an icon.

Bew and Wendy were soon to glimpse that this was not your ordinary wedding. It was a national event—politically and culturally charged to the extreme. For a country that had no personalities or achievements to speak of on the world stage, Miss Universe, Cecilia Bolocco, gave Chile what it so desperately longed for—the international spotlight, even if for only a moment. There, this wedding was being called "the wedding of the century." It was receiving the media attention of a royal wedding.

The event attracted the attentions of the most powerful, successful and ambitious Chileans. Indeed, when Michael and Cecilia announced their marriage, Chilean dictator and president Augusto Pinochet offered to make available the cathedral La Recoleta Dominica—one of Chile's most beautiful monuments—for the wedding and the presidential palace for the reception. Cecilia said that she would only accept this if the newly elected president Patricio Aylwin agreed to it. In the following weeks, Michael and Cecilia were involved in private meetings with Augusto Pinochet and Patricio Aylwin. In the end, all agreed the cathedral and presidential palace would be used for the wedding.

Bew decided to make this trip dual-purpose—before going to the wedding, he would do business with his Chilean colleagues. He and Wendy went to stay on the Chilean coast a few days before the wedding. Bew met separately with Juan Cabesa and Pablo (the man who ran the Chile factory). They spent the time discussing future business. After the factory burned down, Juan's supply of umbrellas was cut off. Pablo was in the process of getting things underway in a new factory. Bew voiced his interest in working with both, but it was apparent that Juan and Pablo were not keen on working with one another.

Business aside, Bew and Wendy enjoyed their experience of the coast and the nearby towns with Juan and Pablo serving as their guides. In a couple of days, Bew and Wendy took the two-hour bus ride to Santiago to the beautiful hotel La Carrera—the hotel hosting many of the wedding's guests.

After settling in, Bew and Wendy embarked upon a motor coach along with Michael Young, Taylor Boyd, Stewart Jackson, Robert Vick and Barry Williams (of Brady Bunch fame), and they went to Viña del Mar (meaning "Vineyard of the Sea")—a beautiful Pacific coastal region in central Chile. They came to the home of the wealthy, well-known Chilean antique dealers and gay couple Victor and Jorge. Victor and Jorge wined and dined the group at their beautiful estate. Sitting at a high elevation, the estate offered a wonderful panoramic view of the coast. Bew and Wendy were especially impressed by the house's infinity pool. This level of wealth and extravagance made Mountain Brook look third world.

The next day—wedding day—Bew and Wendy boarded a waiting motor coach along with Michael and Cecilia's other friends. Embarking from La Carrera, the coach followed the wedding motorcade with the couple, the couple's family and the other wedding guests towards the cathedral La Recoleta Dominica. As they approached the cathedral, Bew and Wendy were astounded to see thousands of Chileans gathered in the streets (there were around forty-eight thousand people). The streets were closed off to all traffic. The crowd cheered wildly as the coach passed them. For security, the Chilean army was out in force.

As the coach got nearer to the cathedral, the crowds became so thick that the bus had to stop and unload its passengers to walk the rest of the way. As Michael and Cecilia disembarked, the crowd let out a loud cheer. The couple waved. Then, for every other person who disembarked, the crowd cheered. When Bew and Wendy stepped out, the crowd gave another loud cheer. Bew and Wendy were wide-eyed. As they all walked towards the cathedral, Michael, Cecilia, and their celebrity friends waved with confidence to the cheering Chileans, as if this were a common experience for them. Seeing the astonishment on Bew and Wendy's faces, Barry Williams chuckled. "Just wave. Like this," he demonstrated.

Bew smiled and shook his head in disbelief, "You're the only famous one here." He was extremely amused by all of this.

"They don't know that." Barry grinned. Bew and Wendy waved as they walked towards the church. They were thrilled at this glimpse into another world. For a brief moment, they were a celebrity couple.

Soon they came to the high iron rod gate leading into the cathedral's courtyard. Modeled after the Roman Basilica Saint Paul Outside the Walls, La Recoleta Dominica was a sight to behold. Bew and Wendy looked up in awe at the cathedral's façade. Six marble Corinthian columns towered before them. As was the custom in Chile, Michael Young and the mother of the bride stood on the stairs greeting the wedding guests—there were one thousand six hundred people in attendance. Michael greeted Bew and Wendy, "Mucho gusto."

Purposely exaggerating his southern accent, Bew said wryly, "Gracias." He shook his old roommate's hand.

Michael smiled and winked as Bew and Wendy passed

through the cathedral's high, ornate double oak doors. They took their seats between fifty-two marble columns which upheld a high decorative dome made of Oregon pine. Behind the guests Chile's largest Catholic choir sang. Finally, when all the guests had taken their seats, and Michael had fulfilled his greeting duties as the groom, the double doors were closed. The roar of the crowd outside subsided, and the Cathedral fell into a hush.

Again, the choir took up its singing with zeal and emotion. Michael and Cecilia walked ceremoniously to the cathedral's altar. As Cecilia walked, the train of her wedding dress trailed behind her. When Michael and Cecilia reached the altar, her train reached from the double oak doors all the way to the altar. Bew and Wendy were breathless at Cecilia's beauty. She wore a gracefully fitted white wedding dress and a bejeweled tiara. Michael and Cecilia stood alone at the front with the justice of the peace. Technically, they had already been married at Cecilia's home in a civil ceremony by this same justice, but now, it was time for the show. This was more than a wedding—it was a moment on the world stage, and many Chileans saw it as such.

Behind Cecilia and Michael kneeled both sets of parents on kneeling benches. The whole wedding was conducted in Spanish. It was a solemn, drawn-out Catholic affair. For two Presbyterians from Alabama, the ceremony felt foreign to Bew and Wendy. This was a cultural event of the like they never thought they would experience.

As the ceremony concluded, the voices of the choir resounded through the cathedral while the couple and their guests exited into the streets. When the double oak doors swung open, the roars of the crowd poured forth. "Cecilia! Cecilia!" The crowd chanted on and on. Bew heard the choir emanating from speakers outside—he realized the crowd had listened to the entire wedding over a speaker system.

As Bew and Wendy came to the doors, people began climbing the courtyard fence. Fearing they might be trampled in the frenzy of the crowd, Bew pulled Wendy back into the church. But they soon realized people were only coming to shower Michael and Cecilia in rice. The newly wedded couple got into a Mercedes bulletproof stretch limo (courtesy of Pinochet) and took off towards the presidential palace.

Bew and Wendy walked back to their coach as the crowds dispersed. Soon, their coach took them to the presidential palace for the reception. As they drove up the long approach, Bew and Wendy took in the sight of the palace. There was no end to this wedding's extravagance. Bew, Wendy, and their group were ushered through the palace and out onto the palace grounds, which were covered in a vast network of tents. Under the tents, there were tables and seating for eight hundred people. At every seat, there was fine china supplied by Chile's largest china manufacturer. About a hundred yards away, a band played an upbeat tune. Bew and Wendy soon found Michael and Cecilia and congratulated the couple. Before he was swept off to speak with some Chilean dignitaries, Michael genuinely thanked his friends.

The reception went on for hours. There was much talking, eating (the bride and groom's families sat at one long banquet table while guests sat at surrounding tables), drinking, and dancing. Important Chileans milked this occasion for all it was worth – networking, politicking, conspiring, and the like—this was happening all around Bew and Wendy. The American government was also aware of the international implications of this event, and they would not let such an opportunity pass them by. Unbeknownst to them, Bew and Wendy were also brushing elbows with American officials and CIA agents who had gotten themselves "invited" to the wedding. But what was this to them? They were enjoying themselves immensely.

At one point in the evening, everyone heard the sound of a distant explosion. "What was that?" Bew asked in alarm. The Chileans around him seemed to show little concern.

It was soon explained to the Americans that such things were not out of the ordinary in this tense time for Chile, but they should not be alarmed. Bew and Wendy were not fully satisfied by this response, but they were soon swept back into the festivities of the reception. Their fears slowly subsided.

Bew and Wendy stayed as long as they could. The reception continued into the early hours of the next day. Finally, at two in the morning, they had to tap out. They tracked down Michael.

"Michael, we're sorry, but we need to go." Bew said ruefully. "Awesome wedding!" he added.

"Billy, Wendy, I am so glad you both came. It means so much to me. Let's catch up again in the States soon!" Michael hugged his friends.

The next day, Bew and Wendy started their return to Alabama. Still, they marveled at this experience of a lifetime. But now, the responsibilities of home beckoned.

AS THE END OF 1990 APPROACHED, Bew cut ties with Mallin —one of those remaining connections to his sales rep days. It was the familiar tale: Mallin was having cashflow problems. Bew had still been buying inventory from Mallin, but recently, sensing that Mallin was having financial troubles, he had delayed in paying them for their most recent delivery of furniture. Sure enough, Mallin's controller called Bew, "You have fifty thousand for the inventory you bought."

Bew was ready, "Well, you guys owe me fifty thousand in commission."

In the end, Bew and Mallin reached a settlement: they would offset. Bew would keep the furniture without paying, and Mallin would keep his commission. Bew was fortunate. Most reps never received their final commission dues. Soon after, Mallin went bankrupt.

In 1991, Bew's business with Chile became complicated. He was still a distributor for Sombra on the east coast. He still placed much significance in his relationship with Juan and the Chile factory, but this relationship was to change drastically. Pablo and his factory cut ties with Juan. Now, Juan was searching for a new factory. Pablo asked Bew to keep working with them, and Juan told Bew he would find a new factory. This was a difficult decision for Bew. On the one hand, he liked the idea of working directly with the factory, but on the other hand, he knew what it was like to be cut out of a deal. He hated to do this to Juan.

In the end, Bew decided to work directly with the factory. Juan warned Bew against this, but he was not angry with Bew. The two of them talked about trying to continue working together as Juan was in the process of getting his product through a new factory. In the end, nothing came of this, and Bew's business relationship with Juan and Sombra petered out.

While Bew remained involved in the umbrella market, so, too, he remained involved with the Base Company, selling umbrella bases. It was a profitable line. Indeed, this year, he acquired a new account—Service Merchandise. They became one of the largest accounts for Summer Classics with orders amounting to over $300,000 in a year.

The seasons passed, and Bew pushed on with his work. He kept up a brutal schedule. For markets, he could be away for three weeks at a time. Additionally, he often traveled to sell Summer Classics. This took its toll on Bew and his family. Bew always dreamed of the day when he could spend more time at home, but Summer Classics required his constant attention. The work was highly dependent on him. He struggled under a constant fear that Summer Classics would not succeed, and he would not be able to support his family.

Wendy and his children remember his long absences well. Walker, William, and Wynne struggled to understand why he did this. Sometimes, they even felt resentful towards him. Like so many children, they longed for their father's love and attention. Bew did love them, and they knew it. Indeed, he could be very encouraging and uplifting, but while he was working, they were growing up. They wanted to spend more time with him. Throughout their upbringing, it was Wendy who raised the children mostly on her own. She gave the children her all, and they knew it. Bew was grateful for Wendy. He knew how much his children leaned upon her. He, too, looked to her for support and encouragement. In his eyes, Wendy was the rock of their home.

Late in 1991, business in Chile took a fortunate turn for Bew and Summer Classics. Business with Pablo had now slowed nearly to a halt and Bew was diverting his attention to domestic manufacturing. Then, another factory in Chile made contact with him. The manager of the factory Sergio Delgado was aware of Summer Classics' involvement in Chile through connections with Pablo. The two negotiated, and Bew planned to come down to Chile to see their operation and meet the factory's ownership.

When Bew went to Chile, he stayed in Santiago. In the morning, Sergio picked him up and drove Bew to the factory, which was about an hour away. Bew and Sergio got on well right away. Sergio was affable, intelligent, and, luckily for Bew, he spoke fluent English.

When they arrived at the factory, they drove through a gate. On the right-hand side of the compound, there were logs stacked two stories high in tin roof sheds. Further along, there was a tin-roof sawmill with no sides and a dirt floor. It was primitive but functional. Sergio parked in front of a shack and welcomed Bew into his office. The office was a wide open, dank room with a single twenty watt light bulb suspended by a wire over a dusty wooden desk.

"Come in!" Sergio said cheerily, walking ahead of Bew. "Coffee?" he asked as he prepared a coffee percolator.

"Thanks," Bew said, scanning the room in wonder. It looked more like an interrogation room than an office.

Soon, they were seated around the desk. Sergio handed Bew a cup of coffee and the two talked business. Bew shared his vision for a new Summer Classics line. He showed Sergio his designs. They talked pricing and delivery. Sergio guaranteed Bew that they could produce the line and deliver product in a timely fashion. Bew was excited. He saw a lot of potential here.

The two spent the next hour or so touring the factory. Sergio acted as Bew's guide and translator as they explored the sawmill and spoke to a few of the workers. The operation was quite active. It seemed sufficient for what Bew needed.

After a few days of further discussion and meetings, which included a meeting with the factory owners at their blueberry farm, Bew returned to Alabama, feeling sure of this new business partnership. The factory got straight to work. In the months that followed, Bew felt validated. Sergio and the Chilean factory produced quality furniture per Bew's designs. Bew loved seeing his vision come to reality.

The year of 1992 was one of promise for Bew and Summer Classics. As the orders grew, so the production volume grew. Bew kept many irons in the fire. He was producing domestically and internationally. The Base Company continued to be profitable. Summer Classics had a wide presence in catalogs and markets.

Yet, there were bumps along the way. Bew received a discouraging report from a loyal customer in Mountain Brook: his domestically produced cypress benches were rotting. Straightaway, Bew went to her house. Sure enough, the benches were rotting at the feet. Bew sawed off the feet and replaced them with new feet. He was alarmed. He kept a couple of these same benches in his own backyard. Going home to check them, a quick analysis confirmed that these benches were rotting as well. Bew knew they had to move away from cypress immediately.

Bew reached out to David Traylor and Bill Davis. He informed them that the cypress wood was rotting. "We need to change woods. We can't use cypress anymore."

Traylor promised to look into a change. In the end, they moved away from cypress to Spanish cedar. Bew was relieved, but this incident got him thinking about his other furniture. He realized that he knew very little about wood. He needed to do his research.

One of the woods Bew discovered in his research was a South American wood called roble. By reputation, roble was extremely durable and high quality. It was as hard as concrete. He would not need to worry about this wood rotting. This would a good material for his furniture. Bew decided to call Sergio to tell him about the rotting of the cypress furniture.

"We use linga here. It won't rot." Sergio assured Bew.

"Yeah, that's what we thought about the cypress." Bew said skeptically. "Can you get any roble wood there? I want to use that. I've heard it has wonderful durability and longevity."

"I can check."

Soon, Sergio called Bew to tell him that it was illegal for them to use roble in Chile. "It is an endangered wood."

Bew went back to the drawing board. Eventually, he settled on pressure-treated pine. Ordinarily, pressure-treated pine required a year to dry out before it could be painted. Bew did not have a year. Because of this, no one was producing pressure-treated pine furniture. But he found a way past this: kiln drying. The wood could be dried in massive kiln ovens and then painted. After much discussion, Bew convinced Sergio to move the factory over to pressure-treated pine.

This was an involved process. It meant the installation of large pressurized tanks and a room-sized kiln. The pine would be treated in these tanks full of chromated copper arsenate until the pine had one hundred percent moisture. Then, the factory would dry the pine in the kiln long enough to take most of the moisture out of the pine. At this point, the pine was ready to be painted. This worked wonderfully. Bew was thrilled with the results. This change put Summer Classics far ahead of its competition.

By the end of the year, Bew had gone to Chile four times. This was to become a trend. He often went to Chile to help the factory with new designs. He and Sergio got on well. Bew became familiar with Sergio and his family, and the two enjoyed getting dinner together. By this point, Bew had also gotten to know the owners of the factory. He didn't much care for them, but it made little difference to him since all of his dealings were through Sergio.

Within only a few years, Summer Classics had doubled its

production volume. With a captive factory in Chile, Bew invested heavily in his relationship with Sergio and this factory. It was a mutually beneficial relationship, where each needed the other to succeed. With this established, Bew felt he could proceed with confidence. Summer Classics grew its line, adding new collections, keeping with (and even ahead of) market demand. Bew was proud that he could pick up any number of widely circulated home catalogs and see his product within its pages.

In the spring of 1993, the southeast was hit by "the Storm of the Century." Beginning on March 12, a blizzard swept across the state of Alabama. The storm raged for two days, and when it was all said and done, Birmingham was covered in nearly thirteen inches of snow. Alabama was sorely unprepared for such conditions, and there was a statewide shutdown for several days. People were stranded at home. Neighbors helped each other, sharing food and supplies. Bew, Wendy, Wynne, and Sergio, who was in Birmingham to conduct business with Bew, were stranded at the White home on Cherokee Road. When things had died down, Bew and Sergio went down to the nearby golf course. Sergio was in awe. "I have never seen anything like this."

By this point, both Walker and William had gone off to college. Walker was in her first year at the University of Alabama, and William was in his second year at the University of Colorado Boulder. They were both grateful for the opportunity to go it on their own. Both Bew and Wendy felt their absence, but Wendy especially. Wynne, who was a good deal younger than her siblings, felt like an only child. She and her mother grew much closer in this time.

Recently, Summer Classics had picked up another product—rocking chairs—from a small, independent manufacturer called Wilder Manufacturing in Westminster, South Carolina. Wilder was owned and run by Wallace Lanning—a truly fascinating character. Bew met him at market and loved the rocking chairs. They were made of American red oak. Bew and Wallace struck up a deal, and soon, Wallace was delivering rocking chairs to Summer Classics by the truckload. At the warehouse, the workers painted the chairs white or mountain green with Sherwin Williams oil-based polyurethane paint.

On the weekend before Labor Day, on a Saturday evening, Bew interviewed Harold Hudson for the position of controller. Harold was good friends with Dan Bundy, Bew's banker at 1st Colonial Bank. Dan put the two in touch. Harold presently worked for the defense contractor Science Applications International Corp (SAIC) in Huntsville, Alabama. While Bew and Harold spoke in Bew's office that evening, they were interrupted by a knock at the door. There was no one in the facility but Bew and Harold. Bew answered the door.

"Hey, I'm here with a delivery of rocking chairs from Wilder Manufacturing. I was supposed to deliver them tomorrow morning, but I'm afraid I need to unload them tonight. Otherwise, I'm going to have to drop the trailer somewhere, and it could be three days before I can bring them back."

Bew shook his head. "No. We can't wait three days. We need to paint them and have them ready to ship at the end of this month. But I don't know how to drive a forklift and everyone else has gone."

"I can drive a forklift." Harold chimed in. "That's how I paid my way through college."

Bew lit up, "Awesome!"

So, Bew and Harold went out to unload the truck. Harold drove the forklift and Bew guided him with a flashlight. Soon, they unloaded all the rockers, and the truck driver left. Bew and Harold stood before the rocking chairs, both feeling satisfied at what they had accomplished.

"Well, I've never driven a forklift for a job interview," Harold chuckled.

Bew laughed as well. He knew he wanted to hire Harold. This was the kind of person Summer Classics needed. Bew needed his employees to be flexible and willing to do whatever work needed to be done. Harold fit this description. Bew conveyed his desire to hire Harold, but he currently lacked the funds for the hire. "We have a massive order coming through at the end of the year with one of our biggest accounts, Service Merchandise. I know I can hire you after that. Can you wait till then?"

Harold thought he could. They agreed to stay in touch and discuss this further.

That fall, Summer Classics received one of its largest orders ever. Gardener's Eden, a Williams Sonoma division, ordered ten truckloads of the Summer Classics Nantucket collection, which included a white-and-blue-striped market umbrella and a white, pressure-treated pine table with four white, cushioned pine chairs. The Nantucket set was to be the cover page of the next Gardener's Eden catalog. Ordinarily, Chile would manufacture product and ship it in a container to Summer Classics, where the product would be painted and shipped to customers. But this order was so massive that Bew felt it necessary that he personally go to Chile to provide direction to the factory. His team didn't have the time or the labor to take on the painting required. The factory would need to do this.

In Chile, Bew worked with the factory, showing them how he wanted them to apply a couple of coats of paint to the product and ship it, and then Summer Classics would apply the final coat. Bew and the factory worked out all the details. Bew even worked out the details with a paint supplier in China – the paint the factory would use. Once Bew was satisfied everything was planned carefully, he returned to Birmingham.

All seemed to go according to plan. The factory manufactured the product, applied two coats of white paint, and shipped the product to Summer Classics. Bew and his team assembled the product in their warehouse, applied the final coats of paint, and shipped ten truckloads of Nantucket to Williams Sonoma. They also shipped Nantucket to several of their other clients —smaller dealerships mostly. Bew and his team congratulated themselves on their accomplishment.

The following week, Bew got a call from a dealer in Marietta, Georgia. "Hey Bew, I got your stuff in, and it looks great. But it rained this weekend."

This seemed like a non sequitur to Bew. "Okay. And?"

"Well, it's already starting to peel."

"Oh! I'm going to get in my car and come see you right away." Bew hung up and grabbed his car keys.

A couple of hours later, he arrived at the dealer's place in Marietta. The dealer took Bew to where the product was displayed on a patio. Just as he had said, the paint was peeling from the rain.

Bew felt his heart beating faster. This was really bad. "Okay, send it back. Call my guys." They shook hands and Bew left for Birmingham.

Upon his return, he went and got Neal. "Neal, we could be in real trouble. The Nantucket in Marietta was peeling from the rain. We just shipped ten truckloads of the stuff. Get Terry and Jerome. We need to hose some Nantucket outside to see if they peel too."

Neal swung into action. He well understood the seriousness of the situation. Soon, Bew, Neal, Jerome and Terry along with some other interested employees were gathered outside. "Okay, Terry. Turn on the hose," Bew ordered.

Jerome sprayed the product, and they watched. In time, they saw what they had so dreaded—it started peeling. "Shit," Bew muttered under his breath.

Bew soon realized that somewhere in the process—whether in China or in Chile—the paint had been switched. Someone had tried to save money and cut corners. The product was not painted as he had originally arranged. Bew knew what he had to do, and it was going to hurt Summer Classics terribly. He called Williams Sonoma straightaway. He was good friends with the buyer. "Have y'all shipped any of the Nantucket yet?"

"No."

Bew explained the problem. He told them to ship everything back. He would order another ten truckloads of the product and send them to Williams Sonoma. It would be another

sixty days until they could get them the product. They agreed—
Gardener's Eden would send the trucks back and they would
wait the sixty days. Bew was grateful.

In a couple of days, Summer Classics received the ten
truckloads of flawed product. At this point, Summer Classics
had grown so much that the Pelham warehouse was full of inventory all the way to the back. Bew was at a loss. He had no
idea what to do with all this product. For the time being, he
leased ten containers from Metro Leasing, filled them with the
Nantucket and stored them in the "backyard," a large lot adjacent to the warehouse where Summer Classics' seconds, returns
and cancellations were kept.

Bew racked his brain, "What am I going to do with this
stuff? I can't sell it. I can't ship this to anybody because I don't
know what's going to happen. Some of it is probably good, but
I don't know which is and which isn't."

For the next several weeks the product sat there as Bew tried
to figure this out. He had reached out to many dealers, asking if
they would pay Summer Classics for the product. They showed
no interest. They would not even buy it at ten cents on the dollar. Bew was left feeling worn and stressed.

His spirits were soon lifted somewhat. That Christmas,
Bew threw a "Magic Christmas Party" at the Mountain Brook
Country Club for his friends and family. If he could afford it,
he would plan such events far more often – ever since his time
as the SAE rush chairman in college, he had always enjoyed
event planning. Yet, such events were costly. For this Christmas
party, several dozen friends and family enjoyed the dinner and
festivities that Bew had arranged for them. Perhaps the most
memorable moment in the evening was the show that a hired
magician put on for them. At one point, the magician did a card
trick with Bew and Wendy's friend, Martha Davis.

"Pick a card."

Martha picked her card, and the magician made some dramatic hand movements, making a show of shuffling the cards.
Then, all of the sudden, the magician threw the cards into the

air. To everyone's astonishment, Martha's card stuck in the ceiling high above them. Everyone applauded and laughed merrily. For some time thereafter, the card remained stuck up there. Everyone enjoyed pointing it out in the weeks to come.

Bew's spirits were lifted yet further when one of their largest orders—the Service Merchandise order—was completed. The order amounted to more than $200,000. Bew excitedly called Harold Hudson when this was done. They had spoken many times since their first eventful interview in September. It had been arranged that Harold would begin after the Service Merchandise order. Summer Classics hired Harold just days later on January 4, 1994.

In the spring of 1994, Bew finally decided to have a sale at the Pelham facility for the Nantucket product sitting in the containers. He was left with no other choice. He called the Birmingham News to see how much it would cost to run an ad for the sale. He was told that it would cost $10,000. He was shocked. "I don't have that kind of money. The only way this is going to work is if I sell enough to pay for the ad and have additional money left over." Bew figured he needed to sell $25,000 for the whole thing to work.

Bew and his team discussed it and arrived at a decision. They would run the ad in the Birmingham News and everyone would come into work on the weekend of the following week to run the sale. The ad would read "Summer Classics opens the factory to the public." Included in the ad would be a map to direct people to Summer Classics.

Throughout the coming days, the team worked hard to prepare for the sale. Their facility was an office and warehouse, not a store. There was a lot of cleaning and moving to do. It took some doing, but by the end of the week, with all hands on deck, they were finally ready.

That Saturday morning, Bew arrived as the sale was beginning. He was surprised by what he saw. Cars were parked everywhere, even dangerously so along Highway 52. Bew was amazed. They had not expected such a turnout. Inside, the

Nantucket product was selling faster than Summer Classics employees could get it out of the containers. People were congregating everywhere. Bew's employees were moving in and out of the facility, trying to supply this huge, unexpected demand.

By the end of the weekend, Summer Classics made close to $50,000 from the sale. Bew and his team were astonished. Summer Classics did not make anything close to this much in the Birmingham market in a whole year. This was a wake-up call. Bew talked to his employees, and they decided to do this again. They did another sale the following month. At the next sale, they made even more than $50,000. Bew was very pleased with this. He decided they would start doing a Summer Classics sale on a quarterly basis. This was the beginning of retail for Summer Classics.

FOR A NUMBER OF YEARS now, Bew had been interested in wrought iron furniture. Outdoor furniture essentially began with the introduction of wrought iron in the 1950s. One of the front runners in this industry had been Meadowcraft – the outdoor furniture company founded by Bill McTyeire, a good friend to Bew Sr. It just so happened that Bew's own vision for Summer Classics was very much inspired by Bill McTyeire's vision for Meadowcraft. As a young sales rep, Bew had made a point of getting to know McTyeire, learning all he could about outdoor furniture. In its heyday several decades earlier, Meadowcraft had succeeded because of Bill's insistence on quality and longevity.

Just as Meadowcraft had been, Bew believed that Summer Classics could be a massive success if they could create quality outdoor furniture that looked just as good twenty years after it had been purchased. He knew this would require patience and a constant focus on the long term (at least twenty years), but he believed that if he could do this, he would build up a strongly loyal customer base.

When it came to outdoor furniture with quality and longevity, wrought iron was considered to be the best. In 1994, the door to wrought iron finally opened to Bew and Summer Classics. Bew received a call out of the blue from Mark Sanders, the CEO of an outdoor furniture manufacturer, Love and Peace Manufacturing, based in Columbiana, Alabama.

Bew and Mark had actually known each other from Bew's sales rep days. In those days, Mark had been the president of Meadowcraft. A New York company called Gulf and Western had purchased Meadowcraft and sent Mark from New York to run the company. Bew had business dealings with Mark as a sales rep, and the two even went on jogs together. Mark had always been fascinated by Bew, and he would invite Bew to Meadowcraft to chat. But, in time, they fell out of touch when Bew and Mark went in new directions—Bew put repping behind him to focus on Summer Classics, and Mark sold Meadowcraft and started his own company, Love and Peace Manufacturing.

The two saw one another again at the High Point Market in 1992. Mark was running a showroom for his new company while Bew was running a showroom for Summer Classics. Bew's eye was drawn to the beautiful wrought iron furniture he saw displayed in the Love and Peace Manufacturing's showroom. He approached Mark and expressed great interest in getting this furniture. Where had he gotten it? From Mexico, Bew learned. But Mark said that he could not sell it to Bew—Mark was partnering with Harris and Company. They sold the furniture for him. Bew was disappointed. Before leaving, he told Mark to call him if he ever reconsidered this.

Now, two years later, Mark was calling Bew. He had reconsidered.

"Bew, this is Mark Sanders."

"Mark, this is a surprise. What can I do for you?"

"Listen, my partnership with Hank has gone sideways. He isn't doing a good job. Do you want to sell my furniture?"

Bew was surprised, "Yeah. I'm interested."

"Good. Can you come to my place in Columbiana to talk?"

"I can come now."

"Good."

After a twenty-minute drive, Bew arrived at Love and Peace Manufacturing in Columbiana. The two got right to business.

"Can you sell this?" Mark asked. Bew and Mark were looking at a stock of wrought iron chairs as they spoke. All of Love and Peace's furniture came directly from a factory in Piedras Negras, Mexico—the factory had a contract to work exclusively with Mark and his company in the US market. Mark quoted his selling price for Bew and Summer Classics. The offer was a great deal. Bew accepted enthusiastically.

These wrought iron chairs became an immediate success for Summer Classics. Bew was able to buy them from Mark and sell them for a great profit. Very soon, Summer Classics was selling the product to Restoration Hardware, Neiman Marcus, Crate & Barrel, Frontgate, John Deere and Gardener's Eden. The demand for this new furniture was even greater than Bew could have expected. He couldn't get enough of these chairs.

The wrought iron furniture of Love and Peace Manufacturing stood out above its competition for one chief reason: its finish. In addition to being the CEO of Love and Peace, Mark was a partner in another Columbiana-based business called Finishing Touch. Finishing Touch was a company that specialized in automotive finish, finishing parts for Ford, Volvo, and Mercedes. Years ago, Bill McTyeire had the novel idea of using automotive finish on Meadowcraft's outdoor furniture. This finish was far superior to any other finish being used on outdoor furniture at the time. It was this that truly gave Meadowcraft's furniture longevity. Mark, who succeeded Bill Mctyeire as president of Meadowcraft, carried this knowledge and practice with him when he started Love and Peace. Because of this, Bew and Summer Classics also became quite familiar and involved in this practice.

Going into 1995, Bew had still been going to Chile four times a year, but he was learning to better delegate. The previous year, Bew had hired Will Clark. Will graduated from Vanderbilt University where he majored in Latin American Studies. After working a few months in the Summer Classics warehouse, Will moved to Santiago, Chile, where he would now live year round. For the next few years, Will visited the factory in Chile every day, giving oversight and help in the production of Summer Classics furniture. This was very significant for Bew. He found it reassuring to have a man on the ground in Chile who could keep him posted and represent Summer Classics.

In addition to this, in 1995, Bew asked Harold to go to Chile in his stead, at least once that year. Harold agreed, and this was a great help to Bew. In time, Bew handed these trips over to Harold. Harold proved to be someone up to the task of handling more responsibilities. For this reason, Bew promoted him to VP of Sales and Marketing.

Bew also made another hire that year—Shane Morrow as his next controller. Shane was a former employee of Love and Peace. Bew would soon see that there was a steady exodus of employees from Love and Peace. Several of them would eventually become employees for Summer Classics. Unfortunately for Bew, his hire of Shane would come back to haunt him.

This year, Bew moved nearly all of their production overseas. Summer Classics orders were so many that only the factories in Chile and Mexico could handle the increasing production volume. This seemed like the right move for Summer Classics, but sadly, their relationship with Chile was to change dramatically.

In 1995, Sergio contacted Bew with some jarring news. "Bew, I'm sorry, but we are going to have to charge you twenty percent more on everything."

Bew was taken aback, "What? Why?"

"The currency exchange is bad. We have to increase our prices."

"A twenty percent increase? That's crazy."

"I'm sorry."

"Can you at least let me get the stuff on the water?" There were containers en route to the US.

"I can ask. But I don't think so."

"Just ask," Bew insisted.

Sergio called Bew back soon with the management's reply, "Sorry. They said, 'No.'"

"How about a gradual price increase?" Bew asked.

"No, they want it all right now." Sergio said. Bew and Sergio had always gotten along. This was a very difficult conversation for them.

Bew took a deep breath. "Okay. I'm going to tell you what's going to happen. I'm not going to drop you right away, but I'm going to start to phase you out."

"I'll let them know, but I don't think it will change anything for them."

Sadly for Bew, the management disregarded Bew's threat. This was a major blow to Summer Classics. For now, he had to pay the price increase. The Summer Classics line was too reliant upon Chile to make changes any time soon, but Bew was now very actively searching for a new producer.

CHAPTER 9

RUNNIN' WITH THE DEVIL

"The supreme quality for leadership is unquestionably integrity.
Without it, no real success is possible."
- Dwight D. Eisenhower

"'EL DIABLO' HAS DONE IT again! That lying son of a bitch!" Harold shouted as he walked into Bew's office. El Diablo is the name they had begun to apply to Mark Sanders to describe his lying, unethical behavior.

For each shipment of wrought iron furniture from Mexico, Summer Classics would pay Mark who would in turn pay Mexico. Mark would then inform Bew when they could expect the shipment's arrival. When the shipment arrived, trucks would deliver the furniture to Finishing Touch where the automotive finish would be applied. Then, Harold would come with a crew to box all this furniture and take it back to their facility in Pelham. This was how things were supposed to happen, but Summer Classics had quickly discovered that Mark Sanders was a pathological liar.

Bew groaned. "What now?"

"Showed up at Finishing Touch with the whole crew. We waited thirty minutes and still no shipment. El Diablo claims we got the time wrong. I assured him we did not."

"What a dirtbag!" Bew fumed.

This had happened several times before, and it was extremely frustrating for Bew. He had employees whose entire job that day was to handle this shipment. He had to send them home when there was no shipment. The shipments always came in the end, but several days later than expected. Very quickly, Bew was learning not to trust Mark. Yet, he needed this furniture—he could not get enough of it.

"Bew, we've got to find a way to verify what this man is saying. We can't trust him."

Bew knew Harold was right. Mark knew how much Bew wanted his product, and he took advantage of this. Bew needed someone on the ground—someone who could set eyes on what was happening in Mexico to verify the truth of what was happening there.

Fortunately for Bew, he found just the man he needed. Thanks to his brother-in-law Mike Goodrich (he is married to Bew's sister Gillian), Bew got connected with Paul Hadley, one of Mike's friends. Paul, who worked at Trinity University in San Antonio, spoke fluent Spanish. Bew hired him to periodically go to the plant in Piedras Negras, Mexico to verify what was happening.

Paul proved to be extremely helpful. He sent Paul without any warning to the factory. This way they could be more sure of catching Mark in his lies. Soon, they discovered this was happening far more than they had even known. Mark would tell Bew one thing – a delivery time or a price – and Paul would find out Mark was lying. Mark was angered that Paul was going to the factory. Bew was not at all apologetic.

"You have to tell me when Paul is going to be there," Mark insisted to Bew after being caught in another lie.

Bew did not conceal his anger. "No. Why would I do that? You lie all the time."

This did nothing to stop Mark. Things between Bew and Mark grew more rocky all the time. By this point, Bew did not even try to hide his disgust for the man. All the same, Bew felt unsure of what to do. While he couldn't trust Mark, the furniture was top notch, and it sold wonderfully for Summer Classics. Because of Mark's contract with the Piedras Negras factory, they had to work exclusively with Mark. If Bew wanted the furniture, he was left with no choice but to deal with El Diablo.

These days, Bew found his outlook darkening. He was not naïve, but he liked to know he could trust the people he worked with in business. His dealings with Mark had certainly punched holes in this expectation. It seemed that every week brought a new conflict. Bew learned to endure Mark, but he was not prepared for a blow that would come from within Summer Classics.

"Yes?" Bew asked after hearing a knock at his office door.

The door opened and Shane Morrow stepped in. "Bew, I wanted to ask you if you wanted me to go to Chile in your stead."

It was the summer of 1996. It was soon time for Bew to make one of his quarterly trips to the factory in Chile. Just the thought of traveling to Chile left Bew feeling tired and frustrated. Summer Classics should have moved on from Chile by now, but still, he had found no other means of maintaining the production necessary to meet customer demand. Shane's offer could not have been more timely. Earlier in the year, after some staff changes, Bew had assigned Shane the role of operations manager, and Neal became the next controller. Not only would the trip suit Shane's responsibilities, more importantly, Bew did not want to go. He did not have to consider Shane's offer long. "Yes."

Bew was pleased to spend a week at home that month. He was away so often. Wendy was pleased to have him home too. He also made efforts to connect better with his now-teenage daughter Wynne. Wynne received Bew's fatherly affections with the skepticism most prominently displayed in teenagers. Wendy was glad to see Bew trying.

The next month, Neal walked into Bew's office with a look of seriousness about him. "Bew, do you have a moment?"

Bew looked up from some designs on his desk. "Sure."

"You know Shane just got back from Chile, and he had your credit card?"

"Yes?" Bew braced himself.

"Well, he spent $2700 on alcohol and hookers."

"You can get hookers with a credit card?"

"Obviously you can in Chile."

Bew shook his head in disbelief. "So, what else?"

"I told him at three o'clock that I would give him two hours to tell you himself before I came to talk to you." It was now five o'clock.

Bew frowned. "Okay. Thanks, Neal. I'll take it from here."

Neal left. Bew called Shane into his office. Shane walked in nonchalantly. "You wanted to see me?"

"Yeah, I've just been talking to Neal about how you used my credit card on hookers and how you're an alcoholic."

Shane's face showed no reaction. "So?"

Bew was shocked. "So, you're not sorry? I thought you might offer to pay me back."

"Yeah, I did those things." There was no remorse in Shane's voice.

"You weren't going to pay me back?"

"No," Shane answered resolutely.

"So, what if we called your wife to see what she thinks about it?" Bew found the number in a directory and dialed.

"Sure. Call her."

Bew held the phone to his ear. It began to ring. He watched Shane with disgust. It rang again. Shane stood there without a care. Bew hung up the phone. "You are a terrible person. Get out of my office. You're fired."

Shane laughed and walked out. Bew was deeply shaken by this. He understood men and their vices. He was not one to jump to judgment, but he had never seen such an unabashed display of human depravity.

Despite such setbacks, Summer Classics continued its rapid growth. Indeed, at its current rate, Summer Classics' gross sales were doubling every three years. As the year of 1996 aged, Bew was realizing that it was time to consider moving. They had now outgrown their facility in Pelham. He began his search, looking at nearby warehouses.

In the following year, Bew found a warehouse in Columbiana. The place used to be an old textile mill. It had one hundred and twenty thousand square feet. The owner, who currently lived in Georgia, offered Bew a great deal. Summer Classics could rent it with an option to buy. Bew agreed to the offer, and Summer Classics moved its operation over to Columbiana. Bew put the Pelham warehouse on the market.

Of course, this new warehouse was also very convenient for Summer Classics considering its nearness to Finishing Touch (it was less than a mile away). As it was, most weeks found Summer Classics employees traveling to and from Columbiana to work with Mark Sanders and Finishing Touch, so this move would greatly decrease the time Bew's employees spent on the road. This had not been the only reason for moving to Columbiana— they had gotten the warehouse for a great deal—but it certainly was a major reason.

Relations with Mark were perhaps more tense than ever. Mark's lying was growing more brazen, and Bew was calling him out more boldly.

"I can't believe you go to church. What do you do there?" Bew said in disgust to Mark on one occasion. But Mark knew how much they wanted his furniture. As long as he was getting their money, he did not care what Bew thought of him.

Not long after they had moved to Columbiana, Mark told Bew that he needed Summer Classics to pay more money and further in advance for their next shipment. Bew was taken aback.

"What? Why?"

"I can't pay it right now and the factory needs the money now before they can ship your container of furniture."

"Okay," Bew consented begrudgingly. This was irregular, but they had orders to fill. Summer Classics needed the furniture as soon as possible.

That same day, Harold took the money over to Mark's office at Finishing Touch. When he walked into the office, he found it mostly vacated except for Rusty—one of Mark's employees. Harold stood in the doorway and made a show of scanning the empty room.

"Can I help you with something?" Rusty asked.

"Where's Mark? I was supposed to meet him here."

"Oh. Well, he's skiing with his family."

"He's skiing?"

"Yeah."

"Tell me how to reach him."

After getting a number, Harold left immediately and returned to Summer Classics. He called Mark.

"Hello. This is Mark."

Harold tore into him. "You're telling me that you have the money to go skiing but not to pay the factory for furniture?"

Mark snapped back. "How dare you! You mind your own f-ing business! If you want the furniture, you'll pay."

Harold began to respond. "You're such a…" He heard the phone slam on its receiver on Mark's end.

Harold immediately related his phone call to Bew. "Why do we work with this guy?" Harold asked incredulously.

Bew was outraged. He, too, had some choice words for Mark. He agreed with Harold. Things had gone far enough. "Harold, we'll pay him this time. We need to fill our orders. But as soon as we can, we're ending our partnership with Mark."

Within the next few months, Bew made sure that all of their furniture had arrived safely, and he made sure that Summer Classics had paid all its debts to Mark. Then, in the spring of 1997, Bew and Harold went to Mark's office to inform him in person that Summer Classics was ending the partnership. Mark did not hesitate to voice his displeasure. Bew and Harold could not have been happier. They were glad to put El Diablo behind them.

Bew knew that Summer Classics would suffer—at least in the short term—for this. This furniture had always sold very well in the Summer Classics line, but Bew could not abide continuing to work with someone so dishonest and unethical. They needed to find someone else who could produce this furniture for them.

Not long after, Bew was put in touch with an entrepreneur in Birmingham—Burt Newman. Burt had a seven-thousand-square-foot space in Birmingham. He was full of aspirations and drive. Hearing of Summer Classics' need for a new producer, he offered Bew his services. Bew and Harold studied the space. Certainly, there was room here to work. Bew told Burt he was interested. "Let's see what you can do."

Unfortunately, Burt underestimated the difficulty of this undertaking, and he overestimated his own abilities. When Burt failed to hire any other employees to help him, he decided to do the manufacturing himself. He presented Bew with samples—samples it had taken him far too long to produce.

"Burt, I'm going to need hundreds of pieces like this. This is more than you can handle." Bew was disappointed.

Yet, Burt played an unexpected and vital role in this endeavor. He had found a way of contacting a steel factory called Ferro Arte in Mexico—the factory which provided steel for Mark's factory in Piedras Negras. "I know how to call them, and they have someone who speaks English."

Bew thanked Burt. Back at his office, Bew called the factory. After introducing himself, he was put in communication with the head of the factory, Enrique. With the help of an English-speaking receptionist at the factory, the two spoke. Bew asked about their operation. Enrique gave a report which satisfied Bew. "Can I come see you?" Bew asked.

"Yes," Enrique replied.

The following week, Bew flew to the San Antonio International Airport. Enrique met Bew there, and Enrique drove them three hours across the border to Ferro Arte in Monclova, Mexico. Upon arrival, Enrique gave Bew a tour of Ferro Arte's operation. The receptionist accompanied them as an interpreter.

The operation was fairly sparse and primitive. If Ferro Arte was to meet Summer Classics' production needs, the factory would need some major improvements.

Yet, in the course of his conversations with Enrique, Bew knew he had found something in Ferro Arte and Enrique—they had a willingness to dedicate the factory's labor and time to Summer Classics. In the end, Bew and Enrique came to an agreement. Up front, Bew and Summer Classics made a heavy financial investment in Ferro Arte to help them improve the factory. Summer Classics transferred all its wrought iron designs to Ferro Arte. They now had a captive factory in Mexico. Summer Classics was committed to the success of this undertaking.

A CELEBRATION
OF LOVE

"Love bears all things, believes all things,
hopes all things, endures all things."
- 1 Corinthians 13:7

BEW HAD DRIFTED Far from his plan to stay at home more. Almost from the moment he began working with Enrique and the factory in Monclova, he was going to Mexico every third week. The Summer Classics operation was ever growing. Perhaps Bew could have delegated more to his staff, but as he had found in the past, this work could be unpredictable. Now more than ever, he felt he needed to head up this new venture in Mexico. Wherever he was heavily invested financially, he would heavily invest his time. With so much at stake, he would personally do all in his power to assure success.

Even though Bew might often be physically absent from his family, his family was not far from his thoughts. He was especially mindful of Wendy this year. July 29, 1997 would mark twenty-five years of marriage for Bew and Wendy. For this landmark anniversary, Bew wanted to make a grand gesture to show his wife how much he loved her.

He spent months planning a party for their twenty-fifth anniversary. He wanted all of their friends and family to be there.

He spared no expense. Perhaps the most significant piece for Bew was the production of a video. This was a costly project back then as he had to hire professionals and a studio, but he wanted to create a video that communicated his love and his children's love to Wendy. Similarly, Bew had created a video for his parents' fiftieth wedding anniversary. This proved to be quite meaningful to his parents and to his family. He wanted to do this again for Wendy.

In the process of this project, he spent a great deal of time reflecting on what he would say to his wife. He compiled old photos from their early years of marriage and family photos. This all had a great impact on him. He was always on the go, always working. It was not often he took the time to reflect like this. Now, thinking back upon his marriage, he was deeply moved. So much had happened over the past twenty-five years. He thought about their time at Auburn. He thought about their first years of marriage in New York and Connecticut. Then, they moved back to Birmingham. Three children, multiple moves and several job changes—so much had happened. There had been ups and downs. Through it all, Wendy was always there—always loving, always supporting, always faithful. He felt such an abundance of love for her as he thought of all these things. How could he communicate how much she meant to him?

On the evening of July 29, Bew's family and friends gathered at the Mountain Brook Country Club to celebrate the anniversary. Bew was pleased to see how many of his friends and family had come from in town and out of town. He was happy for the presence of his friends such as Michael Young, Taylor Boyd, and Danny Lawrence. For Taylor and Michael's part, they both came with a certain sense of curiosity (they were not alone in this)—they could not think of a time they had seen an anniversary celebrated in such a fashion. Yet, in the course of the night, they would be deeply affected.

The evening was an elegant black-tie affair. Bew, Wendy and their family and friends were seated at beautifully set tables around the room. Wendy had personally arranged all the centerpieces with flowers from her garden. The country club's staff waited each table, bringing food and drinks. At Bew's request, Danny Lawrence acted as the master of ceremonies for the evening. Danny was well known for his rich humor. He did not disappoint. He stood at a podium at the front of the room. Behind him, pictures of all the people in attendance cycled on a projector screen to music from the 1960s to the present day. "A word of warning: those of you with weak hearts—please leave now," Danny said. Laughter spread around the room as people settled at their tables. This would not be your average anniversary party.

Danny commenced his roasting—no one and nothing was off limits. "You know, this is a special occasion tonight. I've never seen a happier person than Billy White. The guy is obviously madly in love with Wendy and rightly so. Happiest man I've ever seen. On the other hand, there's Wendy." Danny paused dramatically as everyone laughed and cheered—especially the women in the room. "She said, 'Danny, this is the marriage from hell. He's a bastard. If it wasn't for the children, I'd have left twenty years ago.'" Everyone roared in laughter.

The room was immensely entertained as Danny gave roasts worthy of Don Rickles. "Fifteen years ago, Billy started his business. He's made it what it is today: absolutely nothing." Danny had people laughing to the point of tears (Bew included). "He is a businessman extraordinaire. Billy White is to the business world as Michael Jordan is to baseball."

"I would like to introduce at this time Enrique from Mexico. Will you stand up?" The room applauded as Enrique and his wife rose from their seats. Danny followed his introduction of Enrique with a roast. The room laughed both in amusement and disbelief—indeed, no one was off limits. Enrique laughed good naturedly with everyone else in the room. Bew was pleased to see Enrique included in such a fashion. Of course, this evening was about Bew and Wendy's anniversary—an occasion to be celebrated with friends and family, but if he was going to spend all this money on a party, why not invite his business partners as well? He was not one to pass on the opportunity strengthen his business relationships.

The evening was only just getting started. Danny opened the floor for others. Friend after friend rose to make a toast. One of these friends was Michael Young. Having recently divorced from his wife Cecilia, he was feeling especially reflective and moved in this moment. Rising from his seat at the table neighboring Bew and Wendy's, Michael spoke warmly of his friends, "You're the only people my age I know who are still married after twenty-five years." Michael paused as the room applauded. "And I will bet you that we are all here again for your fiftieth anniversary. That is one thing I will bet on." Everyone cheered in agreement. Michael raised his glass high, "To Bew and Wendy's fiftieth wedding anniversary." Moved by Michael's words, Bew rose to his feet and the two friends clinked their glasses together.

Other friends stood, making their toasts. Bew's old college friend Corky shared an amusing poem he had written himself. Bew's sisters Toody and Gillian entertained the room with a prepared performance, retelling the story of Bew and Wendy's romance, cueing well-known songs on a cassette player at planned points. Bevelle followed her sisters with a humorous speech which she ended with well-wishes to the couple.

Then, Bew and Wendy's friends in the Birthday Club—a group of six couples which formed when Bew, Wendy, and these ten other friends realized they each had a birthday in one of the twelve months of the year—stood together in a semi-circle to sing the "Hula Hop." Once a month, the Birthday Club would gather to celebrate a birthday at the Mountain Brook Country Club. At every birthday, they would sing "Hula Hop" while the celebrated person danced. The group was always amused by Wendy's dance. "Here's to Wendy and the way she dances the Hula Hop," they said. Good naturedly, Wendy rose from her seat and danced while they sang. Everyone laughed and cheered.

Moved by the room's outpouring of love and affection, Wendy's mother joined in the toasting. "I'm so happy for both

GALLERY

Braxton Bragg Comer (Bew's mother's grandfather), governor and senator of Alabama. He Started Avondale Mills which became a Fortune 500 company in the '60s.

Bew's parents, William Bew White Jr. and Gay Comer White.

Billy at Darlington 1968. Headed to Auburn after graduation.

Wendy and Billy at SAE fraternity house 1972. (Note the wide tie)

Wendy and Billy walking down the aisle July 29, 1972.

Top left: Michael Young at their rental house in Auburn. Rent was $65 a month. Bottom left: Wendy at the White House (what they called the rental house in Auburn). Above: Original farmhouse in Boligee before it burned in January 2009. Bew's mother died 2 weeks later.

Clockwise from top:
1) Wendy and Bew at
Christmas with a new
puppy and baby in Wilton,
Connecticut 1975. 2) William
and Walker in Wilton,
Connecticut 1976. 3) Wendy
4) Grandkids Ella and Millie
Martin Dorman at the farm in
2010. 5) William in the post
office Jeep Bew paid $650 for
as a "train car" to drive to the
train station to catch the train
to New York City every day.
6) William (1 year old) and
Bew in 1975.

Left to right: 1) This is what dinner in China looks like - big tables, lots of drinking. (2013) 2) Black tie opening of Chicago showroom. Bew, Honie Weinstein, Harold Hudson, and Jeff Curran. 3) Giving a speech in China in 2004. 4) Bew at the White House. 5) Opening of the new factory in 2013 in north China near Dalian. Christian Given, Grant Yu, Bew and Dillon Yu.

Left to right: Bew and Wendy at the 2019 Garden Party dinner. 2) Wynne's wedding in March 2013 at White River Farms. 3) The rebuilt house at White River Farms.

Left to right: 1) 2016 Grand opening of the Chicago store in Highland Park, Illinois. 2) Gabby showroom High Point, NC April 2017 - Bruce, Bew and Ericson 3) New plant opening north China in 2004.

Left to right: 1) The porch at White River Farms, where all the world's problems are solved. 2) 2012 Society of International Business Fellows meeting in Santa Fe, New Mexico. 3) Wendy's garden in May 2021 with over 600 hydrangeas and 170 Japanese maples 4) The Cake House, built to house the cake at Wynne's wedding. 5) 2016 wedding in Aspen, Colorado.

Wendy and Bew

of you. I wish you both fifty more years of happiness." Others gave a cheery affirmation. "And may you have a lot of pretty grandchildren," she added, smiling at them as she resumed her seat. People laughed and applauded.

Then, Danny Lawrence introduced "Mr. William Bew White II." Bew Sr. rose. Looking at the room, he said with authority, "I'm the real Bew White." Everyone cheered. Bew playfully protested. In a brief toast, Bew Sr. praised Wendy, stating his joy that she was in the White family. Wendy thanked him.

The whole room was swept up in the evening. A feeling of goodwill was shared by all. To the room's delight, Danny returned to the podium and recommenced his roasting. After telling one rather scandalous joke, he raised his voice to speak over the laughter, "If I can be serious for a moment." People laughed and scoffed, knowing that whatever was to follow would not be "serious." "It's a great night for a celebration. For better or for worse, twenty-five years stuff. I asked Billy the secret of his success. And he told me that when he and Wendy got married they made a pact that every night before they went to bed Billy would look her in the eyes and say those three precious words. Y'all know what those are. 'I was wrong.'" This was followed by more applause and laughter.

"Now, I'd like to sing a song in honor of Billy and Wendy, and I would like for Billy to come up." He gave a signal and the song "YMCA" began to play over speakers. Danny got the room clapping as he danced towards Bew.

Bew sat in his seat, shaking his head as Danny strode towards him.

"Go on, Billy!" someone shouted.

Danny dragged Bew from his seat, and the two danced to the front of the room, motioning out "Y-M-C-A." Finally, Bew bent over in laughter, unable to dance any longer. Danny took his bow and ran back to his seat. Everyone applauded loudly as the music faded out. Bew went to the microphone. "Danny said I would never speak to him again after tonight." He paused and gave a wave to Danny, as if to say, "Goodbye."

Composing himself, Bew spoke more seriously. "I want to thank my wife—do you realize that she did all these flowers? And most of them she grew herself." The room showed their appreciation with applause.

"You know, I like material things as much as anybody." The room laughed at this deliberate understatement. "But seriously, the reason I'm doing this is because of you. You're my friends. This is what life is all about to me."

Now, Bew was ready to introduce his video. He nodded, and the projector was turned on, shining on the white screen behind him. "You can't imagine what living with Wendy has been like. I have spent a lot of time working on this, and my children have spent a lot of time working on this. I put together something that I've really got my heart in, and I want y'all to see it. This is a prepared speech, but it's too emotional for me. I can't give it, but…" Bew took his seat by Wendy's side as the video began to play.

A love ballad—"When I Fall in Love" by Natalie Cole—began as old photos of Bew and Wendy displayed on the screen. Transitioning from these, Bew came on, sitting before the camera. "We were married in late July, 1972, and by September, we had moved to New York. And I can never forget… My first boss's name was Dick Maher, and I would go into his office for consultation. I always remember him saying that it just keeps getting better. I was young at the time and didn't understand a lot of things about life. But this statement kept coming back to me. And he kept saying constantly, 'My marriage just keeps getting better.' And I'm in the very fortunate position of saying the same thing: my marriage just keeps getting better. It's incredible, Wendy." Bew faded out.

Now, one at a time, William, Walker, and Wynne appeared, congratulating their parents and expressing their gratitude and love for them—especially for their mother.

"You both possess the greatest, most sought-after relationship. To build a marriage such as this—it can rarely be matched," said William, who had been unable to attend the anniversary's party because of summer school in Colorado.

"I think one of the most important things that has really impressed me is that y'all really enjoy each other," Walker observed.

Complimenting their parents' individually, they commented upon Bew's hard work. "Dad, you built a company from the ground up, and you taught me the meaning of perseverance and integrity," William stated.

"Dad, by watching you I have learned that whatever I decide to do with my life, I should put all my energy into it," Wynne commented.

Their love and appreciation for their mother was especially evident. "Mom, you are without a doubt the kindest, most caring person I've ever known. Your attitude and personality are simply amazing. Your smile lights up every room you enter, and I feel so incredibly fortunate to have you as my mom. You've given me my compassion and sincerity and my kindness and goodwill towards others. You have no idea how much I love you and care about you." This was William.

"I love you, and strongly trust that you will always be there for me whenever I need you. I can talk to you either when things are great in my life or when I'm the biggest slump," Wynne said.

"Y'all's relationship is so wonderful, and I'm proud of y'all for making it these great twenty-five years and for being great parents to me. I love y'all both," Walker said, beaming at the camera.

Bew appeared on the screen once again. "I've always believed that there is one thing that you can do for your children that is more powerful even than spending a great deal of time with them and that is to love their mother."

"I will always love you." The words of Whitney Houston rang in the background.

Bew concluded saying, "Marriage is not a perfect thing. We certainly have our disputes, and hopefully, though, in those times, we actually learn something about each other and we're able to move on. That's somehow made the relationship even stronger. Wendy, I would like to thank you for the greatest twenty-five years of my life, and here's to the next *fifty* years. I love you, Wendy! Happy twenty-fifth anniversary!"

The video concluded with Walker, William and Wynne saying all together, "Congratulations! We love you!"

Applause erupted around the room. People were on their feet. Bew walked to the front of the room and whistled for everyone's attention. "The bar has been opened!"

"Oh, this has been wonderful!" someone exclaimed.

"Now you can see why I appreciate everyone being here," Bew said in reply. Wendy walked to Bew's side, wiping tears from her eyes.

"The band starts. No breaks. Now's the time to have a good time," Bew announced.

"I'd like to say something," Wendy said to him.

"You can't say anything," Bew replied playfully. He wanted this evening to be for her. Nothing was expected of her but to enjoy it.

"Yes, she can!" someone called out.

The room applauded as Wendy went to the mic.

"When he said he was going to have a party, I said, 'Billy, I'm not going to make a speech.'" Wendy laughed and everyone joined in with her. "But- I-" Wendy, who was not one for the spotlight, composed herself. "First of all, I can't thank y'all enough for being here. It means so much to us. And I know some of you have come a long way and had to go through extreme measures to get here, and we do appreciate it."

"Needless to say, I have a wonderful husband. I think y'all can see that now. He is just dear to me. I just can't say enough good things about him. And my children—I'm so blessed. I really am so blessed. And I don't deserve any of this, but I'm so thankful. I'm so thankful." Wendy turned to look at her husband. "I love you, Billy. And I can't thank you enough for this beautiful party that you gave us." Everyone expressed their agreement.

CHAPTER 10

The night continued on. People lingered, enjoying good conversation, good drink and the good feelings that seemed to hang in the air. Soon, a live band began to play. People moved to the dance floor. It was a wonderful night—a night that had impacted them all, but perhaps it impacted no one more than it did Bew.

CHAPTER 11

TIME'S ONWARD MARCH

"MAY WE NEVER FORGET."
- FDNY Memorial Wall, across from the site of
the World Trade Center

THE SUMMER CLASSICS move from Pelham to Columbiana had all gone smoothly. Every day now brought Summer Classics employees to their new office in Columbiana. Operations and routine were soon well established in this new headquarters. Yet, just as Bew had struggled to sell the Pelham warehouse in 1982, he had no success selling it now. In the end, he decided to convert the warehouse into a store. Over the past few years, Summer Classics had continued to open the Pelham facility to the public for sales a few times a year. To his surprise, the sales were continually successful. His hope now was that the Pelham store could profit enough to pay for its own mortgage.

To run Summer Classics' retail, Bew hired an employee from the Vista days—Georgia Minter. Georgia had worked for Bew as a receptionist in those days. She knew and understood him and the business, and she had Bew's trust. Bew was pleased that she was the one heading up retail.

While Summer Classics was now headquartered in Columbiana, Bew continued to keep a close eye on the store in Pelham.

This new venture caused him a good deal of stress. It needed to succeed. He needed the store to be an asset to Summer Classics and not a burden.

That fall, Bew's youngest daughter, Wynne, followed in her father's footsteps and went to finish her last two years of high school at Bew's alma mater—Darlington School—now a co-ed school in Rome, Georgia. Bew was quite pleased with her decision. Both parents agreed to the move, but for Wendy this was exceedingly difficult. Her children had been everything to her. Now, two years earlier than expected, Bew and Wendy were empty nesters. For many weeks following, Wendy was overcome with a deep sadness.

Bew continued to travel to Ferro Arte in Mexico every third week. As the months went by, Summer Classics became ever more invested in Mexico. Slowly but surely, the majority of Summer Classics' production had been moved away from Chile to Mexico. Personally, Bew did much to design new collections there. With years of experience now under his belt, he had come to trust his own instinct and eye. The results of his previous designs were positive and profitable. Between design, quality control and productivity, Bew's work was cut out for him on each trip to Monclova. He also continued to invest personally in the relationship with Enrique. He had come to know Enrique and his family well. In time, he would even attend the weddings of Enrique's children.

In the following year, Bew received a rather remarkable offer. Avondale Mills reached out to Bew and Summer Classics. The once-Fortune 500 company was now greatly diminished. They were looking to sell all their assets and close what had once been the Avondale Mills headquarters in Sylacauga – would Summer Classics be interested in buying it? It was a surreal experience for Bew. Here was the headquarters of the company he had once aspired to lead as president. He had thought this company would be his future, but now, Avondale Mills was offering to sell their former headquarters to Summer Classics – the company he had built from the ground up. Bew, Neal and Harold decided to go look at the property.

Summer Classics was indeed growing, but they had not yet grown enough to need the vast space of this old mill in Sylacauga. Nonetheless, Bew enjoyed touring its familiar grounds. When they learned the cost for electricity each month – one million dollars – Bew and Harold were shocked. If he needed confirmation that this was not the right move for Summer Classics, this was it. Bew passed on the offer, but it still was a significant experience for him. As they drove back towards Columbiana, the mill grew smaller in the rearview mirror. Bew felt no regrets.

"MR. WHITE, THERE'S A CALL FOR YOU. It's a Mr. Don Tickle," Bew's secretary informed him.

"Ah, yes. I'll take it. Thanks." Bew took the call. "Don! This is Bew. It's been a while." Bew knew Don Tickle from his days as a sales rep. Don had been one of his clients.

"Hello, Bew. It certainly has been. How's business?" The two spent a moment briefly catching up, but, soon, Don got to the purpose for his call, "Bew, would you be interested in buying wicker from China?"

"Yeah, I really think I would."

"Great. Can I come visit you?" Don asked.

"Yeah. Come on."

It was now the spring of 1998. Don's call could not have come at a better time. Bew had just begun buying wicker for his store. He had been interested in it for some time now. After struggling to find someone to sell wicker to him (none of his competitors wanted to sell to him), he found two different domestic suppliers—Ebel, a company based in south Florida, and Cebu, a company in Charleston. He was buying paper wicker and resin (which is plastic) wicker. The resin was selling very well. Bew was now ready to design his own wicker.

Soon, Don made the trip from Wilmington, North Carolina to visit Summer Classics. The two spoke in Bew's office. Don elaborated upon his connections with China, "I know someone who makes this stuff. He's a great guy. I've known him forever."

Because Bew had been thinking about designing wicker furniture for some time, he was ready with his ideas. "I want to do something plastic [resin]—something very traditional and something contemporary."

"I think we could arrange that. Can you show me what you have in mind?" Don asked.

Bew drew out some designs, and Don took these back with him to Wilmington, sending them on to the factory in south China. The factory got to work making samples. Things had been set in motion. Bew was excited that he could at long last be producing and selling his own wicker furniture.

But Bew's patience was to be tested. He waited months, and still, no samples. It was four months until the first samples from China finally arrived. Almost immediately Bew saw that they were not quite right. He contacted Don and requested some changes be made. Don relayed these requests to China.

In total, it took about ten months for the factory to get the samples right. In that period of time, Bew had been to Mexico many times and he had visited many markets. In short, in the same time it took China to make samples, Bew traveled extensively—internationally and around the country—designed new collections and did all the work of running a company. This was business as usual for him. He was disturbed by the much slower rate of work in China he was now seeing. It seemed as if Summer Classics would never get its wicker furniture. But in the end, though greatly tried, his patience was rewarded.

In 1999, to Bew's great pleasure, Summer Classics introduced two wicker collections from China. One of these was a resin collection called Classic. The other collection was French Country. This was another resin, but more contemporary wicker collection. Of the two, Classic sold the best by far. Indeed, it remains in the Summer Classics line today. Summer Classics' foray into wicker had been a smashing success.

This step into China was a major move for Summer Classics. Bew had been quite fortunate. As with Mexico, this opportunity had practically fallen into his lap. With its moves into Chile, Mexico and now China, Summer Classics was going international before most of its competitors. This gave them a competitive edge in their market.

Don Tickle became the middleman for all business in China: negotiations, purchases, shipments, design – all of it. Given Bew's past experience with Mark Sanders and the factory in Piedras Negras, he was not particularly fond of doing things this way. Certainly Don was no El Diablo. Bew trusted Don, but he trusted himself even more. In all business – especially in business this important to him – Bew liked to communicate directly with those making his product. Even more than this, Bew liked to see their operation. He wanted to be involved in it himself. This is how he had always done it since his days as a sales rep.

As time wore on, Summer Classics was continually faced with quality control problems regarding the furniture from China. In Mexico, Bew had employees whose entire job was to oversee quality control, but he had no one of the sort in China. Hence, container after container arrived with quality problems. Summer Classics suffered losses when this happened. Whenever such furniture arrived, they were forced to mark it down and sell it at the store—hoping to at least recoup some of their money. Bew took up this issue with Don. "I need you to establish some kind of quality control for me. This is getting out of hand."

"Sorry, Bew. I can't do that."

Bew protested. "Well, you're making money. You're not going to take care of the quality?"

"No, that's the responsibility of the factory."

Bew was exasperated. "But the factory isn't doing it. And you're not doing it. So I'm stuck."

"Sorry."

Bew was unsatisfied with things as they were and knew this

could not continue. If no one else would take on the responsibility of quality control, he would step in to do the job himself. He would personally go to China.

Soon it was arranged. Bew and Don flew to Hong Kong to meet up with Don's connection in China - Winston. Like Don, Winston did not have any ownership or role in the factories. He was a broker, acting as a middleman between factories and companies. Winston and Don were friends, and they both partnered in the business of brokering. Bew did not quite understand why his business had to pass through two brokers, but this was the arrangement.

Winston met them at their hotel, the InterContinental, and he took them out to dinner. Winston was a man of expensive tastes. He wore tailored clothing and enjoyed fine dining establishments. Whatever amount he was making from brokering, it was sufficient to support this lifestyle. Bew could not begrudge the man this and was impressed that Winston had good taste. He was also well educated and well-spoken—in English at least. Bew was glad for this.

Bew and Don stayed in China for close to two weeks and traveled from the city to the factory many times. On every trip to the factory, Winston and Don accompanied Bew. To get to the factory from Hong Kong, they had to take a boat across the water. Bew was pleased to finally set eyes on the operation. He was not surprised to find that the factory was primitive and the work conditions were rather poor (relative to American work conditions), similar to the factory in Mexico.

Bew made the most of his time at the factory. Having spent time at factories in Chile and Mexico, he was quite comfortable in this environment. Indeed, he thrived in it. He knew how he wanted his furniture made and was familiar with the process of production from start to finish. His best designs and ideas often resulted from time spent in the factory, where he made a point of walking around exploring everything, observing all. He solved many quality problems this way. From this trip, Bew was able to refine the production process in ways that would spare him and his team many headaches in the future.

That May, there was a big celebration for Bew Sr.'s eightieth birthday at the Birmingham Country Club. This occasion was very meaningful to the family and their friends. Bew and Wendy were glad to have their children all gathered in one place. Bew was pleased to see his sisters and their families. All were glad to spend time with and celebrate the man who was a husband, a father, a grandfather, a lawyer, and a friend.

For many years, Bew Sr. had been battling prostate cancer. By now, the cancer had spread to the bone. It had been very difficult for his family to watch the man they loved and admired slowly deteriorate before them. Bew owed so much to his father. Bew Sr. had never hesitated to offer his counsel and help (both as a lawyer and a father). What Bew perhaps admired most of all was his father's humility. If Bew Sr. had wanted more from life – more money, greater recognition, or a life of added luxuries and comfort – he could have had it. He was a successful lawyer and a respected member of his community. But Bew Sr. found pleasure in simpler things. He liked his quiet piece of farmland in Boligee. He liked his games of solitaire in the library. He liked a drink in the early evening. He liked the company of his family. Bew Sr. was beloved, and in the view of his family, he deserved nothing less than a celebration that reflected their great appreciation for him.

Now as much as ever, Bew kept a demanding travel schedule, traveling to Mexico every three weeks, to China every three months, and to markets around the nation constantly. This was difficult for him and Wendy, but Wendy had long ago learned to bear with his long absences. She was active in her community and hard at work in her garden. As it concerned his work, Bew felt like things were only getting better. Summer Classics was growing all the time, and he saw all sorts of possibilities before him.

Summer Classics entered the new millennium riding the wave of success. By this point, production in Mexico was full steam ahead. In addition to this, production in China was lifting off. Within a short time, this new venture had produced great results. Bew saw much potential in China. The prices were good, and the profits were high. He wanted to increase his production there, but he knew this would require a great deal of personal involvement, so he committed to traveling to China four times a year.

With production in Mexico and China as it was, Bew was ready to phase out production in Chile. After the Chile factory raised its prices in 1995, he had slowly begun moving production away from them. By 2000, nearly all production had been moved from Chile to Mexico. It was now time to cut ties entirely. As far as the ownership was concerned, there was no lost love there, but Bew, Harold, and those who knew Sergio and the factory management were saddened at this parting.

Production was not the only area of growth for Summer Classics that year. Under the management of Georgia Minter, the Pelham store was growing ever more profitable. What had begun as a means of paying the mortgage had become a reliable source of revenue for Summer Classics. The store benefited Summer Classics in another unexpected way – it gave the company brand greater visibility in the Birmingham market. In times before, it was not unusual for Bew's friends to know little to nothing about his business. But now, the Summer Classics brand was somewhat more familiar in Birmingham, all thanks to the store.

Since this store was doing well, Bew decided they would try opening another. Before long, they found a space in Raleigh, North Carolina. Bew asked Georgia to help open it. She ably trained the store's management and guided them through a smooth grand opening. Bew was pleased with the results.

That August, Summer Classics had its garden party—an annual event where their largest clients came to see the newest line before it was released to the public. Bew had begun the garden party a few years earlier after receiving inspiration from a local competitor. Bew watched as this furniture company flew its biggest clients to Birmingham to show off their new line. For several days they would wine and dine their clients, all in hopes of receiving large orders from them. As Bew observed this, he realized that the company was taking away his own business. Rather than admit defeat, he decided to turn this situation to his own advantage. Discovering the hotel these clients were put up in, Bew sent Harold to go pick them up in their free time and bring them to the Summer Classics plant to show them *their* latest line. This worked brilliantly. Many gladly came, and Summer Classics gained several new clients in the process. Bew's competitor caught wind of this scheme, and they bitterly voiced their frustration to their own clients. But, in the end, nothing was done to stop it.

After a few years of this, the Summer Classics Garden Party had taken on full form. In July or August of each year, Bew flew in Summer Classics' largest clients—hosting them for an expensive party where they could show off the latest line. Then that same evening, Bew, Wendy, the clients and Summer Classics employees enjoyed a nice dinner at the Mountain Brook Country Club. Bew liked to invite his employees to swell the numbers for the evening's dinner, and his employees loved it. This event grew in its reputation and its success was undeniable. It became a staple, exclusive event in the outdoor furniture market.

That December, Bew planned a big Christmas party called Fifty Christmases. As the year end approached, everyone was on edge because of Y2K, fearing that their electricity was going to go out. Bew wanted to plan a special Christmas party, something that could help people turn their focus to more important things, such as the 2000th birthday of Christ. He settled upon the theme of "Fifty Christmases" because he and many of his friends were turning fifty. Bew wanted this to be an "over the hill" celebration and a celebration of Jesus' birth all wrapped into one event. He invited his friends, family and employees—more than a hundred people.

A couple of weeks before the Christmas party, Bew and his father went to spend some time at the farm in Boligee. It was not often that Bew and Bew Sr. got this sort of time together.

On the drive up, they had a very frank and difficult conversation. Bew Sr. knew he was dying. He had known this for some time, but lately the cancer had exacted a heavier toll upon him. Bew Sr. was looking death in the face, and he was afraid. Bew was, too. They both cried together. Bew Sr. was not ready to die. Bew could think of little to say to his father to comfort him. What could one say? "You've had a great life. I would love to have had a life as rewarding as yours," Bew said. This is all he could think to say. Sadness wore heavily upon them.

The Fifty Christmases party came, and it was a special time. Bew and his employees decorated the Mountain Brook Country Club festively. He had his employees put fifty Christmas trees with white lights all around the room along with other Christmas decorations. They had a birthday cake made with baby pictures of all the people turning fifty along with a picture of the baby Jesus on the cake's face. Wendy arranged the evening's flowers. A camera crew was set up to interview people as they came in—give one thought about life. All the responses were filmed.

All the guests were all seated at one long table (this was meant as a sign of unity). Bew looked around the room filled by his family and friends. Conspicuously, Bew Sr. and Gay were absent—Bew Sr. was too sick to attend and Gay stayed home to care for him. The guests enjoyed their dinner and a lovely evening program—the singing of Christmas carols, the reading of the biblical Christmas story, and at the end, the responses filmed earlier were played (in edited form) on a projector screen at the front of the room. It was an unforgettable time. Bew knew how to plan a nice party, and he thoroughly enjoyed doing so. He was happy to make this a special evening for his friends and family.

On January 17, 2001, only weeks following Fifty Christmases, after eighty years of life, Bew Sr. passed away. It was a horrible experience for the family. That morning, his body's functions began to shut down. Learning what was happening, Bew came to the house, but it was too late. There was nothing they could do. Traumatically, Bew watched his father pass away before him. The family was overwrought with grief.

Bew and his family knew this moment might be coming soon, but none of them were prepared for it. Bew would miss walking in to see his father sitting in the library over a game of solitaire. He would miss sharing a drink and conversation with his father in the evening. Most of all, Bew would miss his father's presence. In the time following, Bew felt his absence sorely. The family's faith in God and a life to come helped them face such a loss.

THAT SPRING, BEW WENT INTO A MEETING at the Pelham store with the prospect of a new connection to China. Several weeks earlier, Bew had received an interesting call:

"Hi, this is David from China. Do you want to buy cast aluminum from China?"

Bew had just begun working with Enrique on making cast aluminum in Mexico, but this could be even better. Bew grew excited. "Yeah, because I've seen some Chinese stuff, and it's really cheap. And I'm not going to be able to compete if I buy from Mexico."

"Would you make an appointment with me?"

"Yeah, come see me."

Jim Parker joined Bew for the 9:00 AM meeting. After meeting for three and a half hours in an office, Bew suggested that they all go to lunch.

"Okay. I need to go get Suzie out of the car," David replied.

It was a hot spring day in Alabama—the kind of day that turned a car's interior into an oven. Bew was shocked. "Someone has been in the car this whole time?"

They walked out together onto the front porch of the quonset hut store. David's white Camry was parked out front. David went and got a woman—Suzie—out of his car. He introduced her. Bew and Jim exchanged side glances as they greeted Suzie. "What is going on?" was their unvoiced question.

"Where are you from?" Bew asked Suzie.

"I'm from California," she said.

"California?" Bew's curiosity was further piqued. He turned to David. "David, where did *you* come from?"

"I came from Shanghai."

"Well, who do you work for?"

David went on to describe his boss—a man named Grant. He owned factories in north China. He used to sell armaments to the Chinese government, but he had recently shifted to the furniture business. He sold almost exclusively to Taiwan, but now he wanted customers in America.

"Okay. So how did you get here? Did you drive your Camry from the airport?" Bew asked.

"No. I drove from Los Angeles."

"You drove from LA for this meeting?" Bew asked in disbelief.

"Yes."

"So, Suzie is from LA."

"Yes. She is a friend to Grant."

Bew was fascinated. "Okay. Let's walk through this: so you call me, say, three and a half weeks ago, ask for an appointment, and I gave it to you. How did you get my name?"

"Well, I went through the Casual Living Magazine, and I called everybody in there. I asked them the same thing I asked you—'Are you interested in cast aluminum?'"

"Well, how did that work out for you?"

"You are the only one that would meet with me."

Bew exchanged another look with Jim—both were wide-eyed. "So you called me to confirm, and I moved it back ten days—what did you do?"

"I sat in California and waited for the meeting."

"Okay. Wow. So how did this work? What did your boss tell you to do?"

"He said to me, 'You're the only one that speaks English.

Go to the US and don't come back until you get a customer.'"

Bew shook his head in disbelief. The more David described this character, Grant, Bew could not help but conjure the image of the Godfather, Don Corleone. Who was this guy? After hearing the story, Bew was too interested to simply pass up on this. "This is wild. I'm going to figure out how to do business with you, man. On my next trip to China, why don't I come by to see your plant and I can meet your boss?"

David smiled, pleased that his mission had been successful. He would not be returning to China empty-handed.

Several months later, after first visiting the factory in south China with Winston, Bew and Jim Parker flew to Shanghai. Grant sent a ride to pick them up from the Shanghai Hongqiao International Airport and put them up in the nearby Marriott Hotel. Bew, who had stayed in his share of nice hotels, found this to be the nicest Marriot he had ever stayed in—nothing like any in the States. It had a large and beautiful lobby with a bar at its center, and the rooms were of five-star quality.

After giving them adequate time to rest, Grant and David took them to see the nearby factories. Bew had already sent them designs for product so that they could produce samples ahead of his visit. He was looking forward to seeing their work. Upon arrival, he was not surprised to see that the conditions of the factory were poor. Yet, their work was quality. Bew liked the samples they had produced.

He was interested in making this partnership work. He liked Grant and the people he met there and was ready to invest in this relationship. The issues that he had seen, such as the poor factory conditions, could be addressed and worked upon as he developed a better relationship with Grant. Bew told Grant that he wanted to negotiate a contract.

That evening, Grant, David, Jim and Bew gathered at the bar in the hotel lobby to hammer out the contract. Jim sat taking careful notes of all that was discussed, writing up the contract. He made frequent trips up to his hotel room to use a printer he had brought from the States. Bew and Jim wanted to get a final contract that evening. All the while, Grant was constantly walking outside into the motor court to take phone calls.

With David interpreting, Bew and Grant discussed pricing. At first, Bew found Grant's pricing proposal outrageous. Grant was confused. He restated his price, insistent that this was fair. Bew insisted that it was not. It seemed that they would get nowhere. Suddenly, it occurred to Grant that Bew was misunderstanding him. Bew saw Grant's face light up. Grant said something to David, and David nodded in understanding.

"What did he say?" Bew asked, keeping his eyes fixed on Grant.

"The price is by the kilo," David informed Bew.

"Oh." Bew absorbed this piece of information for a moment. "Can you give us a moment?" Grant nodded. He could wait. Bew and Jim conferred with one another. "So, they're giving us the price by the weight of the product."

"Right. How do we get the price by weight?" Jim thought aloud.

"Let's call the office." Bew got out his cellphone and called Harold. Shanghai was thirteen hours ahead of the time in Alabama, so while it was 11 o'clock in the evening in Shanghai, it was still morning in Alabama. He was glad for the time difference. "Harold, this is Bew. We're talking with Don Corleone and David now, trying to get pricing figured out. Apparently they're pricing the product by the kilo. Jim and I were wondering how to get the price. Don't we have some old cotton scales lying around somewhere?"

"Matter of fact, I think we do," Harold replied.

"Do you think you could figure out what this price would be in pounds?"

"I'll get some guys on it straightaway."

"Okay. Call me back as soon as possible."

Harold got a couple of guys to help him weigh one of their aluminum chairs—samples chairs China had sent earlier—on the scale. Then, they worked out the conversion from pounds to kilos. Harold returned Bew's call a short time later. "Okay,

Bew. We just weighed one of the chairs on the scale and converted the pounds to kilos. This is a really good price, Bew. *Really* good." He gave Bew the numbers.

It took Bew's best poker face to hide his excitement. He spoke in a low tone. "This *is* a great price. A chair that would cost us $120 in Mexico will only cost us about $33 in China."

"Yeah." Neither of them could believe it.

"Okay. Thanks, Harold."

Bew walked back to the bar where the others were seated. "Okay. This price is good for us." Bew watched Grant as David relayed the message.

Grant smiled and nodded. "Good," he said in English.

From then on, things went much more smoothly. They continued to work out some finer points of the contract. Before long, Grant walked outside to take another call.

Bew looked at a clock in the lobby—it was nearly midnight. He turned to David. "Who the hell is he talking to? It's almost midnight!"

"Oh. He works till 2 AM every day," David responded.

"Oh my… We're going to the plant tomorrow, and he's going to get like five hours of sleep."

"Yes. He works very hard. All Chinese work like that," David added with nationalistic pride.

David sat upright as he saw Grant returning. Bew leaned over to Jim. "These guys are going to kill us. They're going to put us out of business." Most people Bew knew in the States just did not have this kind of drive. Jim shook his head in disbelief.

Soon, Bew and Grant finished negotiating the contract. Jim went up to his room to use the printer and returned with the final contract. Bew and Grant signed. They were relieved to make it official. There was handshaking all around. Everyone was pleased with the terms. Grant was excited to have an American customer. Bew felt very fortunate to have gotten into China when they did to get these great prices. He knew it was only a matter of time before all his competitors were doing the same (or else they would be going out of business). He was glad to have gotten a step ahead. But mainly, Bew was happy to go get some sleep. Grant might stay up until 2 AM every night, but he would not. It was time to enjoy that five-star room waiting above.

A couple of months later, on Monday, September 10, Bew and Harold went to the annual Casual Market at The Merchandise Mart in Chicago. With four million square feet of floor space, this art deco building on the Chicago River was one of the largest buildings in the world. As one of the world's top furniture markets, this week-long event held great significance for the business of Summer Classics and another two hundred companies with showrooms there.

Upon arrival in Chicago, Bew and Harold met with Honie Weinstein. Honie, who had worked with Bew in the Vista days, was now responsible for running the Summer Classics showroom in The Merchandise Mart. Since the market was to begin the following day, the three set up the showroom, and then went to dinner and spent the evening catching up.

The next morning, Bew woke up and prepared for the day. He would be meeting Honie soon at the showroom. There was no hurry as the real crowds would not be coming until later that morning. Harold was going to the dock to pick up some packages but would be joining them soon after. Bew turned on the television and let it play in the background. He stood before a mirror as he buttoned his shirt. His fingers stopped on the top button as he heard the morning's news. He positioned himself before the TV. It was being reported that a plane had hit one of the towers of the World Trade Center. Bew, along with so many others, assumed that it was a small, private plane and an accident. Just a little before 9 AM, he arrived at the showroom where he met Honie. They discussed that morning's news as a few people shuffled by.

About thirty minutes later, Harold arrived. "Did y'all hear the news this morning?"

"Yeah, we heard a plane crashed into one of the World Trade Center towers," Bew replied.

"Not just one plane. There's been another," Harold informed them.

Bew and Honie froze. "Another?" Honie asked in alarm.

They stood in silence, absorbing this. "So, this isn't just an accident?" Bew already knew the answer to his own question.

"It's not an accident," Harold said.

Honie turned on a small TV she had there in the showroom. They watched as events played out on live TV. They saw the smoke billowing from the towers. Soon, they started receiving phone calls from sales reps around the country—they all were stuck in airports and could not come to the market. The FAA had grounded all flights around the nation—a decision without precedent. The three of them continued to watch the TV in silence. The South Tower collapsed and thirty minutes later, the North Tower collapsed. They were stricken. Not long after that, Bew, Harold and Honie were informed that The Merchandise Mart was closing down.

Not knowing what else to do, they decided to go get lunch. Out on the streets, the city of Chicago was eerily quiet. There was little traffic to speak of. They found that most restaurants had shut down. They came across an open Cajun bar across the street. Inside, people sat watching the TVs. The mood was somber. They got a beer and a hotdog and watched with the others. Fear was visible on everyone's faces. After the unthinkable had happened, it now seemed that anything else could follow. After lunch, they took a cab back to their hotel. They were all in shock and each took the time to call loved ones and friends to find some solace in one another.

They spent the next few days going to the market although there were hardly any customers and very little talking. That weekend, Bew, Harold and the other manufacturers were all trying to find a way home, which was nearly impossible—no one could get a flight. The vice president of Meadowcraft came into the Summer Classics showroom to inform them that Meadowcraft had rented a bus—would they like to ride back with them to Birmingham? Harold had already made plans to rent a car and drive down with another Birmingham native. Bew decided to stay behind and take a flight on Sunday. They thanked him for the generous offer.

On Sunday, September 16, Bew flew from O'Hare International Airport on a Southwest Airlines commercial jet. The airport's security was heightened, and everyone was on edge. The plane's passengers numbered less than twenty people. Bew sat in silence on the two-hour flight home, reflecting on that week. One thought came into his head—he was glad that his father had not lived to see this horrible moment in America.

CHAPTER 12

TESTED BY FIRE

"A leader has the vision and conviction that a dream can be achieved.
He inspires the power and energy to get it done."
- Ralph Lauren

FOR SOME TIME NOW, Summer Classics had outsourced the manufacturing of its cushions to a plant in Conyers, Georgia belonging to Larry Balkin. Bew had always gotten on well with Larry, who had a great sense of humor, and more importantly, was trustworthy and reliable. But Bew and his team felt that they could cut their margins if they ran their own cushion operation.

In late 2001, Bew made an offer to Larry to buy the plant. Larry was receptive to the idea, and after some negotiation, Summer Classics agreed to purchase the operation for $500,000, paying Larry $50,000 a year until the full amount had been paid. In all this, Bew was actually only interested in one thing: hiring a seamstress—Rita Lopez. Rita was the brains of the cushion operation. She had the work down to a science. After the purchase, a part of the deal was that Rita would be moving down to Columbiana to head up the Summer Classics cushion operation. Summer Classics also acquired the plant's machines and some of its staff.

After the deal was struck, Harold told Bew that he thought they were making a mistake. "We're overpaying. All we need is Rita. Why don't we just double whatever they're paying her?"

"I know." This had crossed Bew's mind. "You're right. I could do that, but we're not going to do that to Larry. I've been on the bad end of a deal before, and it's awful. This is the right way to do it."

Harold admired Bew's integrity. He didn't know many men who would take such a path. Indeed, if Bew had merely hired Rita away, many would have considered it a shrewd business decision. Bew was certainly one for cutting down costs but he wanted to treat others fairly too.

With all parties pleased, the deal was completed. Summer Classics moved the cushion operation to Columbiana. Rita Lopez moved to Birmingham and headed up the operation. Some of the other staff moved down to Birmingham as well.

Since Summer Classics had begun production in north China as well as in south China, Bew's trips there had been much more involved and drawn out. It could be exhausting, but so far the results made it all worth it. Summer Classics was rapidly growing. Bew felt confident that the offerings of Summer Classics—all its collections and diverse styles—put them up with the best in the outdoor furniture market. More and more, he watched as companies moved their production to China. He knew how fortunate they had been to get into China when they did.

Whenever Summer Classics produced a collection, it was always a long process. One of the most difficult parts was the samples which were often a point of tension between Summer Classics and the factories. Many factories struggled to see the profit in making these. Samples were expensive, and they were not sold—the factories got no (immediate) financial return on them. Bew tried to impress upon the factories that this was a necessary part of the business. For Summer Classics to produce new collections, they first needed to make samples. If factories wanted business from Summer Classics, they needed to understand this.

It was not uncommon for Bew to arrive in China only to find that a factory had not made the samples for the latest collections—even though they knew Bew was coming. On one occasion, Bew arrived in south China to find just this—they had not produced the samples yet.

Bew was angry. "I've flown all the way over here, and you haven't made the samples? You've made my trip that much longer. You had the drawings, and you've had plenty of time to make them." In this case, he left early for north China. He would return to south China again after they had finished what he requested. Sadly, this problem would persist for years in the southern factories.

Despite these bumps in the road, Bew knew he could not beat the prices because China was producing quality furniture at a great deal. He was so impressed with what he saw happening in China that he insisted Enrique join him on one trip. After showing him around the factory in north China, Bew told Enrique, "You'd better be careful or these guys are going to put you out of business. I can buy aluminum for less than I am buying steel from you."

Enrique did not share Bew's opinion of the Chinese factory. "No. They're backwards."

"Wow. What a stupid thing to say." Bew felt that Enrique could learn a thing or two from the business here. He was astounded at this ignorant statement.

But it may indeed have been that Enrique saw the truth of what Bew was saying. It may have been fear, not ignorance, that prompted Enrique's statement. Sadly, it was true—China was putting him out of business.

When it came to pricing, China defied so much of what Bew knew about market pricing. As Bew understood it, everyone wants to make a maximum profit. If your competitor is selling a chair for $100 and you are selling a similar product, you want to undercut him with a cheaper price. Therefore, you might sell the chair for $90 (if you can afford to). In Bew's view, China understood the advantage of undercutting the competition with a cheaper price, but he did not understand how they profited. If a competitor was selling a chair for $100, China would sell the same chair for $30. This was the way of things there and it astounded Bew. Yet, now that he was doing business in China himself, he was not complaining.

Soon, Bew decided it was time to open another store. The Raleigh store was not yet producing the results Bew wanted, but this had been the way of things for the Pelham store—it took a few years to start truly turning a profit. Now, the Pelham store was doing better all the time. Bew wanted to invest further in retail. He wanted to see this succeed. They chose to open another store in Charlotte, North Carolina.

As with the Raleigh store, Georgia Minter was very involved in the opening of the Charlotte store. She helped train the management. She oversaw the store's opening. She and her husband Pat even went so far as to personally paint the store's floors. This was the kind of work ethic Bew loved to see in his employees.

In spring of the following year, Bew had one especially memorable trip to China. As usual, Bew and Jim had gone to China to visit the factory in south China with Winston. In addition, they planned to join Winston in the attendance of the Guangzhou Canton Fair in the Guangdong Province which was the largest and oldest trade expo in China.

As they returned to Hong Kong after their final day at the factory, Winston turned to Bew, "You know what, we aren't going to go to the Guangdong Fair. In fact, I think we're done. Why don't you see if you can get an early flight home?"

Bew was surprised but not unpleasantly so. These trips always wore on him, and he had not been particularly keen on attending the fair. "Okay! Yeah, I'm all about that."

Immediately, Bew and Jim contacted Continental Airlines and changed their flight. Surprisingly, the flight did not assess a changing fee.

That evening, when Bew and Jim arrived at the airport, they were surprised to see dozens of people wearing masks. Bew looked around and commented to Jim, "This is weird. They're wearing masks here. Do they always wear masks?"

"Well, some of them do, and some of them don't," Jim responded. Hong Kong was renowned for its poor air quality.

Bew sensed something else might be happening. "I don't think I've ever seen it like this." Soon, they boarded the long flight for home.

Back in the United States, every news outlet was reporting the answer to Bew's question: SARS had hit China. Already, as they had been leaving, there had been an inkling of what was happening, but now it was clear that the virus was widespread. A further piece of news made Bew's heart skip—the SARS breakout point had been the Guangzhou Fair. "Wow. Did we cut it close," Bew thought.

Because of SARS, Bew was prevented from returning to China the remainder of the year. In fact, he only managed to go to China two times that year. This caused him a fair amount of stress. He did not love the travel—it was exhausting—but he felt he needed to go at least four times a year to assure that all was happening as it should. Yet, much to his surprise, this did not seem to affect business. What Bew had dreaded did not come to pass. He realized then that he could cut down on his traveling. From now on, he would only need to go to China twice a year. Bew was delighted at this change.

This year brought another happy change for Bew. His mother wanted him to take over the farm. She was overwhelmed with the responsibility of it and had primarily kept up the farm these years since her husband's passing to honor his memory. All their life, she and Bew Sr. had differed when it came to their preferred vacation destination. For Bew Sr., the farm had always been his haven, but Gay had always preferred the beach. Indeed, when Bew Sr. passed, one of her first acts had been to purchase a condo at the beach. She now spent much of her time there, and only went to the farm occasionally to oversee its care. But she could do this no longer.

When Gay asked Bew to take care of the farm, he considered it for a moment before responding. "Okay. I'll take care of it."

Gay breathed a sigh of relief.

"But," Bew spoke, emphasizing that he had conditions, "I'm telling you that I'm going to do it my way, so don't complain."

Gay gave Bew a dismissive wave of her hand. "Fine. Whatever. Just take it off my hands."

"Okay." Bew spoke with hesitation. He knew his mother. She might claim feelings of indifference now, but if there was one thing Gay White was not, it was indifferent. Whatever the topic and whatever the matter, she always had an opinion.

Regardless, Bew was quite thrilled with this. He had always loved the farm. True, he, Wendy and their children had not gone to the farm all that frequently over the years, but this was to change. Now that he had responsibility for it, he was very interested. There were several major changes he wanted to make immediately.

While the farm sat right alongside the Tombigbee Waterway, one could not actually see the river from either the house or the long approach onto the property. One of the first things Bew did was clear all the underbrush that had grown to block the view. Now, as you drove onto the farm and whenever you sat on the farmhouse's back porch, you could see the river. Proud of his work, Bew thought it looked spectacular.

As Bew had feared when he first agreed to care for the farm, his mother was none too pleased. When she saw the farm after these changes, she confronted him. "What have you done? Why did you do that?"

Bew thought the reason for it was clear and sound. "Well, it seems to me that the river is kind of a critical part of the farm, and it's really pretty when you drive in."

This did nothing to calm Gay. "I can't believe you did that!"

Bew threw up his hands in exasperation. He knew this would happen. "I tell you what. Why don't you take it back?"

His mother's demeanor changed immediately. "No, no, no, no. I won't say anything."

"Okay." Bew was pleased at this turn. Then, he added reassuringly, "I got it. Just come down, enjoy it, and don't complain."

From then on, that is precisely what she did. Bew fixed up the house and made all kinds of changes on the farm (personally paying for it all). For him, this was a labor of love. He thoroughly enjoyed investing in it and had a vision for the property, which he enjoyed seeing come to fruition before his eyes. Now, Bew and Wendy started going to the farm whenever they could. Bew always looked forward to this time. Even Gay came to appreciate all that Bew was doing with the property.

As the year came to a close, Summer Classics' retail continued to grow. Two more stores had been opened—one in Nashville and one in Richmond, Virginia. Bew was amazed to see how far their retail had come. He owed much of this to Georgia Minter who was one of his most dedicated employees.

On the morning of January 25, 2004, Bew and Harold were at the Pelham store when Georgia Minter's husband Pat called Bew—he and Georgia had been in a car accident in a Shelby county intersection. It had been a horrible accident—Georgia was seriously injured.

Bew and Harold drove straight there, arriving just moments before the paramedics. Bew got into the ambulance with Georgia, and Harold and Pat followed right behind in Harold's car. Georgia was in critical condition. Tragically, she passed away not long after her arrival at the hospital. Bew and Harold did their best to console Pat, mourning with him.

Bew and the Summer Classics team sorely felt the loss of Georgia. Taken so suddenly, she had been such a lifeforce among them. The rise of retail was largely due to her hard work. More than this, she was one of the family. Her premature departure left a void among them.

Bew was staggered by Georgia's passing. In all of his experience these many years, nothing had prepared him for this. He felt at a loss. He was especially grieved that Georgia did not have a church there in Birmingham that could conduct her funeral. Bew knew he could do nothing to make the pain go away for her family, but he wanted to do something. Georgia deserved to have a funeral where her family, friends and coworkers might properly mourn her loss and pay honor to the life she had lived. Bew asked his pastor at Covenant Presbyterian, Dr. Bill Hay, if he would conduct the funeral, and Dr. Hay agreed to do it.

They held the funeral at the Summer Classics store in Pelham. Georgia's husband Pat came. Her children made the drive from Oklahoma. All the Summer Classics staff came. Bill Hay conducted the funeral and many employees got up and shared their love and appreciation for Georgia. She had affected them all. Following the service, they spent time together talking and sharing stories of their lost friend.

With Summer Classics ever growing, it was time to move the office once again. Bew actively searched for sufficient real estate in Columbiana or nearby. Quite fortunately, he found the perfect space. It was a warehouse that had previously functioned as a tire distribution warehouse. It would suit Summer Classics fine. The man who owned the building gave Bew these terms: "I'm going to give you the option of buying it for $650,000. If you don't exercise that option in six months, the price is $750,000."

Bew decided to rent the building. The Summer Classics headquarters moved from Columbiana to this warehouse in Montevallo. The cushion operation remained in Columbiana. This move could not have been more timely.

That summer, on a Saturday morning, Bew was enjoying a rare moment of relaxation with Wendy at their house on Cherokee Road when his phone began to ring. It was Harold.

"Bew, I just got a call from the fire department in Columbiana—the plant is burning. I'm on my way there now."

Bew jumped to his feet. Startled, Wendy looked at her husband. "On my way!" He hung up the phone. "The plant is on fire," he called back to Wendy as he grabbed his car keys.

"Oh my…"

In moments, Bew tore down the road at speeds far exceeding the speed limit. He could not get there fast enough. Shaving minutes off the drive time, it still took him close to thirty minutes to reach Columbiana. All the while, his mind raced, thinking of all that was burning—all that was being destroyed. Even before the plant came into view, he could see the smoke billowing. Then he saw it. It was being eaten in flames. There was a flurry of activity—fire trucks were parked out front, firemen were all action doing their best to stop the fire. Bew saw that Harold and many other Summer Classics employees were already gathered. Bew parked and ran to the scene. Many of the employees were crying, fearing they would lose their jobs. Bew approached Harold, "Harold, can we save anything? The cushion patterns—those cost thousands."

Harold ran to a nearby fireman. "Can we get our cushion patterns? They're critical to our business."

"You can't go in there," the fireman stated emphatically.

Harold pled, "Please! I know exactly where they are. Let me take a couple of guys and go save them. Please, before we lose them."

The fireman's face showed conflict, but he empathized. "Okay. Go! Go as fast as you can!"

Harold started for the plant, shouting to Terry and Jerome as he ran, "Let's go! We have to get those cushion molds." Terry and Jerome ran after Harold.

Soon, the three men emerged, personally unscathed, and the molds were intact. "Thank you!" Bew called to the fireman.

The fireman nodded. "Now, everyone stand back!" he commanded.

Bew stood with his team, watching the firemen put out the fire. More of his staff had arrived. His mind worked feverishly. He was already planning for the future. What would he tell his clients? What could he do? How much would this cost them? They needed to find a new building for the cushion plant.

"Mr. White," Bew heard someone say. He turned to see a fireman standing next to him. "I'm the fire marshal—Jack Sanders. Could I have a brief word with you?" Bew nodded wordlessly. The fire marshal led Bew to a parked car, and they got inside.

Bew found this all rather curious. What was going on? What

needed to be discussed so privately?

"Sir, did you burn this warehouse down?"

Bew was astounded. "What?"

"Did you start the fire for insurance?"

"No! No!" Bew was finally coming to grips with the question. "Hell, no!"

The fire marshal put his hands up defensively. "Sorry. Just one of those things we have to ask."

Bew was at a loss for words. He felt like saying any number of choice words, but he could not settle on the one most suited to the occasion. Instead, he gritted his teeth, and then, with some effort, said, "Is that all?"

"That's all."

Bew opened the door and stormed off. He rejoined his staff. He did his best to console his employees. He would do all in his power to keep them. He needed them. By now, the fire was mostly under control, but the damage was done. Summer Classics' days in Columbiana were at an end.

For the next several weeks, everyone worked their hardest. They rallied together as a team. Bew was proud to see his employees' hard work and perseverance in such circumstances. Thanks to the quick work of Harold, Jerome and Terry, much time and effort was spared—with the cushion patterns still intact, the cushion operation, which was moved to Montevallo, would not have to be built from scratch. But there was still much to be done.

They got straight to their biggest concern—keeping their orders. They called all their clients, asking them for patience, explaining the situation. "Wait. We're going to make them. We're just going to be a month late." Amazingly, their clients waited. Bew was very grateful.

When Summer Classics received two million dollars in insurance, this was a huge help. This helped them get their feet back underneath them. Bew also used this to help them acquire more real estate. He found another building for rent down the street in Montevallo.

2004 had been a harsh year for Summer Classics. From all outward appearances, it seemed that they would have a poor year-end, but to everyone's surprise it proved to be a year of growth. Summer Classics grew by 35%. Bew could not believe it. He was glad to be going ahead into 2005. He was ready for a new year.

This year saw one more major change—Summer Classics started banking with Citizens Bank—a subsidiary to the global European bank, Royal Bank of Scotland (RBS). Over the years, Bew had learned much about banks and had formed certain expectations. He knew what he could ask of his bank, and if he felt that they fell short of their responsibility to serve his interests, he was swift to act.

Bew was unsatisfied with his current banking options in Birmingham. He felt that none of these banks meshed well with his business. Summer Classics was always growing, doubling every four years. Up to this point, his banks had struggled to keep stride with this growth. Indeed, they seemed to be averse to it. The banks he knew in Birmingham were very low-risk and conservative, but this was not his world. There were risks involved in his business, but he knew the business well.

Constantly, all his money was tied up in receivables and inventory. Every year, he bet millions. Months in advance, Summer Classics purchased a full season's inventory. This was a gamble, but Bew trusted it. Selling from inventory gave Summer Classics a competitive edge. Timing was key in this work. When orders came flooding in, Summer Classics was ready to ship and meet the demand in a timely fashion. Even further, customers bought their furniture on ninety-day terms. Hence, Summer Classics had to wait several months before they finally got a return on their investment.

Because of this, in order to grow the company, Bew wanted to get his hands on as much money as he could. When banks asked, "How much do you need?" he wanted to ask in reply, "How much will you give me?" But this frightened banks. Since 1997, Bew had banked with First Commercial Bank. He had no qualms with the bank, but Summer Classics was growing beyond them. Their credit line with First Commercial was currently set at nine million dollars, and he needed more. The bank told him that they were at their limit. Bew knew it was time to find a new bank.

In recent times, Bew had instituted an open-door policy with banks. He had learned that the bank-business relationship could be quite fragile. It never hurt to talk with other banks and know what they had to offer. He now opened the door wide, and he got into talks with multiple banks. In short time, he narrowed his search to the RBS subsidiary, Citizens Bank, and Wells Fargo—big banks that would suit his business.

As the two Auburn fraternities SAE and Kappa Alpha had once fought over Bew, now, two Atlanta banks fought over his business. In this period of time, banks like Wells Fargo and Citizens Bank were aggressively giving out new loans. They were searching for a business such as Summer Classics to add to their clientele. For a long time, Wells Fargo and Citizens tried to outdo one another, offering Summer Classics a competitive deal. Bew was thrilled.

In the end, Citizens won out. The bank had about twenty-five southeastern customers at that time. Between all these customers, the bank's loans totaled close to one hundred million dollars. Citizens was pleased to be adding Summer Classics to its portfolio.

It was a great time for businesses like Summer Classics. Big banks like RBS were coming in and doing everything they could to get a competitive edge over local banks. Because of this, Citizens, the RBS subsidiary, was offering Bew unheard-of-terms. Most local banks asked for a personal guarantee on all loans— Citizens waived the personal guarantee. Most banks that worked according to an Asset-Based-Lending (ABL) model would only lend 50% on inventory, but Bew argued that Summer Classics should get 63% because all their product was finished product. Citizens agreed to this.

Bew felt that he had finally found a bank that meshed with his business. Citizens Bank used ABL. None of the banks Bew knew in Birmingham used ABL. This was a good match for Citizens and for Summer Classics. Citizens would lend against Summer Classics' assets—its inventory and receivables, which was perfect—this was Summer Classics' chief collateral.

Best of all, Citizens gave Bew the line of credit he desperately needed. They told Bew they could give Summer Classics a ten million dollar line of credit, and it was likely that they could increase this soon. Bew could not believe his good fortune. It all seemed too good to be true.

CHAPTER 13

THE RECESSION: PART ONE

"Courage is not having the strength to go on; it is going on when you don't have the strength."
- Theodore Roosevelt

WITHIN A SHORT TIME, Citizens Bank made good on their word—they increased the line of credit from ten million to fifteen million. Soon after that, feeling that Summer Classics had the inventory to back it up, they lent Summer Classics close to twenty million dollars. With this kind of credit, Bew and his team felt like anything was possible. Finally, they had a bank that could come alongside them and thrust the company to new heights. Now, they had the room to properly finance Bew's vision. Within the next two years, Bew opened three more stores— one in Atlanta, one in Louisville and another in San Antonio. In addition to this, Bew exercised the option to buy both of their plants in Montevallo. He felt confident in all these decisions.

Summer Classics was not the only one with positive feelings—Citizens seemed to be genuinely excited about their new client. Once a quarter, Summer Classics' CFO Neal Morgan worked with Citizens' field examiner Shannon Connelly to conduct an audit. Each year, Neal would submit yearly projections and a budget to Citizens. On her visits, Shannon and

Neal would go through Summer Classics' receivables, inventory and financials to make sure that Summer Classics was in line to meet their goals. Shannon always returned to Atlanta with a glowing report.

Bew also got on well with the Citizens Bank president—Ethan Price. Bew liked to be able to talk frankly about his business and its needs, and he felt that Ethan could track with his line of thinking. Bew was constantly thinking of better ways to use his banks and finance his business. For example, he also banked with CIT Group, using factoring to finance his company until they had received a return on their inventory. Ethan and his team not only kept stride with Summer Classics in such endeavors, but Bew felt that Ethan was truly invested in helping Summer Classics meet its goals and grow. It seemed to be the very definition of a mutually beneficial relationship.

Even though Bew had this positive impression of Citizens, he still kept his wits about him. He wanted to do all that was necessary to ensure a secure future for Summer Classics. Bew and Neal had come to learn that Citizens was under the control of a larger RBS subsidiary in Boston. When it came down to who was running the show, Boston was running Citizens. Because of this, just before Bew had committed to banking with Citizens, he told Ethan that he wanted to meet the RBS president in Boston.

Bew explained his reasoning bluntly, "I'll bank with you, but you're going to need to bring in the president from Boston. If you get fired, I want to know I have a backup." Ethan arranged the meeting.

Bew met with Ethan and the president from Boston – Phil Gordon—in Atlanta. Phil was cool and impersonal. As they spoke, Bew sensed some tension between Ethan and Phil. For his part, Bew did not much care for Phil. It seemed clear that Phil wanted to keep this as formal as possible. He had come to Atlanta because they wanted the Summer Classics account, but he made little effort to build any sort of relationship with Bew. This disappointed Bew somewhat, but in the end, it mattered little to him. He would be conducting all his business with Ethan. And he knew that he and Ethan would get on well.

Already, Summer Classics had been in the process of phasing Mexico out. China's prices could not be matched. Bew did not consciously decide one day that he wanted to be done with Mexico, but as things worked out, Summer Classics was taking most all of their new collections to China. Without new collections, Mexico was losing Summer Classics.

Yet, if there was an incident that changed Bew's relationship with Enrique, it was when Enrique hugely misapplied funds from Summer Classics. Enrique had told Bew that he needed a loan of $100,000 for the factory. Summer Classics duly provided it. But when Bew came down to pay a visit, he saw that Enrique had added a beautiful and expensive patio to his house. Bew started piecing things together.

"Enrique, how much did that cost?" Bew asked.

Enrique observed Bew for a moment, debating how he wanted to respond. "$110,000," he finally admitted.

Bew felt his suspicions confirmed. "So, that's what you did with the $100,000 I lent to you? I am so pissed at you. You took my money and built this?"

Enrique protested, "No. No, I used my wife's money."

Bew did not believe him. "Dude. No. You used my money. That is so unethical."

Bew returned to the states with ill feelings regarding his relationship with Enrique. He vented to Harold. "Harold, he is so unethical. He thinks my money is his money."

While Summer Classics was growing and changing, there was still much that had not changed. Business with China proceeded much as it had in previous years. Between Bew and Harold, the two split up travel to China. In south China, Winston had formed a relationship with a second factory, so Summer Classics was soon producing in this factory as well. As always, samples and quality continued to be a sticking point—in south China and north China. Bew and his team had grown accustomed to this issue, but they never liked it.

Naturally, as the company grew, Summer Classics increased its personnel. Bew now had hundreds of men and women in his employ. He was very mindful of this. He was glad for the growth—this is what he had always wanted—but he could not help but consider Summer Classics in its beginnings when it was just him and a few others. Things had been simpler then. Now, the livelihood of so many people relied upon the success of his business. Summer Classics was not just his dream anymore—it belonged to them all now.

FROM THE MOMENT BEW STARTED banking with Citizens, Summer Classics entered into a new phase. It felt like the culmination of all the hard work that had come before. They had clawed their way to this point. Now, it was as if Citizens had given Summer Classics all the money they could ever ask for, saying, "Dream bigger." Whatever Bew might envision, he only had to reach out and grasp it.

For Bew and Wendy, this had a direct impact on their financial stability. For the ten years leading up to 2005, Bew had paid himself a salary of $41,000. In addition to this, year after year, he pulled most all the equity out of their house yearly and put it into Summer Classics until customer payments starting coming in, at which point he took the money back and put it into his home equity again. He was so fearful of failure that he signed the house over to Wendy. Imagining the possibility that repo men might come to take all he owned, he told her, "This is your house. I just hope you'll let me live in it." Wendy playfully agreed Bew could continue to live there.

But these were new and fairer times. Now, Bew could pay himself a proper salary. He was not burdened by the same fear of failure. Summer Classics was not as dependent on him as it had been. He and Wendy started to invest more time in enjoying their life and their marriage. They spent more time together at the country club and at the farm. Life was good.

In 2007, something happened which Bew had long hoped for—William wanted to join Summer Classics. Ever since college, William had chosen to go his own way. Up to this point, he had not shown a personal interest in Summer Classics. At the time, William was working for the large German chemical company BASF. It was a good job, but now he was interested in one of Bew's latest projects.

That year, Bew had purchased Brooks & Collier in Huntsville. He greatly admired the company's store model. The owner had indoor furniture mixed in with outdoor furniture. The owner was well traveled, going to countries such as India, the Philippines, and France. Borrowing various styles from these cultures, he gave his store an international, exotic character. Bew loved the look. He felt it complemented the outdoor furniture and made the product more appealing to customers. He bought the company with the plan to adopt a similar model with all of his stores. Now, Summer Classics would start a new division called SC Home, producing indoor luxury furniture.

William had observed this latest venture for Summer Classics, and he saw a lot of potential in it. He had many ideas for how this could be done. He told his father about his interest, and Bew was thrilled.

While William wanted to come on board, he wanted to make something clear, "I want to do my own thing. I'll do indoor. You do the outdoor." He added, "But I need you to help me with it."

Bew was enthusiastic, "Great. When I go to China, you go to China. We can meet and you can go see some of your suppliers."

William joined Summer Classics in January of 2008. Only days later, Wynne joined Summer Classics as a sales rep. This was mostly coincidental. Neither of them had spoken to each other about joining. Their timing and decision had been independent.

Whenever Bew was traveling to China, William accompanied him. Bew taught him how to meet with suppliers and everything else he thought might serve William in starting SC Home. The plan was that William would spend whatever time was necessary to prepare and begin the new indoor division.

Over the years, Bew had invested so much time and effort into the company. He had learned much in the process. His dedication to Summer Classics was such that his children had long called it his fourth child. He knew he had often been absent as a father, but he liked to think that much of what he had done—the company he had created—was for them, for his family and not just for him. For this reason, Bew was happy that he could invest in William like this. For the most part, William worked independently at Summer Classics. William had his own ideas and vision. Bew wanted to respect this, but he also wanted to offer William all the help he could.

Bew had so many reasons to feel excitement for the future. Summer Classics was on an ever-upward trajectory. Every year seemed to bring new and exciting advances in the company. All his staff carried themselves with more confidence these days. Wherever Summer Classics went, success seemed to follow, and everyone was excited to be a part of it.

Despite all this, when the summer of 2008 came, Bew felt a rising sense of unease. He could not find a specific reason for this feeling, but he just had a premonition. For years, he had been an avid watcher of CNBC. Every day, he stayed up to date with the latest Dow numbers. He was personally quite invested in the stock market. From all outward appearances, everything seemed great. Everyone felt that the economy was as strong as ever and only getting stronger. But he sensed that something was happening on the peripheries.

At first, Bew tried to dismiss this feeling. Why was he worried? No one else was. But he could not shake this feeling. He started to take preventive action. He had learned to trust his gut in these matters. By the time the Casual pre-market in Chicago rolled around, his unease was deep-set. That July, at the pre-market, they all had a sales meeting. "I've got to say something," Bew thought.

He moved to the front of the room and got everyone's attention. "Guys, I don't want to scare you, but I just feel like something terrible is coming. And in preparation, I have shorted a lot of stock. I've sold a quarter of a million dollars in stock. I've refinanced my house. I've taken a quarter of a million dollars out of my house." Everyone listened with raised eyebrows. "But frankly, I don't think it's enough. I don't know what it is. I don't know why I feel this way."

Almost in unison, they replied, "We're doing great. Stop worrying." William and Wynne, who were also in attendance, sat and listened in silence.

Bew could tell everyone thought he was crazy. "Okay. Well, I hope y'all aren't wrong, but I'm not changing my mind until I see the coast is clear."

"We're fine," some of them repeated. Seeing that none would take his concerns seriously, Bew grudgingly moved on to the business of the market.

These days, Bew struggled to find sleep. His anxiety kept him up at night. He found himself fluctuating back and forth between panic and positivity. Business seemed to be great. So, what was wrong? Why couldn't he shake this feeling of dread?

The annual Summer Classics Garden Party was held at the end of July. It was very well attended, and all went as well as they could hope. This certainly was as good a garden party as any before it. "Maybe I am wrong. I still feel like something is wrong, but I don't know what it is. I don't know why I feel this way." Hesitantly, Bew let himself enjoy that day's festivities. Everything was all right.

But the previous month's order activity told another story. No one had been watching it. If Bew had looked at the June order activity, he would have seen that it had dropped dramatically. It was as if their clients were collectively bracing for something.

In the first week of September, Bew joined a group of other leaders in his industry for a hunting trip on Nicholson Island, a small island used as a private game preserve on Lake Ontario.

They flew on a private jet to a small airport. To reach their island, they took an amphibious vehicle called a DUKW (more commonly known as a "Duck"). They were all greatly amused as the Duck drove down a ramp into the water, floating them the short distance to their island hunting lodge.

The following morning, Bew rose before the others. Grabbing a cup of coffee, he sat down before the TV, watching CNBC. Now, he was not the only one with a premonition. Others were growing alarmed. The signs were clearer now: the stock market was in steady decline. Something was happening. Bew sat glued to the TV.

For every morning on this trip, this was Bew's ritual: he rose early to watch CNBC, doing his best to discover what was happening. This trip was supposed to be an escape from work, but Bew could not escape. The others began to take notice. One morning, they rose and came to join him in front of the TV.

"What are you doing?" Leib Oehmig, the president of Sunbrella, asked Bew.

Bew turned in his chair, "We're getting ready to get a major disruption. This is going to be the biggest f-ing disaster ever."

Leib sank into a chair next to Bew, his face showing alarm, "Damn. Really? What's wrong with the stock market?" The others stood listening.

"It's going down the limit like ten percent a day," Bew stated.

They all began to mutter. Some pulled out their smart phones, their thumbs quickly working their Blackberry keyboards. A cloud fell upon the remainder of the hunting trip. Everyone feared what reality might be awaiting them back in the States.

Only days later, on September 15, Lehman Brothers filed for Chapter 11 bankruptcy. It was (and still remains) the largest bankruptcy filing in US history. Lehman Brothers held over $600 billion in assets. Their collapse rocked the US market and caused wide-spread panic. A market that had seemed so solid now threatened to crumble and bring the fabric of the US economy down with it. That day, the Dow had its sharpest single-day drop since September 11, 2001. Fear and panic were ruling the day. Bew watched in horror. His mind was filled with this one thought: "This is the beginning of the end of the world as I know it."

The very next week, Bew and his team attended Casual Market in Chicago. Bew could not help but think of their last visit to Chicago during pre-market. He had a premonition then that something awful was coming, but this was far worse than he had ever imagined.

Taking the flight of fifty stairs up to their floor, Bew studied the faces of people going by him—he saw panic. They were all going into survival mode.

All of a sudden, he felt a great shortness of breath. He braced himself on the railing and stood there for nearly two minutes, trying to recover himself. "What is happening?" Bew thought. He had always maintained an active lifestyle, running six miles a week and playing tennis at the country club frequently. Bew called his doctor in Birmingham.

"Get to an emergency room—stat!" his doctor told him.

He called his staff in the Summer Classics showroom to tell them he was going to the emergency room. He assured them he could get there himself. Under his own power, he went to the emergency room at Northwestern Hospital.

A nurse beckoned him back to a room, where they took his heart rate. "Man, your heart rate is 45. You must run a lot."

They asked him to run on a machine while they hooked him up to an electrocardiogram to measure his heartbeat. Bew ran on the machine for them, and he felt fine. There was no shortness of breath.

Bew was pronounced healthy. "Man, you are in great shape. You must work out! You have the heart rate of a marathoner."

Bew could not make sense of this. His best conclusion was that whatever had happened to him, it must have been stress-induced. He wasn't sleeping, and the stress was getting to him. In short time, he put this incident behind him. It must be an anomaly. He had enough to worry about as it was.

As was often the case, Summer Classics was in a vulnerable time. They were highly dependent upon their line of credit— credit which Citizens had doled out so liberally. Citizens' biggest draw for Summer Classics had been flexibility, but it was now becoming clear that big banks like Citizens (and RBS by extension) had overextended themselves. There had been such an unquestioning confidence in the current economy. Banks knew they were being liberal and flexible, but everyone felt secure in doing so. Now, they were paying through the nose for this mistake.

The previous year, Ethan Price, the president of Citizens, had been fired. This had been a blow to Summer Classics. Bew and Ethan had been on good terms. They had established a good working relationship. But now that Ethan was gone, Bew knew that he should prepare for Citizens to become more inflexible and soon. He had no one on the inside to help him now. Summer Classics owed Citizens over fifteen million dollars. Bew told Neal that they needed to start looking for a new bank, just in case.

Sure enough, in the first week of October, Citizens Bank began to apply pressure. Bew had not expected this so soon. Shannon Connelly, who had once been a field examiner, was now Summer Classics' loan officer at Citizens. Bew and Neal had always gotten on well with Shannon. Now, she bore the role of messenger. Increasingly, she would be the bearer of bad news. Shannon reached out to Bew, "What are you going to do? You need to do something."

"What are you talking about? Like what?" Bew asked.

"Go raise some money," Shannon replied.

Bew was dumbfounded. "In this market? Are you freaking crazy? I would have to give my company away to raise money. Nobody wants to give money to a company like ours in this market. They think everyone is going to go out of business. But we're not going to go out of business. Don't worry. We're fine," he added.

Shannon hated this. Over the years, she had built a good relationship with Summer Classics. But recently, the RBS branch in Boston had imposed itself on everything at Citizens. Orders were coming in from the top, and Boston guys were being sent to Atlanta to manage things. Credit officer Mason Roach was set over her. It was his job to scrutinize her portfolio and "encourage her" (more like pressure her) to make cuts. Wanting to keep his job at the bank, he was encouraging her somewhat strongly lately. She, too, was afraid to lose her job. The bank and everyone in it were going into survival mode. She did her best to keep her tone cool and professional, "You need to start raising money."

Bew was overwhelmed. It was hard to know what to do. One thing Bew knew for sure: he had to give this situation his complete attention. He dropped by William's office. "William, I hate to do this to you, but I can't help you. I have to save the company. I'm going to be primarily working on money—how we can keep enough money and keep the bank off our butts."

William understood. "It's okay. I got it. I'm fine."

Survival would require a great deal of forward thinking. While they tried to figure things out with Citizens, Bew and Neal also kept looking for banks, but, so far, no banks would talk to them. Most were too busy trying to save themselves to even consider taking on another account.

Bew was especially concerned about one thing: Summer Classics was going to break its covenant with Citizens. In bank loan agreements, covenants are a normal practice. With every bank there is a ratio which has to do with assets and liabilities. The business and the bank negotiate the ratio number, and whatever is settled upon becomes a covenant. To go below this settled number is a covenant break. A bank covenant is a very serious thing. Indeed, this had been yet another competitive advantage for Citizens: their covenant with Summer Classics had been far more flexible than those of their competition.

One of these covenant agreements stated that Summer Classics could not lose money two quarters in a row. Looking ahead, Bew knew that they would break this covenant. They would not make money in the final quarter of 2008 (October-December) or in the first quarter of 2009 (January-March). Bew decided to get out ahead of this. He contacted Citizens Bank, "Hey, I'm going to break a covenant. We're not going to make money for two quarters in a row."

"We'll cross that bridge when we come to it," was the reply.

"I'd rather know now than wait until we cross the bridge. You can start foreclosing on me if I don't know what's going to happen." Bew wanted to be able to take a more aggressive stance if he knew this might be coming.

But their reply remained unchanged, "No. We won't worry about that till we come to it."

This was utterly unsatisfactory for Bew. If he broke the covenant, there was no knowing what Citizens Bank would do to Summer Classics. This is what Bew hated about this situation: Citizens held all the power. But Bew would not sit back passively. If there was anything he could do to better his situation, he would do it.

Burdened with anxiety, he felt like he was being slowly crushed to death. He longed for sleep at night, but it would not come. When his mind was not working to find an escape for his company, he was kept awake by an overwhelming feeling of fear. Not wanting to keep Wendy up, he started sleeping on the couch downstairs. Night after night, he quietly moved from their room to the couch. In time, he simply remained downstairs, knowing he would end his night there anyway.

Wendy felt burdened for her husband. "What can I do? What can I do?" she asked Bew.

"A lot of praying. Lots of praying," Bew replied. If Wendy could be relied upon for anything, above all else, it was this— she was a prayer warrior.

Wendy had indeed been praying, and now she prayed even harder. She also began to lay out a blanket and a pillow on the couch for Bew each night.

Just as Bew had predicted, Summer Classics passed through the final quarter of the year without making any money. They had to make money in the next quarter, but he knew they would not. He continued to press Citizens Bank—what would happen if he broke the covenant? They would give no reply. Meanwhile, Citizens continued to pressure Bew to raise capital. But now, they moved from subtly suggesting he do this to practically threatening him. Bew continued to protest—how was he supposed to raise money in this market?

He did not know what he was supposed to do. He needed someone on the inside, someone he knew. Boston was running this show. "Let me call the president—Phil Gordon. He'll understand," Bew said to the bank.

Bew was told emphatically that he could do no such thing, "Do not call him."

"He'll understand," Bew insisted.

"If you call him, we will foreclose."

Bew was stunned, "Are you serious?"

"Just raise money." The call ended.

"Why don't they want me to call him? Now, it seems like I need to call him. He's my only hope," Bew thought to himself. But he never made this call—he was too afraid of the consequences. If they had been trying to scare him, it worked—he was terrified.

In January of 2009, Bew began to meet with Summer Classics management multiple times every week. They had to start letting people go. Every day in every meeting they were asking, "What can we do? Who can we let go?" They all hated it. The stores took the first hit: they had to let go of all the assistant managers in the stores. The managers would have to run the stores alone.

Whenever they let someone go, Bew tried to be personally involved in these meetings or else to at least call that person. "You haven't done anything wrong," he would tell them. "You've been a great employee. We just have to make a cut because the recession is killing us. The only way we can reduce our overhead is letting people go. I don't want to do it. I just have to do it to save the company." Bew hated this, but if this had to happen he knew it was best if it came from him.

Spirits were heavy at Summer Classics. The energy and enthusiasm that had so characterized their work only a year ago
was now all but gone. Now, they worked to survive. Many went
into work fearing that any day may be their last day of employment. But the work had to go on. Bew did his best to motivate
and push his team. They could not give up.

In early February, Bew and William took a number of Summer Classics clients to hunt at the farm. They were hoping to
rally up more business. The hunt lasted the weekend. At its end,
Bew made his way back to Birmingham, hoping that it had been
worth their time. They needed to bring in more new orders.

Soon after he returned to Birmingham, he prepared to join
his family for a birthday dinner at the Mountain Brook Country
Club. Every month, his mother liked to gather all her family to
celebrate the family birthdays occurring that month. As Bew
was preparing to leave, he received a phone call from their care-
taker at the farm—Willy.

"Mr. White! The farmhouse! It's burning down," Willy
blurted out.

"What? Burning? Can you stop it?" Bew froze.

"I can't stop it! It's burning down!"

"I'm coming." Bew felt desperate. He was going back to
Boligee. He called William, frantic. "William, the farm's burned
down! The farm's burned down!"

William and his fiancée Laurie were on their way to the
birthday dinner when Bew called. William could not keep up
with all his father was saying, but he understood enough. They
ended the call, and William sobbed. It was the first time Laurie
had ever seen him cry. They did not go to the birthday dinner.

At the country club, all the family was seated for dinner.
Wynne and Walker were there. Gillian, Toody, Bevelle and their
families were there. Gay White was there. Bew, Wendy and William were conspicuously absent. Mike Goodrich, Gillian's husband, took a phone call. Everyone saw his face go white. He put
his phone away. Leaning in his chair, he said something to Gay.

Instantly, she burst into tears.

A hush came over the room. Mike rose to his feet. All eyes were upon him. "The farmhouse has burned down. Billy just called me." There was a collective gasp. It was an awful moment.

A couple of hours later, Bew and Wendy arrived in Boligee to find the farmhouse all but destroyed. The fire had spread to every corner of the structure. Here, his family had made so many memories—memories from his youth, memories of his late father. This—his father's haven—*his* haven was now only a charred remnant. Bew broke down crying. It was one of the saddest days in his life.

In the days following the fire, Gay's health went into decline. The fire had devastated her, and she would not recover. Two weeks later, Gabrielle Comer White passed away.

CHAPTER 14

THE GARDEN

"God is our refuge and strength, a very present help in trouble.
Therefore, we will not fear though the earth gives way."
- Psalm 46:1-2

BEHIND BEW and Wendy's house, spread across several acres on a hill bank, there is a garden. This is Wendy's garden. In this garden, there are hundreds of hydrangeas, over a hundred Japanese maples, and various kinds of flowers. In the midst of all this, there are close to one hundred stones, each with a different Scripture engraved upon its face. The stones are placed carefully in the garden. Every Scripture is for meditation and prayer. Every Scripture marks a significant moment in Wendy's life. This garden is Wendy's calling.

Nearly two decades earlier, Wendy began to feel that there was something that she needed to do to honor the Lord. She had been praying, asking him how he wanted her to honor him. Around this time, Wendy and Bew had dinner with their friends Whitney and Adair DeBardeleben at the DeBardeleben house. While the men spoke in the other room, Wendy and Adair went into the dining room. A beautiful arrangement of flowers on the dining room table caught Wendy's eye. "Where did you get those?" Wendy asked. "They're so pretty."

"Oh, I just took them from my mother in-law's cutting garden," Adair replied.

Wendy looked at these flowers, and for the first time, she wondered, "Could I ever grow a flower?" She had never tried gardening before. Years ago, at their home in Connecticut, she had laughed at Bew when he tried to grow a vegetable garden. Watching him labor in the yard with a hoe, she thought it looked boring and tedious. But now Wendy wondered if God was calling her to start a garden.

The hill bank behind Bew and Wendy's house was overrun with poison ivy, weeds and kudzu. Wendy was not sure if she could even have a garden. She asked her friend Karen Chapman, a landscape architect, to come over to look at it. Wendy followed Karen as they walked among the overgrowth – Karen giving everything a careful study. "Could I grow flowers up here?" Wendy asked.

"Oh yeah," Karen confirmed. "You've got sun coming in under the power lines."

Wendy decided she would try. Standing in the middle of the kudzu on the bank, she prayed, "Lord, if it's your will for me, I would love to have a garden for your honor."

Wendy got right to work, and this soon took up a great part of her time. She was constantly checking garden books out of the library. She labored on the hillside with her own hands day after day. She weeded the garden, pulling out the kudzu and the poison ivy. She made garden paths, laying down wooden beams to mark the way.

For years, Wendy labored in this garden. Wendy's children—these children who were her life—were growing up and leaving the house. She toiled in the garden. Before long, it was only her and Wynne. Bew was gone all the time. When he was home, he was always stressed, always worried about money. She toiled in the garden.

As a child, Wynne felt no fondness for the garden. She was jealous for her mother's attentions and time. The garden took her mother away from her. As Summer Classics was like a fourth child for Bew, the garden was for Wendy. But, as Wynne matured, she came to see the garden in a new light. It was in the garden that Wendy poured out all her stress, all her worry, all her suffering. To the casual onlooker, the garden was just a garden, but when Wynne beheld the garden she saw her mother's inner turmoil.

Wynne saw something that few could see, but there was more to the garden than even this. For Wendy, the garden was as she had first conceived it—the garden was her offering to God. She gardened to honor and serve him.

> *And this is eternal life that they know You,*
> *the only true God,*
> *and Jesus Christ whom You have sent.*
> *John 17:3*

Wendy was not just sowing seeds for the flowers, she was sowing seeds for the gospel. Throughout the garden, Wendy carefully placed Scriptures engraved upon stones. Every Bible verse bore a special meaning for Wendy. Throughout her life, the Lord had impressed Scripture upon her heart—Scripture which the Lord had brought to her in a moment of trial or in a moment of need. Before it found its way into the garden, each one had been meditated upon in Wendy's heart. As the years rolled by, she placed more and more of them in the garden. To see the garden is to see a life of faith—it is to see Wendy's walk with the Lord.

> *Let everything that has*
> *breath praise the Lord.*
> *Praise the Lord.*
> *Psalm 150:6*

For herself and for her family, she wanted nothing more than that they please the Lord. But so often, she and her family were overcome with the stress and worry of life. Wendy was hard on herself, feeling that she failed God much of the time. She poured herself into the garden. She wanted it to be a fitting offering for him. Like the worries that could so easily crowd upon her, she tirelessly purged her garden of growing weeds. Sometimes, she felt like the struggle was in vain. The weeds and her worries always returned, threatening to choke out life.

In time, the garden gained recognition in the Birmingham community. It was added to the Birmingham Gardens Tour. Groups of people would come to walk the three-acre garden on a hillside. Churches would call to schedule times of prayer for their church groups. Wendy hoped the garden could inspire them and enrich their souls.

All through their marriage, in times of trial, Bew had been sustained by the faith of his wife—her faith sustained his faith. Her longsuffering, her constant love and support, her vigilant prayer on his behalf—none of these things went unnoticed or unappreciated. When Bew first married Wendy, he did not realize the support she would give him. He did not think of this, but she did. When times had gotten hard, he had often felt like giving up, but she was always there to support him. "No, you can do this. I believe in you," she would tell him. And Bew would keep going.

Over the years, as a rule, Bew did his best not to talk to Wendy about the problems of his work. He was always worried, but he felt that it was unfair to burden her with this. Whenever he did share all his worries and stress, he saw how it weighed on her. He always felt guilty. "Why am I doing this to her? She has enough problems on her own. I don't want to dump this on her," he thought.

But Wendy knew her husband. Whether he talked to her about his problems or not, Wendy knew. She saw the constant worry on his face, and he was right—it weighed upon her. But whatever it was that weighed upon her she brought before the Lord in prayer and supplication. She prayed constantly and she meditated upon Scripture fervently. She toiled in the garden.

The garden displays Wendy's faith in a loving and mighty

God. She believed in a God who watched over her family – a God who cared for their every need. Burdened by the cares of her family, she poured out her heart to the Lord. Whenever a family member was going through a time of crisis, Wendy silently burdened their suffering and cast it upon the Lord. She begged his protection and care upon her family.

Seek the Lord and His strength;
seek his presence continually!
1 Chronicles 16:11

In 2008, Wendy's heart ached as she watched her husband downtrodden with worry and fear. Night after night, he slept on the couch downstairs, and night after night, she prayed. As the year went on, things only got worse.

"What can I do?" she asked Bew.

Bew longed for his wife's support. As he had so many times before, he leaned upon her faith. "A lot of praying. Lots of praying."

"Yes, we will pray," Wendy replied.

The worry could not be held at bay. Like weeds, the worry overwhelmed Bew. He began to pray, "God, give me wisdom to figure this out. I don't know what to do. I thought I'd been in every situation. I can't figure this out on my own."

The farmhouse burned down. Gay White passed away. Their dear daughter Walker was struggling through her own personal crisis. Wendy begged the Lord to provide peace in the midst of the storm—peace for those she so loved. She poured her heart out to God. She toiled in the garden, finding hope in the Word of God and its promises.

Whoever dwells in the shelter of the Most High
will rest in the shadow of the Almighty.
Psalm 91:1

CHAPTER 15

THE RECESSION: PART TWO

"Through perseverance many people win success out of what seemed destined to be certain failure."
- Benjamin Disraeli

THE DAY AFTER Gay White passed away, Bew met with some of his family to plan her funeral. Bevelle, who lived with her family in Chattanooga, had come to stay at Bew and Wendy's house during this time. While they were talking, Bew's phone rang. He stepped outside. Bevelle could not hear the conversation, but she saw that Bew was visibly upset. He paced back and forth outside.

The bank was still applying pressure. "We don't like your space." This was Brian Clark with the bank's Special Assets department in Boston.

"What do you mean?" Bew asked. "What do you mean 'my space'?"

"That's the business you're in. We don't like the business you're in. You're a discretionary," Brian explained.

Bew was dumbfounded, "Well, you lent me twenty million dollars. You should have said that before you lent me the twenty million and not after."

Brian was unperturbed, "You need to be raising money."

Bew struggled to keep his tone civil. "How?" he asked incredulously. "Look, we won't make money this quarter, but I still have plenty of assets to cover that." Wendy and Bevelle watched as he gestured animatedly. "I'm going to be fine. Hold tight." Bew was ever mindful of the bank covenant—Citizens Bank still would not say what would happen when the covenant was broken—something terrible he was sure.

Brian held firm, "We just need to see you taking action to raise capital."

The call was over. Bew walked back inside. He felt downtrodden and worn down, and he looked it too. Bevelle and Wendy looked at Bew in concern. "The bank is threatening me. They're telling me to raise money. How am I supposed to raise money in this market? We are so screwed." Bew sank into a chair. His world was crumbling around him. Wendy put her arm around his shoulders.

Despite the tragic nature of recent events, somehow there was still a certain sweetness to the following days. Bew came home often to visit with Bevelle and Wendy at the house. Bevelle remembers this time fondly. This was a rare opportunity— she and her brother did not get to talk often. She cherished their conversations. Bew, too, enjoyed their conversations—they gave him comfort in an otherwise tumultuous time.

Soon, the funeral came. Bew and his sisters and their families gathered with friends to honor the memory of their mother. It was a time that brought them all together and made them all mindful of the gift of family. They were not a perfect family, but they had each other. It was a sad but meaningful occasion for them all.

Soon, the time came for Bevelle to return to her home in Chattanooga. She packed her things, thanked Wendy for her hospitality and love, and she left. She was on Old Leeds Road when her phone rang. It was Bew.

"Where are you?" Bew asked. He had just come home.

"I'm leaving," Bevelle replied.

"You're leaving?" Bevelle could hear the sadness in Bew's voice.

But then they kept talking. Bew and Bevelle still had their conversation. They talked for a long time over the phone while Bevelle drove back to Chattanooga. It warmed her heart to have this time with her big brother.

Surprisingly, Summer Classics lost no money in 2008, but they did not profit either. Bew knew they would not get by so easily in 2009. Not only were they were passing through the first quarter of 2009 without making money, they were starting to lose money. They were about to break the covenant.

That March, only a couple of weeks after Gay's funeral, Citizens Bank asked Bew to come to Atlanta for a conference meeting with their Special Assets group from Boston. They did not outline the purpose of the meeting—they just emphasized that it was very important that it happen. Bew was scared to death, "Are they calling me to Atlanta to take me out?" They still would not tell him what would happen when Summer Classics broke the covenant.

Bew would soon learn that Citizens Bank was already taking action regarding the oncoming covenant break. Most bank loans are graded on a risk rating system. The more risky loans a bank has, the greater the loan loss provision a bank is required to allocate and the greater the loan loss reserves a bank must set aside. Even when a bank has not actually realized any losses, it still has to create a reserve for potential losses. Therefore, the bank makes less money.

In the recession banks fell under severe scrutiny. For many years, banks had done pretty much as they pleased with little oversight. Negligence was widespread because everyone had such confidence in the strength of the economy. There was nothing to worry about. But now that it had become clear that everyone—the banks more than anyone—had been playing with money they did not actually have, the bank examiners began to tighten the screws on the banks. With the feds breathing down their necks, senior bank executives started pressing everyone beneath them to unload high-risk loans, irrespective of the relationship or history the bank might have with that client.

They would do whatever they had to do to save their necks and get the feds off their back.

A loan could be downgraded for many reasons—one of the reasons was the breaking of a covenant. This almost always downgrades a loan. Whenever a commercial bank like Citizens Bank has a problem loan, it reports that loan to Special Assets, the bank department responsible for handling the negotiation and management of the bank's forbearance agreements. Also known as the "Bank Workout Group," most clients assume that Special Assets will do everything it can to "work out" the problem and get their loan back on track. But in practice, Special Assets is a bank's hit squad. When the loan passes to Special Assets, they usually get to work unloading it from the bank's portfolio. If Special Assets can "squeeze" some money from the client before killing their loan, this is always best. Special Assets' involvement in the Summer Classics loan meant Citizens practically considered the covenant broken and the loan downgraded.

Bew drove to Atlanta with Neal and Tommy Clement for the meeting. Tommy was a store licensee for Summer Classics in Mobile. Bew thought the two of them could be helpful in the meeting, but at the very least, he just wanted as many people with him as possible. He had no clue what to expect, and it was nice to have numbers on his side. But they did not even have this. In Atlanta, Bew was ushered into one of the bank's conference rooms where eight people were already seated around a conference table. "Shit," Bew thought. This was foreboding.

One man spoke, introducing the others in the room. One of the eight was their loan officer Shannon Connelly. Bew was glad to see at least one familiar face. "Brian Clark." Brian, the man in charge, extended his hand. Bew knew Brian—they had spoken over the phone the day after his mother's death. He tried to conceal his dislike for the man. "We're with Special Assets in Boston," Brian continued, pointing to two other men with him. They had flown to Atlanta specifically for this meeting. The other two introduced themselves. Bew, Neal and Tommy introduced themselves in turn, and they took their seats at the table.

Brian started right in, "We need to reevaluate your loan. These are hard times. You're a discretionary, and people just don't have that kind of money to spend right now."

Bew did not know these guys from Boston, and they did not know him. He liked to know his bank. For him, building personal relationships with his bankers was key. For years, it seemed this had been Citizen Bank's mentality as well. He had gotten on well with Ethan Price and Shannon Connelly. But recently, this had changed. Boston stepped in, and they only seemed to see numbers—Summer Classics was just a number.

Bew listened to Brian and his Special Assets group as they coolly painted a damning picture. Summer Classics was on trial, but the verdict had been decided from the outset. Impersonally and professionally, they were tightening a noose around Bew's neck. He looked to Shannon for aid. She knew Summer Classics. Maybe she would defend them. But she kept her eyes downcast, not wishing to make eye contact. She felt mortified. As Summer Classics' loan officer, Special Assets had required her presence in this meeting. She did not want to be there. She knew this was a hit job.

Finally, Bew could take it no more. This was not fair. He interrupted Brian, "Why don't you guys come over to the store and see what we actually do? Y'all are just making judgments, saying you don't like our space, but you don't really know our space. You're saying that people don't have the money to spend, but I disagree with you. I think we are going to have a good year."

Summer Classics had not come into their season yet. He did not actually know whether or not they would have a good year, but he wanted to exude nothing but confidence right now. He could not show weakness or doubt. These Boston guys were just looking for a way to save their own asses. They didn't know him or his business. If he could get them to the Atlanta store, maybe this would become more personal. At the very least, this could make a hatchet job more difficult to perpetrate.

Brian and the others agreed to go along with them to the Atlanta store. Bew thought that if he could just show them his product and explain it to them, they might change their tune. Pulling from his long experience as a sales rep, he gave his best pitch. He guided them through the store, explaining his product. He told them how well certain collections had done. He talked about everything that set Summer Classics apart from all its competition. Yet, it seemed that nothing could change their minds. They were negative the entire time. They balked at the prices. They looked at it all from a cynical perspective.

Bew felt both despair and rage. It was clear that they had already made up their minds, and he could say nothing to change this. What was the point of the meeting if they already knew what they were going to do?

Before he returned to Birmingham, Bew made a point to ask about the covenant. They had not yet broken the covenant. "Please, let's go ahead and decide what we're going to do with the covenants." But they would give him nothing conclusive. They simply encouraged him to go raise money.

After this meeting, Citizens handed Summer Classics off to Jarred Manning in their Workout Group. Jarred flew down from Boston to meet with Bew at Summer Classics. He made a survey of their financials and inventory. Bew took him to the Pelham store.

As he walked through the store, Jarred paused before a dining chair, turning the price tag in his hand. "$1500!" he exclaimed in surprise.

"Well, yeah. This is not unusual. Our clients readily pay this," Bew explained. "Do you have any outdoor furniture?"

"Yeah, I have a lobster trap with a piece of glass on top," Jarred stated.

"We're dead," Bew thought. Jarred seemed like a nice guy, but this was not the person they wanted handling their loan. He clearly had no understanding of their industry.

Following this, Citizens mandated Summer Classics to have a third-party audit. A firm from Charlotte came down and conducted a field exam. The field examiner visited the Summer

Classics office and three stores. Bew and Neal watched this in horror.

"No way they can do this in three days and come away with the right valuation," Neal said. He had worked with Shannon when she had been a field examiner and the audit had been a very involved and lengthy process.

"They're just trying to evaluate our inventory to see how much they can dump it for. We're screwed. They're already planning to foreclose on me," Bew despaired.

A couple of days later, Citizens sent Summer Classics an invoice for $15,000—it was the invoice for the audit. Bew and Neal were furious. Neal called Shannon angrily, "What the hell is this, Shannon? What is happening over there? Why didn't you warn us? We're expected to pay for this? We didn't even want it!"

"I'm sorry. No one told me about it. I'm really sorry," Shannon said sincerely.

As Bew had long expected, Summer Classics passed through a second quarter without making any money. The covenant was now broken. He sat in dread, awaiting the death sentence at any moment.

In early May, it finally came. Citizens made contact with Neal, and he came to Bew's office. Seeing Neal's face, Bew knew the dreaded moment had arrived. "Citizens just dropped our inventory balance from 63% to 47%," Neal informed him.

Bew groaned. "Shit! That's two million dollars. They're going to pull two million dollars?" He bent over in his chair. "How are they going to do this?"

"They're going to pull it out of our account. They say we have thirty days."

"They're going to pull two million dollars out of our account in thirty days?" Bew agonized.

"I asked them to give us more time, at least three months— or to at least make the decrease gradual."

"And they won't do it?"

"But they won't do it."

"Shit." Bew rose to his feet. "Okay, we need to figure cash-flow out or move money to another bank." His mind began to race furiously. "We have to do something or we aren't going to have any money to operate on."

Neal nodded his head solemnly. He had reached a similar conclusion.

Soon, they arranged a meeting with Bew's friend and lawyer Jim Rotch. Bew explained the situation, "We need to raise two million dollars."

"I know someone who might be able to help—a Birmingham investment bank, Jones, Reese and Bentley. Let's call them." Jim called one of the partners—Ward Jones—and they set up a meeting.

Bew, Neal and Jim met with Ward and his partners. Ward explained that they would do their due diligence, put a package together and try to raise money for Summer Classics. Neal would work closely alongside his partner Ed Reese, providing them with the financials and the necessary help. The fee would be $25,000. They sent a letter confirming this amount. Bew did not want to hire an investment bank in the first place, but he had to do it. He agreed. Ward passed a document around and they all signed it.

Since September of the previous year, Summer Classics had been forced to steadily release more and more personnel. Retail and wholesale had been the most severely hit. In the end, retail would be cut by 50% and wholesale by 30%. As he had in the beginning, Bew tried to be personally involved in each meeting. He let them say whatever they needed to say. Some had choice words for him, and he understood. He did his best to console them and offer them what help he could provide.

He and his management continued to meet week after week. "What can we do?" they kept asking, leaving no stone unturned. But more often than not, they were left with no alternative: they had to let more people go. As time wore on, even the management in these very meetings fell under consideration. By the end, Bew was forced to let management go, some who had been with Summer Classics for as long as twenty years.

By this point, Bew was breaking down in all these meetings. He felt so spent and raw. He was burdened with all these people he was putting into unemployment. What was going to happen to them? How would they provide for their families? Was he doing the right thing? He felt like they were slowly bleeding to death.

In these later meetings, the roles were reversed—now they were the ones consoling him. "You haven't done anything wrong. It's okay. It's okay. I understand," they consoled him as he cried.

"When is this going to end?" Bew wondered. "I'm firing people who are working their asses off. This is crazy."

For those who had a long history with Summer Classics— those who had been with the company for twenty years or more—he let them gather the whole management team (if they wanted to) to say whatever they wanted to say. "Cuss us out if you want to," Bew told them.

Some gathered the team just to share a parting word, and others took him up on his invitation, cussing everyone out. This was always difficult and upsetting, but Bew understood. He just sat there and let them vent. "No. You're right. I don't know what to tell you."

Every night, Bew went home to lay on the couch. He tossed and turned, and sleep did not come. Wendy comforted her husband as best she could. And she prayed. As anxiety wore her husband down, she lifted him up in prayer. She knew that it would take an act of God to save them from this.

Now, perhaps more than ever, work had to go on. They needed to bring in more orders. That May Bew was in Las Vegas, showing along with many other manufacturers at the May contract event. Sunbrella was also there showing. While Bew was in the Summer Classics showroom, Leib Oehmig, the president of Sunbrella, came by to see him. The last time they had seen each other was on their hunting trip in September of the previous year just before the recession started. Leib remembered how Bew had predicted the coming disaster. It had jarred him and perhaps gave his company critical advance notice of what was coming.

The two of them talked. There was only one thing to talk about – what are you doing to survive? After a brief exchange, Leib said, "Hey, go to dinner with us tonight."

"Okay," Bew accepted the invitation.

That night, Bew, Leib, Allan Gant—the Sunbrella CEO— and several other Sunbrella executives had dinner together. "Bew, what can we do to help you?" Allan asked.

"Tell me what to do," Bew said. "I've never been in a situation like this. I'm panicked."

"We're going to do everything we can to help you," Leib assured him.

If they were offering, Bew decided he would ask. He needed whatever help he could get. "Well, make it where I don't have to pay you. I don't mean never but just whenever I can. I will pay you. I'm not going to screw you."

Bew was surprised to see Allan's brow furrow in thought. Was he seriously considering this? Allen looked at Leib who nodded, and he turned back to Bew, "Okay. I think we can work something out."

A smile broke across Bew's face, "Really? Thank you!" He shook both men's hands vigorously. They returned his smile.

True to his word, Leib had it arranged that Summer Classics could pay Sunbrella in ninety days, and even if they could not pay within this period, Sunbrella would work with Summer Classics. This freed up a much-needed half a million dollars for Summer Classics to apply to payroll. Bew was immensely grateful for this act of generosity. In this time of crisis, almost everyone was in survival mode, fending for themselves. Allen, Leib and Sunbrella had done a rare and wonderful thing.

Bew wondered, "Could this be how we survive? What if I called more people—more of our vendors—to ask them if they could wait until we could afford to pay them?"

Bew started to call all their vendors. One of his first calls was to Winston in China, "Hey, I don't know what to do. The bank is taking two million dollars away from me. I need to do something."

"Don't pay me," Winston replied.

"Okay," Bew said excitedly. "Ever?" he added jokingly.

"No." Winston shut that down immediately. "Just pay me when you can. We've got your back. Don't worry."

"Thank you," Bew said with genuine gratitude.

Next, he reached out to Grant, explaining his predicament. "Can you help me?"

"Yes. I'll give you one million," Grant replied.

"Thank you!"

Bew called every other vendor. "Hey, I need extra terms. I normally pay you in thirty or sixty days. Can I pay you in ninety or one hundred twenty days?"

There were a few vendors who declined to help, but, in one way or another, almost every vendor agreed to extra terms. Bew was amazed. Summer Classics' vendors were basically taking the bank's place—they were lending Summer Classics the money it needed. But this was even better because there was no interest.

Bew went to Neal's office. He was beaming. "Okay, Neal. I got the money."

Neal was amazed, "Thank God!"

"Yeah, just don't pay these guys." He handed Neal a list of the vendors. Neal took the paper, shaking his head in disbelief and smiling from ear to ear.

Bew walked out of Neal's office with a lightness in his step. All of a sudden, the world seemed a better place. All these people had agreed to help them. He knew they were far from safe, but he felt hope again. He said a silent prayer of thanks.

He hardly had time to enjoy this turn of good fortune before Summer Classics suffered another blow. Still an avid watcher of CNBC, Bew learned that CIT Group was going the way of many banks—it was on the verge of bankruptcy. He was greatly alarmed. CIT was in charge of Summer Classics' factoring, and they still owed him three million dollars. Immediately, he started shorting all his contracts, and he looked to his lawyers and consultants to try to help him help get out of this situation—this in itself was very costly. Without CIT, he was not sure if Summer Classics could make payroll.

Morning after morning, Bew watched the CNBC show Squawk Box. He always appreciated the insights of show hosts Becky Quick, Carl Quintanilla and Joe Kernen. But in this case, Bew felt like they did not seem to understand how devastating it would be for small businesses like Summer Classics if CIT collapsed. He reached out to CNBC to share his thoughts. To his surprise, they asked him to come on the show for a brief segment to discuss this on July 16.

After introducing Bew and his company, they asked him to explain what the collapse of CIT might mean for small businesses across America. Bew got right to his point. He felt that most did not grasp the seriousness of the situation. Joe and Carl felt it would be simple for a company to just move their line to a new bank, but Bew (who was struggling with this very thing) explained that this was hard enough in the current climate and near impossible considering the fact that thousands would be forced to move their lines simultaneously. Further, Bew explained that CIT was a primary source of credit for most companies because this was their only bank.

They finally understood Bew's point—the collapse of CIT could lead to many businesses shutting down. Without the cash-flow which CIT provided, many companies would not be able to make payroll or get the product necessary to run their businesses. It was a brief segment, but Bew had made his point well. He was comfortable and articulate before the camera. They thanked Bew for his time.

Just as Bew had said on Squawk Box, CIT's threatening collapse could have massive consequences for Summer Classics. Without CIT, they might not be able to make payroll or get vital product. CIT was not their main source of credit, but this just compounded an already horrible situation.

This merely served to further impress upon Bew how desperately they needed to find a new bank. They had been trying for months, but no bank would talk to them. With saving help from their vendors, Summer Classics was surviving, but how long would this hold? Eventually, they would have to pay their vendors. If they did not find a new bank soon, things would be as bad as before or even worse.

With no banks speaking to them, Bew was left to do what he could with the bank they had now. Citizens Bank had been pressuring Summer Classics to raise money, so he had been forced to hire the investment bank, Jones, Reese and Bentley. For a long time now, Neal had worked closely with Ed Reese, poring over financials in order to build a package. Bew needed this package to prove to Citizens that he was raising money like they asked. Perhaps this would placate them for a time.

He asked Ed Reese for the book—was it ready? Ed told him that they would give it, but Summer Classics needed to pay first. He sent Summer Classics an invoice for $125,000. Furious, Bew went to Jim.

"This is utterly unethical," Bew fumed.

Jim agreed. They were just taking advantage of Summer Classics at their lowest point—when Summer Classics could not fight back. Jim swore he would never work with them again.

Bew contacted Ward Jones. "This piece of paper is meaningless. You agreed to $25,000, and we signed it. I'm not paying you this."

Bew was told in no uncertain terms that he could not have the book until he paid $125,000. Summer Classics was without options. They had to pay it because they had to give the book to Citizens to prove they were trying to raise money.

A final meeting was scheduled where they would exchange the money for the book. Bew refused to go. He asked Jim and Neal to go in his stead. He was so infuriated that he did not know what he might say or do if he was brought face to face with them. Summer Classics got the book, and Neal took it to Citizens in Atlanta. From all appearances, it seemed to help some, but still, Citizens was reserved. Summer Classics' future remained unclear.

A couple of months passed and still they had gotten nowhere. They could not find a new bank, and Citizens Bank had gone silent. This was ominous. Then, Neal finally got a phone call from Shannon. "Shannon, what's going on?" Neal asked. "We're freaking out over here."

"Neal," Shannon hesitated. "We need you to find another bank."

Neal almost laughed. "What did they think Summer Classics had been doing?" he thought to himself. They had been looking for another bank since the summer of 2008.

"We'll work with you until you find another bank, but you need to find one," Shannon reiterated.

It was a somber moment for both of them. Each felt empathy for the other. News had come to Neal that RBS was cleaning house at Citizens in Atlanta. Many people had already been fired. Neal knew that things were getting really bad over there.

For Shannon's part, she hated the role she had played in this. She liked everyone at Summer Classics. For years she tried to do a good job, and doing a good job had always been knowing her clients and serving them well. In the past year, all of this had been flipped on its head. Now, they were expected to throw all this out the window. She had passed most nights sleeplessly. She hated having to tell her clients that they were useless to the bank. She admired the resilience of Summer Classics. Where so many had failed, Summer Classics pressed on. She sincerely hoped that they would make it.

"All right," Neal sighed. "Thanks, Shannon."

Neal called Bew, "Shannon just called us and said we need to find another bank."

"Wow. What do they think we've been doing?" Bew replied.

"Right. I thought the same thing."

"Well, is that all?" Bew asked.

"She said they'll work with us until we find another."

"That's huge. At least they aren't foreclosing on us right now," Bew attempted to find a silver lining. He took a deep breath. "Well, let's keep looking, Neal. We have to find someone who will talk to us."

They redoubled their efforts. For several weeks, they reached out to bank after bank but with little success. They tried Regions. They tried Synovus. Neither would sign. BBVA called but they offered Summer Classics a terrible deal. "No one would do a deal like this, nobody in their right mind unless they were desperate," Bew angrily told them.

All their efforts seemed to be in vain. Then, suddenly, in mid-October, Wells Fargo showed a willingness to talk. Bew was thrilled.

A short while later, a broker from Atlanta contacted him. "My name is Jake Andrews. I'm with Cole Taylor."

"I don't know them. Tell me who they are," Bew said.

"Cole Taylor used to be a part of LaSalle Bank."

Bew knew LaSalle. "Okay. Let's talk."

He allowed a ray of hope to break in upon his otherwise pessimistic (and realistic) disposition. "Okay. They're going to talk to us now. This is huge," he thought.

Over the following months, Bew got into separate negotiations with Wells Fargo and Cole Taylor. The talks shifted from initial meetings to hot pursuit on the part of the banks. It was an incredible turn of events: banks were competing for Summer Classics.

Bew used this competition to improve the loan agreement, and this helped immensely. He went back and forth between the two banks. He would negotiate with Jake, and then he would take this deal to Wells Fargo. "Cole Taylor has offered this." Wells Fargo would match it. Bew would take this back to Cole Taylor. Negotiations went on and on like this, and the loan agreement terms steadily improved.

The bank negotiations carried over into 2010. They were not at the point of signing yet, but they were getting ever closer. Through this competition, he had managed to eliminate most of his personal guarantee, increase the line of credit, increase the debt against inventory and more. Bew wanted to see how much further he could take this. Certainly, it would not be like the deal he negotiated with Citizens Bank back in 2004 (no bank could offer this sort of deal in the day's climate), but he knew there was still more he could get. Time ticked on, and as it did, his anxiety grew. They would need to sign soon. Their current loan agreement with Citizens was due to end on June 1.

Bew felt it was time for another step. Since January of 2008, William had been doing all he could to prepare the indoor division for its launch. In the summer of 2009, in honor of his late grandmother, William decided to call it Gabby, instead of SC Home. While Bew had been grappling with Citizens, William had been working hard to get Gabby underway. Timing did not seem to be on his side. It was a hard time to be starting a new company, but William had not given up. Bew felt they could wait no longer. William agreed. They signed a lease for a showroom at the Atlanta show.

Just as Gabby was nearing its launch, Restoration Hardware released a new line that was incredibly similar to Gabby's. Bew thought this might actually help Gabby. "Wow. We're going to be right on top of Restoration Hardware. I think that's kind of good."

But William's instincts told him otherwise. "I'm going to change it all," he informed Bew.

Bew was shocked, "We did all this work and you're going to change it?"

"I'll change some of it. I don't want to look like Restoration Hardware. I'm going to do something more petite, more feminine, more French, and more European." So William changed the whole line. Bew had his reservations.

In January of 2010, William showed the Gabby line for the first time at the Atlanta show, and that January, Gabby outsold Summer Classics in show orders. At that moment, Bew realized that they had something remarkable. "Okay. This could be great," he thought. He realized the timing was actually perfect because no one was starting new businesses at this time. This set Gabby apart. Also, while many other companies were releasing furniture that mimicked Restoration Hardware, Gabby introduced something that was fresh and distinct. Bew admired his son's instincts—William had made the right call.

By March of 2010, Summer Classics finally had its deal with a bank—Wells Fargo. Bew felt confident that they had negotiated the best possible deal in this climate for Summer Classics. Pitting the two banks against one another had been the key. They were ready to sign, but for some reason, Wells Fargo hesitated.

Bew grew impatient. Their neck was on the line. "What are we waiting on? Let's do this." But Wells Fargo would not sign.

Fortunately for Bew, he knew the head loan officer in Birmingham—Austin Davis. As a child, William had carpooled to school every day with Austin and his own kids. Austin vouched for Bew, contacting the Wells Fargo in Atlanta, saying, "Hey, these are good guys. It'll be fine. I'll take care of them over here." Austin kept in close contact with Bew during the bank negotiations.

Now that Wells Fargo hesitated, Bew was calling Austin often. "We have to get this done by May 31, or I'm going to have to go to the other bank to close this." Austin promised to do what he could.

This dragged on for weeks. Bew stressed as May 31 grew ever nearer. He feared that Citizens could foreclose on Summer Classics at any moment. He contacted them, assuring them that he had a bank lined up.

Right around this time, Bew sensed that First Commercial Bank was getting nervous. All of Summer Classics' real estate loans were with First Commercial. Just in case, he decided to check on how things stood. As he feared, they told him that he would need to find a new bank when his loans came due—all five of them on the distribution buildings Summer Classics owned and the Pelham store. The thought of moving five real estate loans left Bew feeling exhausted. Shopping banks had become like a second job for him.

Fortunately, Oakworth Bank, a Birmingham bank which had formed in 2008, had already voiced interest in working with Bew in real estate. Bew reached out and asked them if he could move his loans there. The answer was affirmative. He managed to move all five loans in fairly quick succession, and he even managed to get better interest rates on these new loans. "Thank God," Bew thought. "I have a bank that will work for me." He was very glad to have found Oakworth.

By this point, Summer Classics had paid off close to seventeen million of its loan with Citizens Bank, but the deadline was fast approaching. They had a couple million left to pay, and still they had not signed with another bank. He feared that Citizens could come at any moment, take what was owed them, and shut down Summer Classics.

May 15 came, and still Wells Fargo had not signed. All the while, Bew tried to keep Cole Taylor on the line. He called Wells Fargo, trying to emphasize the urgency of their situation, "Hey, it's May 15, guys. I've got two weeks. These guys are going to shut me down if we don't do this."

The entire time Wells Fargo had been nervous, but this last push finally had its desired effect. On May 31, Summer Classics and Wells Fargo signed a loan agreement. This was one day before their loan with Citizens Bank was due. That very same day, Summer Classics paid Citizens its remaining debt. Immediately, a peace came over Bew. They had done it! He thanked God with all his heart. That night, he got into bed next to Wendy, and he slept as he had not in over a year.

CHAPTER 16

WHEN DEATH COMES KNOCKING

"The great use of life is to spend it for something that will outlast it."
- William James

NOW THAT SUMMER CLASSICS had finally signed with Wells Fargo, there was much that needed to be done. One of the first things they did was pay all their vendors—everyone who had so graciously helped Summer Classics get through this. Bew thanked them all.

He also made sure they reached out to Jake Andrews at Cole Taylor. They could not have gotten this deal without him. Bew felt sorry for him. He knew how hard Jake had worked for this deal. In the end, Summer Classics chose Wells Fargo because they needed a 'too big to fail' bank. They had learned their lesson and they wanted a bank that wouldn't fail and do the same thing that Citizens Bank had done.

"Jake, we're going with Wells Fargo, but you've really worked your butt off here. We want to do something for you. We'd like to give you a set of Summer Classics furniture."

While this must have been hard to hear, Jake took it all in stride, "I'm glad you got a good deal."

In mid-June, not long after signing the loan, Bew and Neal met their new Wells Fargo loan officer Tricia Powell and a Wells Fargo sales rep Larry Sweeney at the Mountain Brook Country Club for lunch and a round of golf. The purpose of this meeting was simply to get acquainted with one another. Bew was glad to have a bank where the relationships seemed to matter again. After a pleasant lunch, they got on the golf course.

When they reached the back nine, Bew asked a question he had wanted to ask for some time. "Now, Tricia, we started talking to you guys in September of 2009, and y'all didn't close this loan until May 31. And our last day on the Citizens Bank line was June 1. It was like the last minute. I see your CEO on TV all the time saying, 'We're lending tons of money. We're doing all this banking.'" Tricia nodded to indicate that she was following. Bew came to his question, "What were you guys doing from that time—from September of 2008—till now? Had you made any loans?"

They parked the golf cart and walked towards the tee. "No," Tricia replied. "You are our first loan." She lined up at the tee. The driver club made a ringing sound as it made contact with the golf ball. Tricia was a fine golfer. She shielded her eyes from the sun as she watched her ball soar through the air and land on the distant fairway.

Bew stood dumbstruck, absorbing what Tricia had just told him. Her whole job was to make loans. This was the job of her whole department, and they hadn't been fired. He caught Neal's eye. Neal was clearly following a similar line of thought—surprise showed on his face.

Soon, they were all walking down the fairway towards their balls. "What were y'all doing in all that time?" Bew asked.

"We were sitting under our desks shivering, scared to death," Tricia said frankly. "Weren't we, Larry?" she called out to him over her shoulder.

"That's right, Tricia." Larry nodded in confirmation.

Bew swore in anger, "Son of a bitch."

Bew was angered by how unethical the banks had been in

this time, and this conversation sent him over the edge. He had seen the Wells Fargo CEO on CNBC, lying, saying that the bank was lending all kinds of money. Bew realized what the CEO was really saying was that the bank was renewing lines because they couldn't get them placed anywhere else. The BB&T CEO had been saying the same thing. According to them, they are all lending money, and everything is fine. "But," Bew thought, "They're not lending money. They're just taking care of their regular customers until they can get rid of them like they did me."

Bew's experience with Citizens Bank had shaken him. He had invested so much time and effort into his banks, and where had it gotten him? All the relationships, all the history and all the good faith had counted for nothing. He had learned his lesson. From now on, he would do whatever he had to do to protect his own interests and the interests of his company. The banks could promise what they wanted, but he had seen what banks would do when the chips were down. He wanted to believe this would never happen again, but from this time forward, he would harbor a healthy level of concern towards banks.

One lesson Bew learned was that there needed to be a covenant break fix. He was emphatic on this point to Wells Fargo. This had been his downfall with Citizens Bank.

"What are you talking about?" they asked him.

"I want something in there for when these covenants don't work so I can do something to fix it," he said.

In these times, banking would need to be different. The old rules were not enough. Banks like Wells Fargo understood that they must do more to earn the trust of their clients again. So Wells Fargo came up with something. They presented Bew with three things he could do in the case of a covenant break. Bew was pleased. Things would not be as they had been at Citizens Bank where he had nothing in writing and he had no way to fix a covenant. He insisted this all be put into writing, and it was.

As things settled, Bew was pleased to see some normality return to Summer Classics. His team carried itself with more confidence. They were more cheery. Once again, ambition and drive characterized their work. The company had suffered losses in volume as high as 30% in the previous year, but here they were, still standing. Bew recalled their growth pre-recession. He knew what they were capable of. They could rise once again.

Later that year, he went to China to visit the factories. He was especially set on introducing a new collection. He had a design he had been contemplating for some time now. He thought of how when he was sixteen he had gone to Hawaii with his parents. Every hotel they had gone to had the same furniture. When he got older, he had discovered that it was a company called McGuire that made this product.

At one of their factories in south China, Bew gathered some of the factory staff, his designers and Winston around him. "Do you guys know who McGuire is?"

"Yes. They're from the Philippines," one of them replied.

"Well, they had a group with an edge on it that was braided," Bew continued.

As Bew spoke, a designer did an internet search on his laptop. "Is this the one?" He turned the laptop to face Bew.

"That's it." Bew got excited. He began to draw some designs to show what he was envisioning. His designers studied it carefully and got to work sketching it out with variations for Bew to consider.

Later that day, Bew was walking around the factory when he saw an interesting material lying about. "What's this material?" he asked.

"That's sica," they told him.

Bew studied it. At this time, everyone was using small wicker, but this material was thick. "What's sica?"

"It's not really what we use for wicker. It's a reed that grows in the jungle."

"Can we get some?" Bew asked. They said they could.

The next day, they brought Bew some sica in the design room. "That's it!" Bew said excitedly. "Can we make resin that looks like this?"

"Yeah," they nodded.

Bew sifted through some drawings and pictures on the table, and he grabbed a picture of a McGuire chair. "Then, can you make me a chair that looks like that?"

They nodded. "Yes. We can."

Bew's designers were standing next to him. Seeing their questioning looks, he outlined his vision more clearly for them, "Listen, I'm doing a new group, and it's going to be a major winner. I'm drawing from a time in people's youth when this product was everywhere. But it had only been an indoor product then. It's in the minds of people. They may not remember the product exactly, but it's in their memory. They'll be drawn to our new product."

The result of this was the Sedona collection. It was a major success—one of their best collections to date. Just as Bew had predicted, when people saw it, they felt drawn to it. Bew was glad to be doing what he loved once again.

For Bew, the end of 2010 felt like the closing of a chapter. Summer Classics had come out of the valley. They were back on firm standing. By hard work, supporting one another, the help of friends and family and, chiefly, by the grace of God, they had come through to the other side alive. More than this, they had shockingly managed growth—they had begun Gabby Home. Gabby's first year proved to be profitable one. Bew was proud of William for this accomplishment—he had shown good instinct and resilience in a trying time.

Bew spent the next few years trying to push Summer Classics to new heights. His company had a history of two decades behind it. Just as he had envisioned in the nineties, his product now had a reputation for its quality. It looked as good now as it had two decades earlier. There was a timeless quality to it. Bew believed they could build upon this. Summer Classics had yet to realize its full potential. He had a new goal on the horizon: reaching $100 million in sales.

Bew was always busy. He was still traveling plenty. Every day was filled with meetings. Even on a day clear of meetings, he always found something that needed to be done. He checked on the stores. He stopped by the cushion plant. He liked to know what his employees were doing. He needed Summer Classics to work like a well-oiled machine.

Yet, he also managed to find time to enjoy himself. He always looked for reasons to go to the farm whenever he could. If he was not there on a personal vacation, he was taking clients there to hunt. If he could mix business and pleasure, he would.

After Gay White passed away, the farm had passed to Bew. He invested heavily into it. He rebuilt the farmhouse, moving it closer to the river. It was a beautiful two-story house with high picture windows which allowed plenty of natural light inside and offered a good view of the river outside. The house had a great room with a high ceiling and large wooden beams. The walls were bedecked with animal mounts. Attached to the house was a large screened-in porch, furnished with Summer Classics furniture and a large stone fireplace. This place was his haven.

In March of 2013, the farm was set to be the venue of his youngest daughter's wedding. In preparation for it, Bew had a new building constructed—a half glass, half screen house. They called it the Cake House because it would be housing the wedding cake. The house sat adjacent to one of three lakes on the property. Bew was very pleased with it, thinking it added a lot to the farm.

On the day of the wedding, family and friends drove up for the occasion. The wedding was held outdoors. To everyone's dismay, a heavy Alabama rain came to pass on the same day. Cars had to park near the farmhouse, which was about a quarter of a mile from the wedding setup. Everyone trudged through the rain and mud. They scrambled to move the wedding under a tent which had been set up for the wedding reception.

What was stressful at the time merely served to make the wedding more memorable. The wedding was a sweet one. It involved all of Bew's favorite things—his family, his friends, and the farm. He was happy for his daughter.

For some time now, Bew had been wanting William to become more involved in Summer Classics. There was a separation between the operations of Gabby and Summer Classics. Obviously, Bew was very focused on the operation of Summer Classics and William on the operation of Gabby. Bew wanted William on board with everything that was happening in both operations. He wanted him to understand how to run the company, and he hoped that one day William might succeed him as CEO.

William, however, did not have these aspirations for himself. He did not envision taking his father's place at the helm of Summer Classics. Not only did he feel unprepared for this, it did not interest him—he enjoyed the work he was doing. But Bew did not give up. He continued to broach the subject, hoping that William might change his mind.

In the midst of this, something strange began to happen: Bew felt like something was about to happen to him. This feeling did not come all at once. It stemmed from a common theme which filled his dreams almost every night now—the theme of death. These were not nightmares, only dreams. He did not know what to make of all this. He just had this premonition.

This feeling was like the one he had in July of 2008 just before the recession. At that time, he felt like a disaster was coming. He could not say why he felt this, but he did all he could to prepare for something terrible. Then the recession came. Just as he could not shake it then, he could not shake it now.

This dragged on for months. Night after night, he dreamed about death. Day after day, this premonition lingered. He kept all of this to himself, not even sharing it with Wendy. As he did not know what to think of this, he did not want to needlessly worry her. It might be nothing.

But then he felt physical changes. He started to have shortness of breath. Just a simple climb up the stairs left him feeling winded. The last time he had felt like this was in September 2009 in Chicago, but the hospital had pronounced him healthy. He had assumed this incident was an anomaly. Now, fear gripped him. What was happening? First, there was this feeling that he could not shake and all these dreams of his death, and now these physical changes. He started to grapple with the actual possibility that he could die.

He had to walk slower now. He started to feel a throbbing pain in his leg, and it was only getting worse as time went on. Others began to notice that he was struggling. Bew could not hide this from Wendy. Finally, he began to open up to her. He told her about the pain his leg and his shortness of breath. He did not tell her about his dreams or that he thought he might be dying.

Wendy was worried. Bew was usually so full of energy. He lived an active life. He did not have a history of health problems. "You need to see a doctor," she urged him.

"I will. I'll try to set it up soon," he assured her.

The days went by. The dreams continued. An ominous feeling lingered. His leg still hurt. It felt like an incredible strain that he couldn't stretch out. But he was busy. He put off making the doctor's appointment. He would find time soon.

Again, Wendy urged him, but now more seriously, "Billy, you really need to see a doctor."

"Okay, I will. I'll make an appointment next week." The following week, he was going to the farm for planning meetings with the staff. He would make an appointment for when they got back from Boligee.

The next day, Wright Currie stopped by Bew's office. Starting with Summer Classics in 2006, Wright was the company's head designer. Since then, he had traveled with Bew to China and worked hard through the recession. Wright was someone Bew could rely on. He gave a knock on the open door before stepping inside. "Hey Bew, I'm setting up a meeting with Emily Cosgrove next week in Atlanta to look at some Sunbrella designs. Can you come?"

"When?" Bew asked.

"I was thinking the day after we get back from Boligee."

Bew thought a moment. "Okay. I have a doctor's appointment at three o'clock that day. Can we make it so we finish early so we can get back in time for my appointment?"

"I'm sure we could. I'll plan an earlier time with Emily."

"Great. Thanks, Wright."

Going into the next week, Bew's shortness of breath was even worse, and his leg pain had increased. Sitting on the couch in his home library, he extended his leg to stretch it. He did his best to look calm, but he was afraid.

Wendy sat across from him, watching him. "Are you sure you should to go to the farm?" she asked. Her concern for Bew was ever growing.

"Well, I already have a doctor's appointment for when I get back. I'll be okay. We're just going to the farm for our yearly management meeting."

Wendy sighed and nodded. She hated to see her husband like this—he was clearly enduring a lot of discomfort and pain.

Bew went to farm with the Summer Classics staff on October 6 for a couple of days of planning meetings. He was always glad to escape to the farm. He enjoyed sitting on the porch looking down on the river. He enjoyed sitting in front of the fireplace with a nice cigar in the evening. Here, he could rest, and rest he needed badly. But even the peace and the rest did not seem to end his pain and discomfort.

On October 8, their last day in Boligee, the staff was set to meet in the farmhouse early that morning. Bew had set the agenda for that day's discussion: "What if Bew dies?" The staff found this phrasing rather morbid, but they understood the gist of it—they needed to have a clear, thought-out plan for the company's future. Bew had been encouraging his staff to think in this way for many weeks now.

Everyone gathered around the table, ready with notepads, pens and coffee. Bew was late. A few moments later, he came out of his room. Joining them at the table, he looked pale. They exchanged worried glances with one another. He had been complaining about shortness of breath and pain in his leg the other day.

What had been morbid a moment ago, now felt strange – "What if Bew dies?" Surely not. Bew was a machine that never stopped. Yet, a seriousness entered into their discussion – a seriousness that would not have been present without seeing Bew as he was that morning. He was clearly struggling.

As they spoke, Bew looked across the table at William. He could not say it, but this discussion was for him. He wanted William to be ready to take over. He had wanted this for so long now, but now, more than ever, he wanted to prepare William.

After their morning meeting, they all went to enjoy lunch in the Cake House. As they ate, they enjoyed the view this place afforded of the lake. Finishing his lunch, Bew walked down to the dock and took a seat in a Summer Classics chair looking out on the water.

He was glad he had come up. He needed the peace and quiet. He needed an escape from the city. The escape had also given him space to reflect. He was finally processing everything that had happened these past few months. This premonition, these dreams and now the pain and shortness of breath. This morning's discussion had not been a hypothetical one for him, as they all might have presumed—he was finally coming to grips with the fact that he might be dying. He needed to prepare them.

William told the others to go on to the house without him. He wandered down to the dock to join his father, seating himself in the adjacent chair. William's sudden presence jarred Bew from his deep thought.

"What's wrong, Dad?" William asked.

"William, I know this is going to sound crazy—I haven't even told your mother—I'm going to die and it's going to be soon." It felt strange to hear himself say aloud what he had been thinking for so long. It was like he had not believed it until he heard himself actually say it. Bew felt a sudden heaviness.

"You're crazy, Dad. Why would you say that?"

Bew nodded, "I know it sounds crazy. I've been wanting to tell someone." They both looked forward, watching the sunlight glisten on the surface of the water. "Right now, it seems so real. I've been to the emergency room several times. They can't find anything. Tomorrow, they're giving me a pulmonary test. I can't breathe."

"Forget it, Dad. That's nuts!"

They had told Bew this at Chicago pre-market in July, 2008—they told him he was crazy. He had a premonition then, too. "I hope you're right, William, but I don't think so. I think it's going to be soon. We need to prepare. You need to prepare. I don't think we've thought this through. We don't have a concrete plan to make sure this works if something happens to me."

Memories of Bew in the recession played in William's mind. His father had overcome much that would have brought down most (and did bring down many) people. Bew was a fighter. But then William considered their discussion that morning—Bew really thought he was dying. "Dad, this is crazy. You're not going to die."

"Okay, but we've got to pretend it might happen. And soon. You'll see. When we walk back to the house, you can see that I run out of breath just walking short distances. I don't know how to talk to Mom about this. It's really bugging me."

Bew thought about the woman he loved so much. He didn't deserve her love and support, but she gave it to him anyway. She had suffered much with him. He knew she would willingly suffer with him now, but he didn't want that for her. She deserved to be happy.

"Why are you thinking this, Dad?" William knew there must be more to this than Bew had let on. What was he not saying?

"Well, I'm having this dream every night that I'm dying. I think it's been going on for about five months—maybe longer. After a while it gets to you. You think, 'Is this for real? Is God trying to tell me something?'"

This didn't happen to people. You don't know when you're going to die. His father was going to be okay. "You're not going to die, Dad. Get that out of your head." William fought back tears.

"All I want you to do is to be prepared to take over if something happens to me." Tears welled in Bew's eyes now.

He had wanted William to take his place, but not like this. They were supposed to do it together. William was supposed to come alongside him. Bew would teach William everything he knew, and he would do all in his power to put William and the company in the best possible place for success. They needed time. But now that he had made his thoughts audible, he felt certain that he was going to die.

William rose from his chair, and Bew followed suit. They walked slowly back to the house, attempting to speak of lighter things.

The next morning, Bew rose early from bed at his house in Birmingham. Wright was coming to pick him up to drive them to the meeting in Atlanta.

"Do you have to go to Atlanta?" Wendy pled.

"My doctor's appointment is at three o'clock this afternoon. We'll go to the meeting, and we'll be back before three." There was a knock at the door. "Wright's here. Gotta go." Bew gave Wendy a kiss. He grabbed a cane as he walked out the door.

All the way up to Atlanta, he sat with his leg elevated on the dash while Wright drove. Sitting in the car like this was agonizing. His leg killed him.

"Are you okay, Bew?" Wright asked.

"Yeah, my leg is killing me. I just need to stretch it. I've also been dealing with shortness of breath. We just need to be back in time for my doctor's appointment at three."

"We can make this brief. We should be back in plenty of time," Wright assured him.

"Great."

They arrived at the Atlanta Decorative Arts Center (ADAC) at 9 AM. They found Emily waiting to greet them. She had flown from Burlington, North Carolina specifically to meet with Bew and Wright to review the Sunbrella fabric designs displayed there. She led the way into the showrooms.

With the support of his cane, Bew trailed behind. Wright and Emily walked out of the first showroom. He attempted to push through the pain, but there was no way he could make it through a long meeting on his feet.

Realizing Bew was not with them, Wright turned around. "Bew?" By the look on Bew's face, he could tell that something was seriously wrong. "Is everything all right?"

Bew shook his head, gritting his teeth. The pain was intolerable. "Wright, give me the keys to the car. I've got to go to the emergency room. Something is terribly wrong with my leg."

"I can drive—"

Bew cut him off, "I know where the hospital is—it's very close. You two can finish up. I should be done by then or you can take a cab to the hospital. I will text you my progress." He took the car keys and left.

He drove as fast as he possibly could to Piedmont Atlanta Hospital. He parked nearby and went into the emergency room. Within the hour, he was taken into an examination room. A nurse rubbed some gel on his leg and ran a Doppler ultrasound on his skin. He knew she was checking for blood clots. Not seeing the screen, he tried to read her face—she looked very concerned. This done, she ushered him back into the empty waiting room, promising to come get him soon. He feared the worst. Almost immediately, he was summoned back again, "Mr. White."

Back in the examination room, he sat across from the nurse. "I've got them, don't I?"

"I'm not supposed to tell you that." The nurse was studying a chart.

"Yeah, but I need to know. I've got them, don't I?" Bew continued to press like this until she finally cracked.

"Yeah. You have them, and you have a lot of them. We need to put you on heparin right away." She started Bew on a heparin drip to break down the blood clots.

Bew tried to collect himself. He was having more difficulty breathing. "Nurse, I can't breathe."

"Oh. Then we need to do a CT scan on your lungs to see if you have any blood clots there."

Blood clots in his leg and lungs? Bew felt overwhelmed. He was given a CT scan and asked to wait. The nurse returned.

"Mr. White, you have five blood clots in your lungs. Any one of those could have killed you. We've got to admit you and keep you for observation."

Bew sat in his bed, trying to absorb the news. He thought about his premonition of death. Just then Wright and Emily arrived.

"Did they find anything?" Wright asked.

Bew nodded. "Blood clots in my legs and five more in my lungs," his voice tremored.

Seeing the seriousness of the situation, Emily quickly excused herself. Bew and Wright waited in silence for some moments. Wright didn't know what to say. He never expected to be sitting with his boss in the hospital.

"Wright, can you contact Wendy and the family for me? I don't know that I could speak to them right now."

"Of course, Bew."

In Birmingham, Wendy was occupied with the responsibilities of keeping a household. All morning, she had been worrying about Bew, praying, "Lord, please give us some answers. Let us know what we're facing here." Her cell phone rang in the next room. She answered it, "Hello?"

"Wendy, this is Wright. Bew is being admitted to the Piedmont Atlanta Hospital. They found blood clots in his legs and lungs. I'm here with him now."

Wendy braced herself on a nearby chair. "How is he?"

"He is very upset. We're waiting here in the emergency room for him to be admitted."

"Okay. I'll pack some things and head up right away."

"I'll stay here with Bew until you get here," Wright assured her.

"Thank you, Wright."

As Wright hung up the phone, Bew asked, "Is she on her way?"

"She is leaving from your house now."

Bew took a deep, shaky breath and nodded. "Wright, take my keys and drive my car back to Birmingham. Wendy will be here. I'll be fine."

Wright shook his head. "I'm not leaving until Wendy gets here.

Bew was touched, but he insisted, "I don't want you to be here for this. I think this is it. I don't want you to see me die."

"It's okay, Bew. I'll stay with you in case you need anything and in case anything else happens."

Bew conceded, "Thank you, Wright."

"I'll call William."

Calling William, Wright was immediately impressed by William's presence of mind. William was concerned but in control of himself—as much as anyone might be in such a situation.

"Thank you for staying with him, Wright. Is he receiving good care?" William asked.

"I would say so."

"Good. Tell Dad I can take care of things here. I'm ready for whatever comes. Tell him. He'll understand."

William thought of their conversation the other day. Bew wanted William to be ready to take over. If this really was it, if Bew was about to die, William wanted to give his father a sense of peace. He wanted Bew to know that he would put everything he had into making sure that Summer Classics was sustainable. He would take the helm.

"I will," Wright promised.

"Thanks Wright. Call me if anything else happens."

Following the call, Wright told Bew, "William wanted me to tell you that he's ready to take care of things."

At this, Bew sat up. His eyes welled with tears.

"William said you would understand," Wright added.

"Yes," Bew said softly. Then he told Wright about the conversation he and William had at the farm the day before.

Wright's eyes widened. "Wow."

They sat in silence for some time. Bew's mind was reeling from everything that was happening. He longed for his wife by his side. He broke down into tears. "Wright, I'm sorry. This just seems so real. One blood clot in your lungs can kill you—I have five! I think this is it."

Wright was starting to believe this was true—that Bew would die. He felt heavy. "Bew, I'll call the rest of your family. If you need anything, let me know."

Bew nodded, "Thank you."

Time rolled by. Still in the examination room on a heparin drip, Bew was waiting to be admitted and he was waiting for Wendy. He was struggling to breathe. "Wright, I'm scared. Several years ago I watched my own father die right in front of me at the dinner table. It was horrible. It's the first time I'd ever seen someone die. I'm not ready to die."

Wright didn't know what to say, "That's horrible. I can't imagine."

Bew could not help but go into the gruesome details of his father's passing. Death was on his mind, and his thoughts were dark.

Then the two sat in silence. His vivid recollection of his father's death and his own confrontation with death took a toll on him.

After some time, Bew looked at Wright gratefully. "Wright, you've worked for me for a long time now. You've always done great work. You could still do even more. I know you could. You have a promising career ahead of you. Every chance you get, be sure to take on more responsibility," Bew went on to encourage Wright, counseling him on how he might grow further.

Wright listened in wonder. Here Bew was at death's door, and even still, he was thinking of another's future welfare and career. Not taking the moment for granted, Wright sat attentively.

The two talked in this way for two hours until Bew was finally admitted into the hospital. Just as he was being moved up to the fifth floor, Wendy arrived. She embraced Wright. "Thank you." Then she went to Bew's side and clasped his hand tightly.

"They're taking me up, Wendy," Bew told her. Turning to Wright, he said, "Wright, you're excused! Thank you, thank you for staying with me today!"

Wright took Bew's keys and left for Birmingham, and

Wendy followed Bew's bed and an orderly up to the fifth floor of the hospital.

Settled in his room, Bew had wires and tubes hanging off his body—the heart monitor, an IV of heparin. A nurse gave him some pain medication, and he felt almost immediate relief. While the nurses saw that Bew was settled and cared for, Wendy took the opportunity to update family.

A doctor entered the room. "Mr. White, my name is Dr. Chad Miller. I'm a pulmonologist here and I'll be helping take care of you. Are we feeling any better?" Dr. Miller scanned Bew's charts.

"Certainly better than I was, but I'm still worried," Bew responded drowsily. He was worn out from the eventful day and the effects of the medication.

Dr. Miller spoke reassuringly, "Don't worry, Mr. White. This happens all the time. We'll have you out of here in a day. We just want to be on the safe side and monitor you overnight."

Bew still felt some reservation. "Okay. I don't think so, but okay."

"I'll check in again soon. Get some rest."

"Thank you, doctor," Wendy said gratefully.

Wendy sat down and responded to texts from family. Within minutes, Bew fell into a deep sleep. Fixing his blanket, she breathed a sigh of relief. What neither Bew nor Wendy knew was that one of the blood clots was dangerously situated between Bew's heart and his lungs.

Lying on the sofa, Wendy woke up the next morning. It was still dark outside. Bew was sleeping soundly. She looked at the time. It was just after 5:30 AM. Wendy was glad to see Bew resting so well. "He's gone through so much," she thought. "I'll go downstairs to get some coffee and breakfast and be back before he wakes."

Downstairs, Wendy had just seated herself with a bagel and coffee when she received a text from Bew, "Help!"

Wendy figured he must have lost something. She texted back, "What's up?"

His response made her blood go cold. Throwing her breakfast in the trash, Wendy ran for the elevator.

Not long after Wendy left the room, Bew had been awakened by a pain in his chest. At first, he felt groggy, but he was quickly jarred to full consciousness—it felt as if the life was being sucked out of him. He looked around for Wendy. Not seeing her, he panicked. He picked up his phone and texted her. At the same time, he jammed the nurse's button repeatedly. There was no answer. Where was Wendy? Where was a nurse? Somebody!

Wendy texted back, "What's up?"

Bew typed furiously, "I don't know and the nurse won't answer. This may be it?" He jammed the nurse's button more.

"On my way," Wendy replied.

He attempted to reply but only managed, "on hitjnyh." His mind raced. "Oh God, will I ever see her again? Is this our last communication? It can't end like this! What have I done?"

He gasped for air. He was overwhelmed with a deep feeling of failure and loneliness. Would he die in this bed alone, never seeing Wendy again? What a mess! What had he done to her? The person he loved more than anyone in the world would be left in his disastrous wake. "You selfish bastard! How could you do this to her?" He was tormented.

He tried to sit up, but it hurt and brought no relief. He tried to text her again, "I pxctyh."

He knew he only had minutes left—if even that.

A nurse spoke over the intercom, "What's wrong, Mr. White?"

"I think I'm going to die. I am dying! Help! I'm going to die soon! Help!" Bew felt sure this was it. He felt his brain signaling his imminent death.

In moments, six nurses rushed into the room. "Mr. White, what's wrong? Tell us what's wrong," one of them said as the others acted swiftly.

Bew gasped, "I can't breathe. I can't breathe."

"Okay," one of the nurses looked at the others and shouted instructions. Then, she spoke again to Bew, "We need you to lie still, Mr. White."

"I need my wife," Bew said. "Where's my wife?" He tried to prop himself up.

"Mr. White, lie still!"

There she was! Bew saw Wendy walk quickly into the room. "Wendy! I love you! I'm so sorry! I'm going to die! I'm so sorry! I'm so sorry! I'm so sorry!" He reached out for her.

"Keep him down!" The nurses pushed Bew down.

Wendy stood where she could remain in his line of sight. She couldn't allow herself to panic. She needed to be calm for him. "That's ok, darling. I love you. You're going to be fine. Don't worry, everything is going to be okay. Everything is going to be okay." She was trying to convince herself as much as she was trying to convince him.

"I'm sorry, Wendy. I'm so sorry," he cried out.

Wendy wanted so desperately to hold him in her arms. "Honey, you didn't do anything. There's no need…"

"Lie down, Mr. White," a nurse commanded. "Put that in his IV. Push him down!"

Another nurse spoke as she held him down, "You're going to be okay. You're going to be okay."

"No, I'm not! I am dead! I know I am dead! I have a minute or so. I feel it! Seconds!" He was turning white. His heartbeat was slowing.

"Lie down, Mr. White."

Watching her husband turn white, Wendy fought to hold back her tears. He couldn't leave her. He had to be okay. He just had to.

"We have to take him to ICU! Take him to ICU!"

Bew interrupted, "ICU? Are you guys kidding me? I am so dead! I won't make it to the elevator! I have only a minute or two! We'll never make it to the elevator and then wherever the heck ICU is! Oh God this is it!"

"His blood pressure is 70/30. Get the dopamine!"

The nurses began lowering his bed so that his head was lower than his heart. As his head descended, he was losing sight of Wendy. He craned his head. "Wendy, I'm sorry. I'm so sorry. I'll never see you again. You're beautiful, you're everything, you're my life." His vision was blurred with tears. His heart was full of fear and regret.

"Stay down," a nurse said gently, pushing his head down onto his pillow.

Wendy was stunned. One of the nurses, a young man, looked up. Wendy gave a hopeful look. In response, his face was grim. He dropped his gaze. Wendy's heart sank.

"Wendy! I love you!" Bew shouted, his head was now lower than his heart.

"Honey, I love you. It's okay. It's okay," she called out.

"Mrs. White..." The nurse spoke imploringly.

Wendy understood. She stepped into the hallway to give the nurses space to work. Tears streamed down her face. "Where's my wife?" she heard behind her. She closed her eyes and began to pray.

A nurse in the room came out. "Are you okay?" she asked.

Wendy shook her head, the tears flowing more freely. "No. It's kind of hard when you're about to lose your husband of forty years."

The nurse put a hand on Wendy's shoulder, "It's going to be okay." The nurse went back into the room.

"Please save him, Lord. Please save my husband," Wendy pled.

Inside the room, color slowly began to return to Bew's face. He was soon drawing in more air. He breathed deeper and deeper with every breath. He sucked in oxygen, trying to restore the life he had moments ago felt leaving him. His fight was returning. He would not resign himself to death. He would live. He took an even deeper breath. The nurses slowly raised his bed into an upright position.

The same nurse stepped back into the hallway. Wendy was still praying. "He's going to be all right," she said reassuringly. Wendy turned around. "He's okay. He's going to be okay," she repeated, smiling.

Wendy rushed into the room. Bew began to sob uncontrollably. She went to his bedside and grabbed his hand. His hand grabbed hers back and squeezed it tightly. Bew never wanted to let her go. He never wanted her to leave his side.

Wendy's tears of sorrow turned into tears of joy. "Thank you, Jesus!" she prayed.

Soon, they returned to a somewhat cautious stance. They were optimistic, but still, they had thought the same the night before. The rest of Bew's family arrived later that day. Bew was still recovering from that morning, but he was glad to see them. They all treasured one another's presence.

As Bew gained strength, they began to feel more positive. They were told that he should be able to leave the hospital the next day. Aside from Wendy, the rest of the family returned to Birmingham. Some friends of Bew and Wendy who lived in Atlanta invited Wendy to come stay with them that evening. Wendy declined. She would not leave Bew's side. Bew was comforted. He did not want her to leave. He needed her there with him.

Bew was discharged from Piedmont Atlanta Hospital the next day. By the hour, he was gaining strength. Jealously he sucked oxygen into his lungs. His will to live was strong. More than anything, he felt a desire to remain present with his wife. She was his life. When death threatened to tear him from her, it had been the most horrible thing he had ever experienced. He had faced the prospect of never seeing Wendy again. As they walked to Wendy's car, he clutched her hand tightly.

In the past few years, Bew had passed through fire. His world had threatened to crumble around him. He faced the prospect of losing Summer Classics—the business he had worked so hard to build. He endured a time when men and women were turning on one another, doing whatever they had to do to survive. When it seemed like there could be nothing worse than this, death came for him. Faced with death, his entire life had been put into perspective. In this moment, he knew what really mattered to him in this world—his wife, his family and loved ones.

They were his life.

In time, Bew and Wendy would process so much that had happened through their lives. They thought about their own meeting and eventual marriage. They thought about Bew's leaving Avondale Mills. They thought about the pregnancy and birth of Wynne. And they thought about Bew's premonitions—first in the recession and most recently, the premonition regarding his death. They considered all these things, and they arrived at one firm conclusion: God's hand was apparent in it all.

When it came to the premonitions, Bew came to understand that God had been preparing him for what was to come. God had given him these for good. In the recession, this premonition had helped him and his company survive. The premonition of his death seemed to be so much more. God wanted Bew to know what it would be like if everything he ever had was taken away. He had received a gift—he was able to face death and walk away with the understanding of all he had, and he realized that he had so much—much that he had taken for granted.

Since that day, since the day that he almost died and lost it all, he determined that he would not take his blessings for granted any longer. He had worked so hard to build Summer Classics, and he was proud of all he and his staff had accomplished. Yet, without his wife, without his family and without loved ones, what did any of this count for? All he did needed to be for them. He would love his wife. He would love his family. He would strive to be a better husband and a better father. He would lead his company well, caring for his people. These relationships were what really mattered. In the end, these formed the substance of his life.

EPILOGUE

"But God said to him, 'You fool! This very night your life will be demanded from you. Then who will get what you have prepared for yourself?'—Luke 12:20

IN 1963, when William "Billy" Bew White was thirteen years old, he and his family were going on vacation to Panama City Beach, Florida. Avondale Mills owned a place called Camp Helen on the Phillips Inlet. Camp Helen had cabins where all the textile mill workers and their families could enjoy free lodging at the beach and get cheap food in a community cafeteria.

This was a time before the construction of Interstate 65, so the only way to the beach was on the two-lane Highway 31. Once you passed out of Vestavia the landscape was all rural, bare of urban infrastructure, until you reached Montgomery. As the car was leaving Pelham, the young Bew noticed a sprawling facility on the right side of the highway.

"Oh my gosh, Dad." Bew pointed out the window. "What is that huge building?"

Bew Sr. glanced quickly out the window to see what Bew was pointing to. "Oh. That's the Moore-Handley building," he informed his son.

"What's a Moore-Handley?" Bew asked.

"They're in the hardware business."

"What's hardware?"

"Well, that's like hammers and nails and things like that," Bew's mother, Gay White, chimed in.

Bew's eyes widened, "Does somebody need that many hammers and nails?"

Bew Sr. chuckled. Then, he explained the two-step distribution process to his teenage son. Small hardware stores like Little Hardware in Mountain Brook didn't want to keep inventory on every single item. So you had these companies like Moore-Handley who bought all the inventory and put it in a warehouse. Whenever Mountain Brook's Little Hardware needed hammers, nails, glue and the like, they could call Moore-Handley and come to pick up what they needed the very same day.

Bew's eyes glazed over. This was far more information than he wanted. The Moore-Handley building disappeared behind them. "How long till we get there?" Bew asked.

Today, the Moore-Handley building serves as the headquarters for Summer Classics. The 500,000-square-foot building has been completely remodeled into a state-of-the-art facility. Almost all of Summer Classics operations happen under a single roof now. It houses the vast majority of Summer Classics' massive inventory, an impressive cushion operation, and more than a dozen separate loading docks. Hundreds of employees come to Summer Classics every day to work in the many offices, the warehouse and the cushion manufacturing facility. There is a sharp-looking cafe, furnished with Summer Classics' own tables and chairs, where employees can go to get their lunch and coffee. Attached to the main facility is a 10,000-square-foot showroom, open for the public and for trade. Bew's own office has mahogany wood paneling around the room and bookshelves lining the walls. He sits at a large oak desk with a window at his back and two comfortable chairs in front of his desk where staff members can come to speak with him.

At the age of 70, Bew remains the CEO of Summer Classics. Ever active, his days are filled with meetings. He stays atop all that happens in his stores across the country, his facilities in Montevallo, the store in Pelham and their main base of operations in Pelham on Highway 31. He prides himself on the purchase of the Moore-Handley building. They managed to get the property at less than $6 per square foot—an unheard of price.

As Bew had hoped for so long, William stepped forward to take the mantle of responsibility. Today, he currently serves as the president of Gabriella White (the parent company set over Summer Classics, Gabby White and other newly formed divisions). Bew and William work side by side, leading the company towards a bigger and better future. Whenever his time comes, William is ready to lead and succeed his father at the head of the company. Bew could not be more pleased or proud of his son.

Though still busy, Bew has taken a step back. He does not travel as he once did, now leaving most of these responsibilities in the hands of capable employees such as Harold. These days, Bew spends more time with his wife at their farm or at their condo at Ponte Vedra Beach when they can. There are even some days that Bew does nothing but relax. Accustomed to her husband's constant energy, Wendy is not sure what to do with the new Bew. She is delighted at his clear enjoyment of and love for her. Indeed, the two are more in love with each other now than they have ever been.

If you ask any of Bew's children today, they will say they have noticed a change in him in recent years. After all he went through in the recession and in his near-death experience, he has become a better father, a better grandfather and a better husband. Over two decades ago, at their 25th wedding anniversary, Bew said, "I've always believed that there is one thing that you can do for your children that is more powerful even than spending a great deal of time with them and that is to love their mother." His children have seen him loving their mother more and more every day.

In December 2018, Summer Classics passed $100 million in sales. This was a huge accomplishment for Bew and Summer Classics. To celebrate this achievement the Summer Classics staff rented a theater auditorium to show their appreciation to Bew for all of his hard work.

Bew's employees and family took their seats in the auditorium as William spoke to them from the front of the room. Wearing tan slacks, a tan blazer and a red tie, William, now gray haired, looked every bit the part of president. Bew was seated in a raised chair in the front of the auditorium to William's left.

William raised the mic in his hand, "This is just a moment I want to take to honor my father for all the work he's done. There's really no greater indicator for the success of a company than the person who leads it. The fact that we are successful is because of this guy right here." William pointed to his father. Bew playfully raised his arms in triumph. William threw his hand up in summons. "Come on! Round of applause!" William directed the auditorium. Everyone applauded. Bew smiled.

"Suck up, as he says, right?" William joked. Bew laughed.

"So what I want to do here is bring up my sisters and my mom. We're going to read some letters that we wrote to dad, and then we'll close out."

Bew raised his own mic. "Geez, this is the 'make Bew cry' deal." There was laughter.

Bew's eldest daughter, Walker, came up first. She embraced her father on her way to the microphone in the front. She stood at the mic with a black blouse and white jacket. A cross necklace hung about her neck and her brunette hair fell to just above her shoulders. She exuded kindness and warmth.

"Hello. I know most of y'all, but I am Walker." Bew took a seat on the front row and William went to join his family a few rows back. "I am Bew and Wendy's first daughter. I am Gabriella Walker White."

"I just wanted to speak to Dad about some qualities that he has. But I want to make sure that y'all—if you're here for just a little while, that y'all see this, because it's rare, and I realize that my father set quite a standard and example as a man, as a father, as a husband. I think all of this is about perseverance." She swallowed. "I've certainly learned a lot of that in my life. It's interesting how—when I read this letter—how my life has really kind of followed the company's up and down. But as I have persevered through trial I know that my character has been refined and that I've become a different person and I like the person I am now." Walker clutched the cross on her neck as she said this.

"People ask me if I'm jealous that I'm not working for the company or if I wish I was." She held up her hand and in a thick southern accent, said, "I've had my time." Everyone laughed.

"But the thing is my passion is ministry. That's just my heart. It's all about relationship, and I wanted everybody to know that every person that works for this company, my father cares about you. I know that because I've seen him through hard times really just be overtaken with grief having to let people go. He cries, and *they* try to encourage him."

She unfolded some pages in her hand. "I'm going to read this letter, and it will help you understand what kind of guy my dad is." She began to read, "Dear Dad, congratulations! This accomplishment is truly a testimony of your perseverance. I know that you can remember as if it was yesterday—the recession, the loss of the farmhouse, and Granny's passing. I will never forget how difficult it was to watch you go through such a trying time. Even though you'd experienced tremendous personal loss, what grieved you the most was having to let go of loyal employees due to losses incurred during the recession. You grieved for them, for their families and what they would have to endure without an income to put food on the table.

"Dad this is such a tremendous accomplishment to have weathered the storms over the years that have led to this day of celebration. To me, your greatest success is, though at many times you have felt like you were walking in the wilderness, you maintained your commitment to God's leading and you refused to compromise your integrity. What a testimony of God's faithfulness in your character. You have endured trial and persevered in the face of difficulty, and now, generations will receive the fruit of your faith."

Walker looked at her father, "Dad, you have a wonderful spirit of true generosity, a huge heart and you're a wonderful father. God is faithful to give rewards here on earth, just as he will do in heaven. He brought you out of the hard times, and now, he is walking with you into the reward that he promised you."

"This company was built with your vision, integrity and deep love for and belief in God and people. May it continue to prosper for generations to come. I love you, and I'm so proud that you're my dad."

The auditorium applauded. Bew rose, and he embraced his precious daughter. Walker took her seat, and Bew resumed his own.

Now, Wynne took her turn at the mic. She was wearing a green blouse with a fur coat vest. Her brown hair went past her shoulders and a necklace hung from her neck. "So mine's going to be a little different," she joked. Wynne had her father's sense of humor. They laughed.

"So I'm just going to read this." She lowered her gaze to some pages in her hands and began to read, "Dad, a hundred million! To say I'm proud is the ultimate understatement. I'd like to say I knew you could do it, but I didn't." The auditorium laughed heartily.

"I remember when I was a kid, I used to pray that you would change your mind about this patio furniture gig and be a lawyer like Papa. He was home every night (at least I think he was), and he gave much better Christmas gifts." More laughter. "So, he had to be doing something right. I guess I'm glad that my prayers weren't answered because the future me would definitely be out of a job and on your and Mom's couch if you had taken the lawyer path more traveled." Wynne had them laughing again.

She continued to read. "It is an inspiration to watch your mind at work, and how you can turn an idea into actuality. It is only with your tenacity, judge of character and creativity that this business has flourished the way it has. Well, I take that back—if you didn't have Wendy White by your side, I'm pretty sure none of this would be possible." Bew turned to smile at his wife.

"I'm proud to call you 'Dad.' I love you more than words can describe and here's to a *five hundred* million dollar idea." The room applauded. Bew embraced his daughter and comedian, giving her a playful smile.

William walked to the front holding his own young son in his arms. "Okay. It's my turn. You've heard enough from me. I know you're thinking, 'Get him out of here.'" People laughed. They liked their boss William's good nature.

William began to read the letter in his hand, "Dear Dad, your extremely proud family has been watching you grow this company since I was his age." William tilted his head towards his own son. "All the way from zero dollars in 1978 to this incredible landmark. My proudest achievement is that I've done my best to help you and that I got to work closely with my dad for over a decade. I'm excited to work by your side for years to come, and hopefully someday my children will be alongside of me, and that they will know that their awesome grandfather founded this company and poured everything he had into it." Bew beamed at these words.

William continued, "It's impossible for anyone today (except maybe my mother) to fully understand what you've been through to get to this point—the hurdles, challenges, sleepless nights, poor health, things that didn't work, a fire in the old building, the recession, the ones who never got on board with the plan, inevitable loneliness at the top, the ugly stuff that people haven't seen, or that they don't understand that has helped mold you into the success you are." William had just given a succinct summary of Bew's entire career. Bew gave a knowing nod.

"Your tireless effort, your passion, your ability to endure challenge after challenge, your grit, your will of leadership, your ability to connect with others has built a special place where we get to follow our passion and make a living for our loved ones. You're a great gift to us all. You're the reason we are all here today. This company supports hundreds of families. For this we are forever grateful. I am honored and privileged to call you my dad."

"Let's do this again when we reach…" William looked up from his letter and used his most dramatic voice, "One *billion* dollars." Everyone laughed and applauded as William stepped away from the mic and walked back to his family.

With all the style and grace of Laura Bush, Wendy walked to the front. She wore a red blouse with a red cardigan and a chain necklace. Her black hair was in an elegant bob cut. Her glasses were hooked on her collar. She raised her letter, cleared her throat, and began to read, "My dearest Billy, congratulations on the huge accomplishment of getting one hundred million dollars in sales for all the companies under the Gabriella White brand. I'm so proud of you. I am not surprised that under your leadership, the companies were able to hit this milestone. Though, I've always known you were capable of great things, and you've told me a few times that I'm always right." At this she smirked, and everyone laughed.

"I remember the many nights the alarm would go off in Pelham at 2 AM and you would get up and drive to the office to meet with the police, the terrible night the plant burned in Columbiana, and, of course, the financial downturn in 2008. Many people would have given up, but you were such a special person. You just kept working hard, figuring out solutions to each problem."

"The company has grown so much and added so many divisions it is hard for me to keep up. I know you're thrilled that William and Wynne are working with you now. You've done a wonderful job of laying the groundwork for the next generation. You've given our children a real gift and an example to live up to. You're not only a very good businessman, you are also a man of faith and integrity."

"I thank God for you and for giving us this incredible life together. I thank him for how he has blessed this company and been with us not only in the good times but also during the difficult times."

At this point, Wendy paused. She looked up from her letter and looked at Bew with all her love. It was clear to everyone that Wendy loved this man with her all. "Thank you for marrying me," she said. Then, she began to cry. "I love you very much." She signed off, saying, "Wendy."

Bew had tears in his eyes. He rose from his seat and walked to his wife. She looked up at him, gazing into his loving eyes. Bew wrapped Wendy in a tight embrace.

ACKNOWLEDGMENTS

I AM GRATEFUL to have had the help and encouragement of so many in the writing of this book. First of all, I want to thank my father, Larry Alex Taunton, who is a much more established author than I, for lending me his expertise and for motivating me and helping me develop the story arc. Secondly, I want to thank my mother, Lauri Taunton and grandmother Judith Taunton for reading the book and giving me valuable feedback. I am grateful to my brother Michael Taunton for his professional expertise. I also want to thank my editor, Sharon Herbitter, for her keen eye, encouraging words and more thorough knowledge of the technicalities of English grammar.

I am grateful to Bew and his family for all their cooperation, help and confidence in me. All my conversations and interactions with them were nothing but pleasant. I thank the employees of Summer Classics for talking with me and giving me helpful insights. I am grateful to Bew's friends and business acquaintances for doing the same.